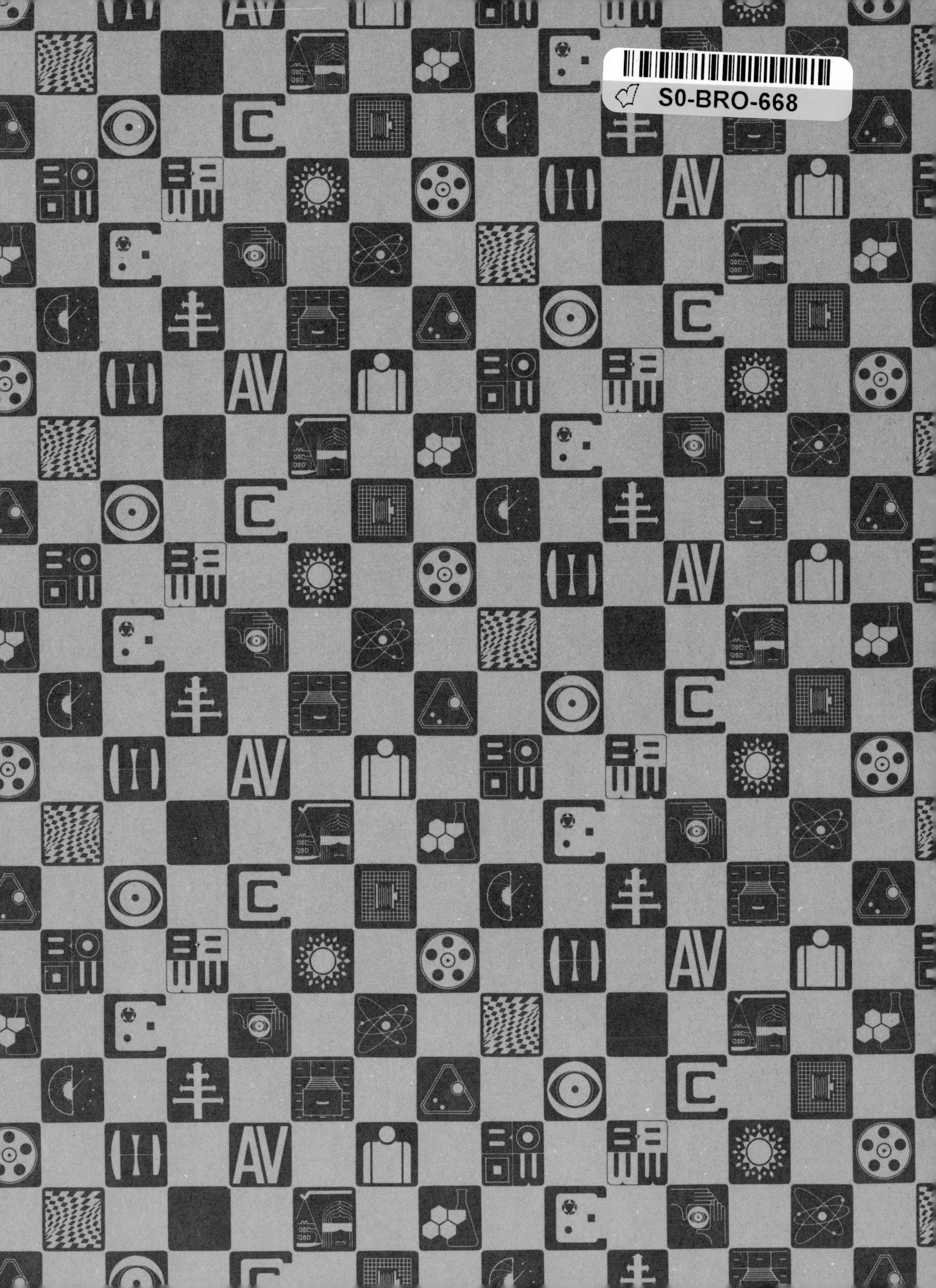
AV
C
S0-BRO-668

Encyclopedia of Practical Photography

Volume 2

Bac - Cha

Edited by and published for
EASTMAN KODAK COMPANY

AMPHOTO
American Photographic Book Publishing Company
Garden City, New York

Notes on Photography

The cover photos and the photos of letters that appear elsewhere in this encyclopedia were taken by Chris Maggio.

Library of Congress Cataloging in Publication Data

Amphoto, New York.
Encyclopedia of practical photography.

Includes bibliographical references and index.
1. Photography—Dictionaries. I. Eastman Kodak Company. II. Title.
TR9.T34 770′.3 77-22562

ISBN 0-8174-3050-4 Trade Edition—Whole Set
ISBN 0-8174-3200-0 Library Edition—Whole Set
ISBN 0-8174-3052-0 Trade Edition—Volume 2
ISBN 0-8174-3202-7 Library Edition—Volume 2

Manufactured in the United States of America

Editorial Board

The *Encyclopedia of Practical Photography* was compiled and edited jointly by Eastman Kodak Company and American Photographic Book Publishing Co., Inc. (Amphoto). The comprehensive archives, vast resources, and technical staffs of both companies, as well as the published works of Kodak, were used as the basis for most of the information contained in this encyclopedia.

Symbol Identification

Audiovisual

Biography

Black-and-White Materials

Black-and-White Processing and Printing

Business and Legal Aspects

Chemicals

Color Materials

Color Processing and Printing

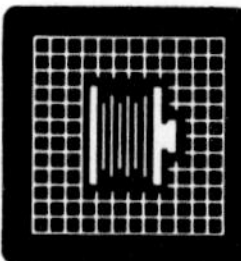

Equipment and Facilities

Exposure

History

Lighting

Motion Picture

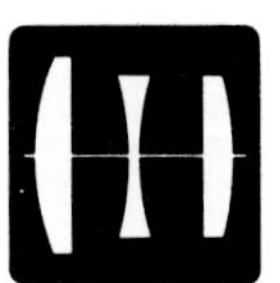

Optics

Picture-Making Techniques

Scientific Photography

Special Effects and Techniques

Special Interests

Storage and Care

Theory of Photography

Vision

Guide for the Reader

Use this encyclopedia as you would any good encyclopedia or dictionary. Look for the subject desired as it first occurs to you—most often you will locate it immediately. The shorter articles begin with a dictionary-style definition, and the longer articles begin with a short paragraph that summarizes the article that follows. Either of these should tell you if the information you need is in the article. The longer articles are then broken down by series of headings and sub-headings to aid further in locating specific information.

Cross References

If you do not find the specific information you are seeking in the article first consulted, use the cross references (within the article and at the end of it) to lead you to more information. The cross references can lead you from a general article to the more detailed articles into which the subject is divided. Cross references are printed in capital letters so that you can easily recognize them.
Example: *See also:* ZONE SYSTEM.

Index

If the initial article you turn to does not supply you with the information you seek, and the cross references do not lead you to it, use the index in the last volume. The index contains thousands of entries to help you identify and locate any subject you seek.

Symbols

To further aid you in locating information, the articles throughout have been organized into major photographic categories. Each category is represented by a symbol displayed on the opposite page. By using only the symbols, you can scan each volume and locate all the information under any of the general categories. Thus, if you wish to read all about lighting, simply locate the lighting symbols and read the articles under them.

Reading Lists

Most of the longer articles are followed by reading lists citing useful sources for further information. Should you require additional sources, check the cross-referenced articles for additional reading lists.

Metric Measurement

Both the U.S. Customary System of measurement and the International System (SI) are used throughout this encyclopedia. In most cases, the metric measurement is given first with the U.S. customary equivalent following in parenthesis. When equivalent measurements are given, they will be rounded off to the nearest whole unit or a tenth of a unit, unless precise measurement is important. When a measurement is considered a "standard," equivalents will not be given. For example: 35 mm film, 200 mm lens, 4″ × 5″ negative, and 8″ × 10″ prints will not be given with their customary or metric equivalents.

How Articles are Alphabetized

Article titles are alphabetized by letter sequence, with word breaks and hyphens not considered. Example:

Archer, Frederick Scott
Architectural Photography
Archival Processing
Arc Lamps

Abbreviations are alphabetized according to the letters of the abbreviations, not by the words the letters stand for. Example:

Artificial Light
ASA Speed

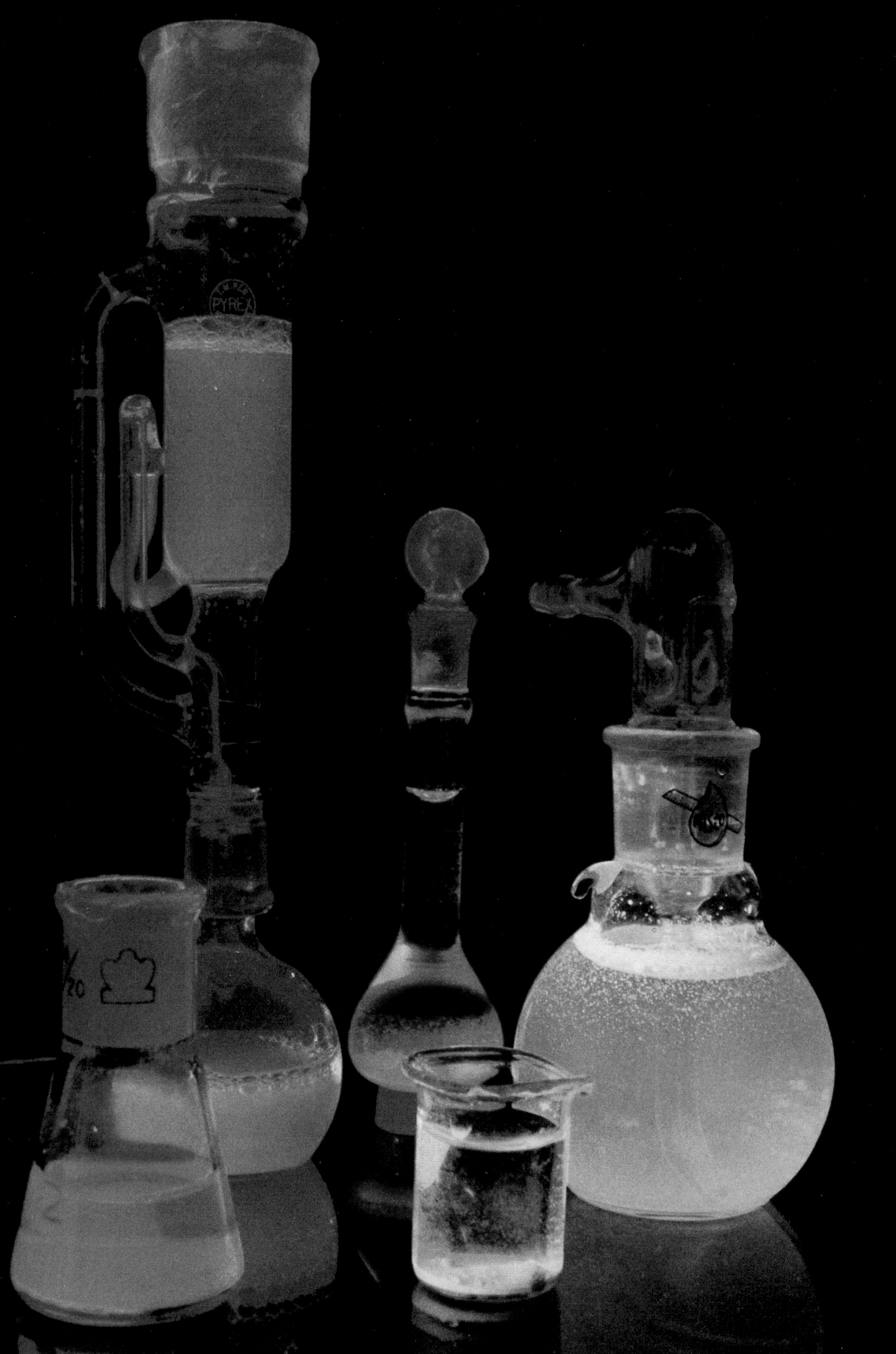
PYREX

Contents
Volume 2

Back Focus

When a lens is focused at infinity, the distance measured along the lens axis from the center of the rear lens surface to the focal plane or film plane is called the "back focus." It is not directly related to the focal length of the lens. In the case of telephoto lenses, the back focus is considerably less than the focal length, while with the inverted-telephoto type of wide-angle lens, the back focus is a good deal greater than the focal length. The importance of the back focus is that it provides data for the use of a given lens on a camera having limited bellows extension (as in the case of the telephoto) or where considerable clearance between the back of the lens and the shutter or mirror mechanism is required, as in motion-picture and reflex cameras.

• *See also:* LENSES; OPTICS.

Backgrounds

The background, or better, *ground,* of a picture is the visual material that is seen around the main subject—above, below, and to either side within the picture area. When space, perspective, and physical details are realistically represented in a picture, the background is perceived as being behind the subject, at a greater distance from the viewer.

Some subjects, such as landscapes or a crowd, are continuous in depth and thus do not have a background in a picture. But photographs of a single object or person, or a group, do have backgrounds, which in turn have a great effect on how the pictures communicate. When the subject does have a background, be aware of the *entire* background. The ground should complement the subject and not detract from the picture's main elements.

The top diagram of a telephoto lens and the bottom diagram of a reversed telephoto lens show the back focus distance for these two lenses. With a telephoto lens, the back focus distance is less than the focal length of the lens. With a reversed telephoto lens, the back focus distance is exceptionally long, often as long as or longer than the focal length of the lens.

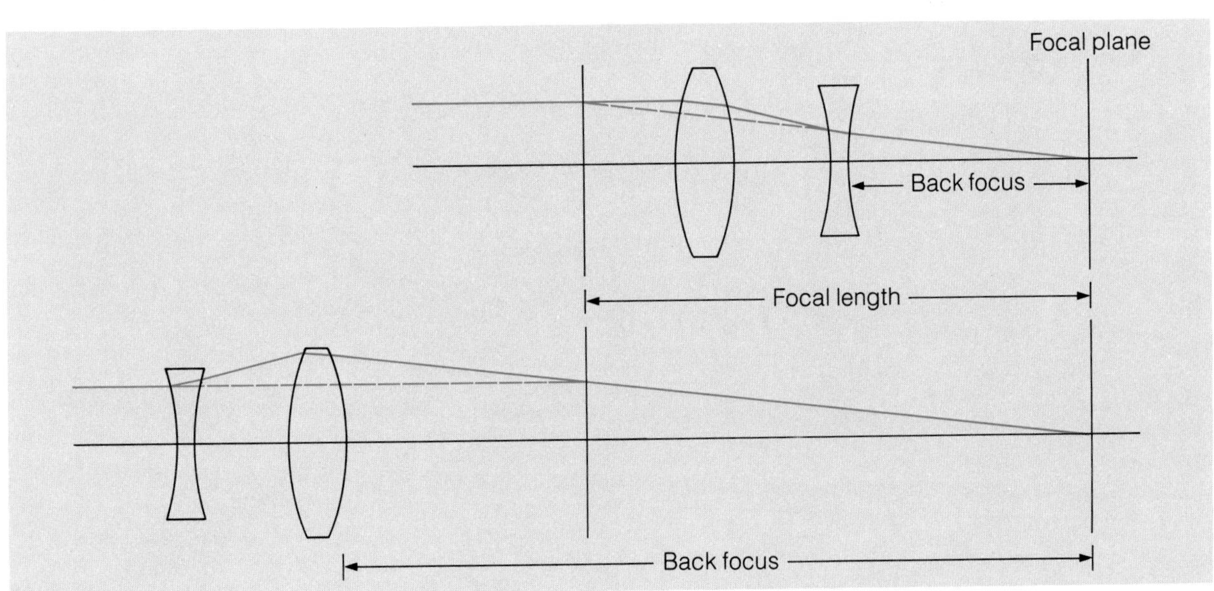

Background Functions

The background does three things:

1. It makes the subject visually distinct so that its shape or outline can be seen clearly. Therefore, the background must contrast sufficiently in tone or color so that it does not seem to merge or blend with the subject tone. And it must not be so detailed or "busy" that it camouflages the subject by confusing or breaking up the visual line of the subject edges.

2. The background helps establish the volume of space in which the subject is located. When the background is close behind the subject, the space seems shallow, even cramped. As subject-to-background distance increases, the apparent space also increases.

3. The background establishes the character of the locale. It indicates the environment and the mood or atmosphere of the setting. This is as true of featureless, single-tone (or color) backgrounds as it is of those backgrounds full of realistic details.

Background Problems

As a photographer, you must see and evaluate background problems each time you look through the viewfinder. Obvious distractions, such as trees or

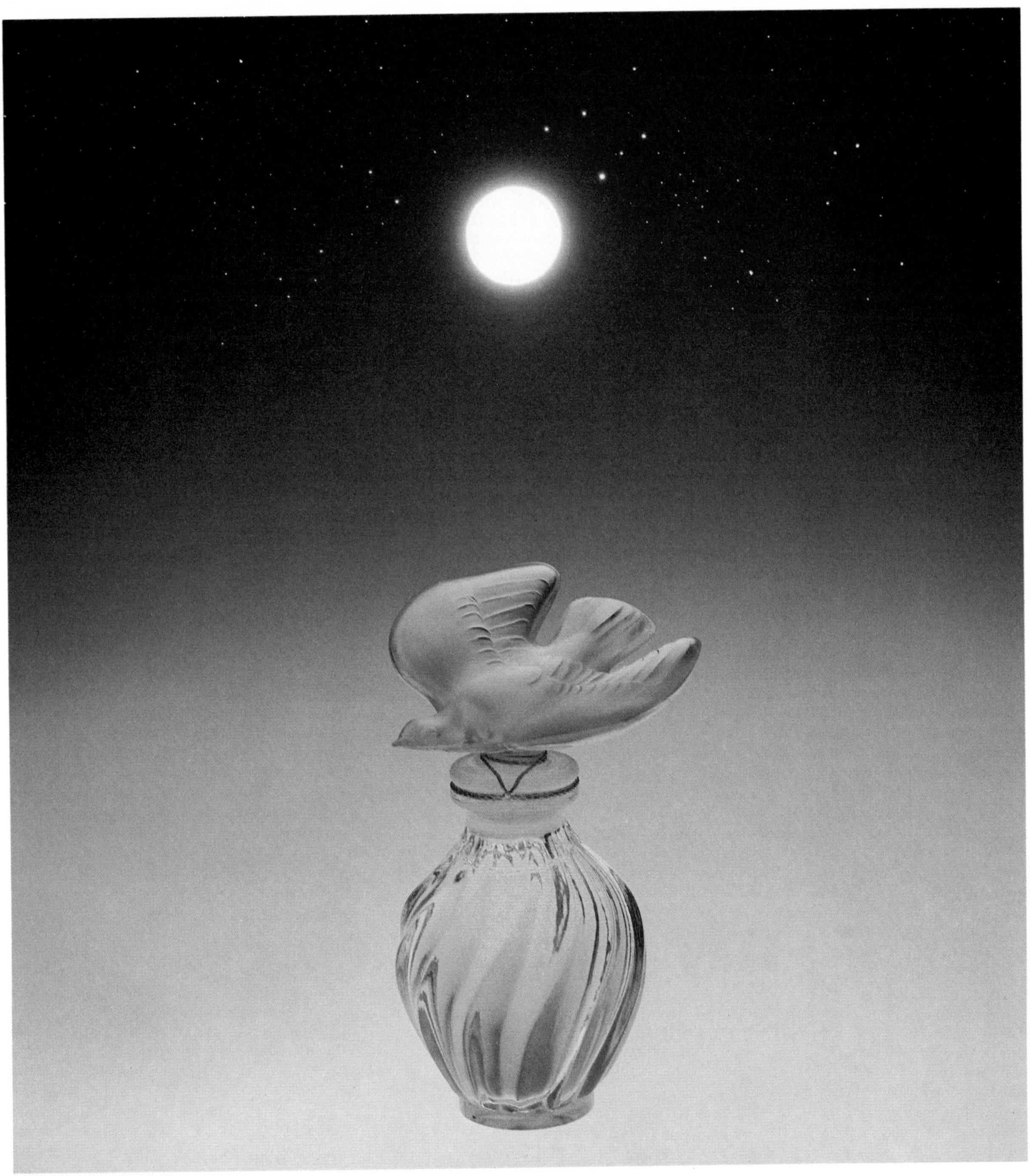

(Left) Every element in this background contributes to the subject illustrated. This composition, created for a cookbook, displays the subject close to its source. Photo by Albert Gommi. (Above) A double exposure was used to combine subject and background. The bottle was photographed first, resting on a piece of curved Plexiglas lighted from below. The moon and stars, cut and punched from black paper, were lighted from behind. Photo by Jerry Sarapochiello.

lampshades that seem to rest on top of the subject, must be eliminated. Remove them, or move the subject or the camera—or both. To subdue busy backgrounds, throw them out of focus so that the sharp details of the subject stand out in clear relief. You can add back- or rimlight to clarify the edges of the subject.

Watch out for bright spots of warm hues (red, orange, yellow) in the background of color pictures. Because these colors are usually perceived as being closer than cool colors, they may work against the sense of space, even when out of focus. Of course, backgrounds that are very bright or vivid will make it hard to see a less intense subject.

Controlling and Creating Backgrounds

To control the amount of background in the picture, move the camera closer or farther away, or change to a lens with a narrower or wider angle of view. But keep in mind that these changes will also change the size of the subject.

When shooting in actual locations, indoors or out , your primary control over the background is through subject and camera placement. The surroundings are there, and you must determine what and how much to include. Besides moving side to side, check the view from higher and lower angles. You may discover a broad expanse of undistracting rug or floor, or an even-toned sky.

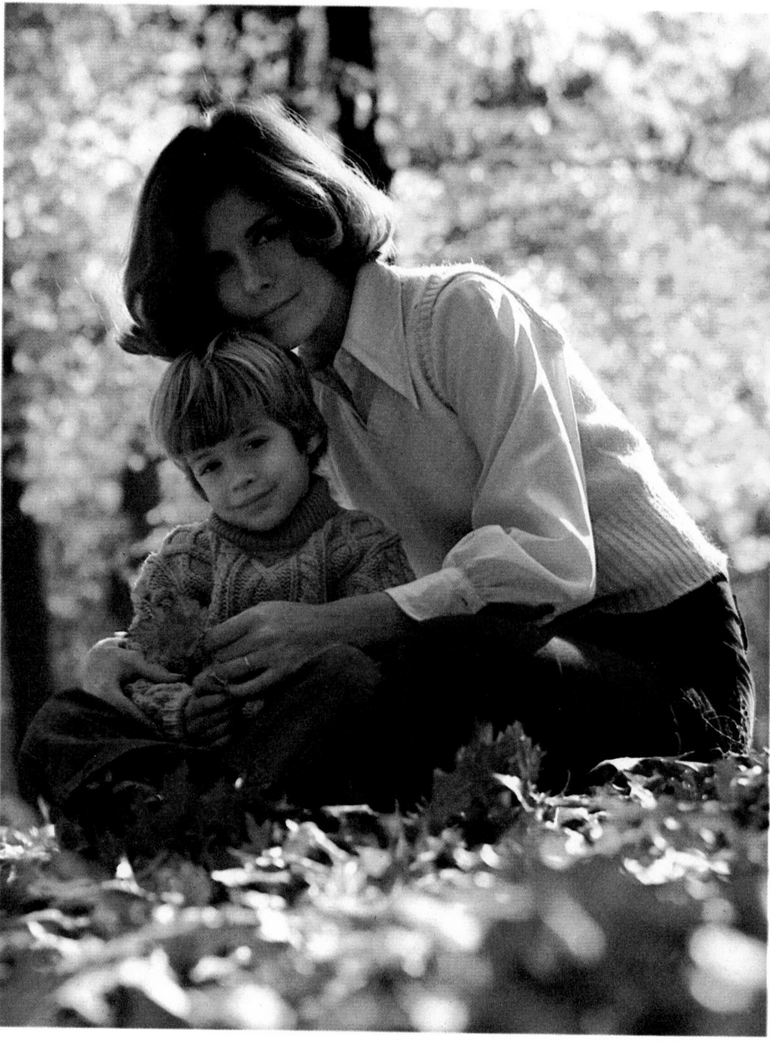

A background of autumn leaves makes a colorful and harmonious setting for this informal portrait of a mother and her young son. Because the patterns of the leaves might have appeared too busy if they were in sharp focus, the photographer used shallow depth-of-field to throw both background and foreground into a blur of color.

(Below) For location portraits, the photographer must learn to work with the backgrounds at hand. This requires eliminating distracting elements and positioning camera and subject carefully. (Right) Light filtered through a sheer white curtain provides soft illumination and an unobtrusive background. Photo by Al Gilbert.

Studio Backgrounds. In the studio, you have complete control, for you must create the background. It may be as simple as a single color or tone that harmonizes with the subject—a treatment common in much product and fashion photography—or it may be a full-scale setting, complete in every detail, for an editorial or advertising illustration.

Seamless Paper. The most common studio background materials are long rolls of seamless paper in 9- or 12-foot widths. They are hung on a rod well above subject height, and pulled down as needed. When curved at floor level and pulled forward under the subject, the horizon line is eliminated. Use weights at the corners and along the edges, out of camera range, to hold the paper in place. Step on the paper only in stocking feet, to avoid creasing it or leaving tracks when making adjustments.

You can buy seamless paper rolls in many colors, or you can use colored light on white paper. In black-and-white, you can make light-gray paper photograph as any shade simply by adjusting the light intensity falling on it. A level two to three stops greater than the strongest light on the subject will make the background print white. For middle and darker tones, be sure that light on the subject does not spill on the background and weaken or completely wash out the tone you want. Settings can be suggested by shadow patterns on a seamless paper background. Use cutouts or actual objects, such as branches, in front of a spotlight or a slide projector to create the shadows.

Other Background Materials. Settings can also be created from actual furniture and objects, or from substitutes and imitations constructed by common theatrical techniques. Often, a combination of these methods is practical. Outdoor scenes, and especially elaborate backgrounds, can be created with photographic realism by projecting an appropriate slide. Realistic foreground elements add to the illusion. Projected background methods may also be used to contribute to the scene. (*See:* FRONT PROJECTION; REAR PROJECTION.)

Studio Portrait Backgrounds

The choice of a background is critical. Generally, you should strive for simplicity in the background. Not only does simplicity yield more artistic results by maintaining the accent on the sitter, but it is a practical fact that the repeated use of a background with a definite or easily recognizable design

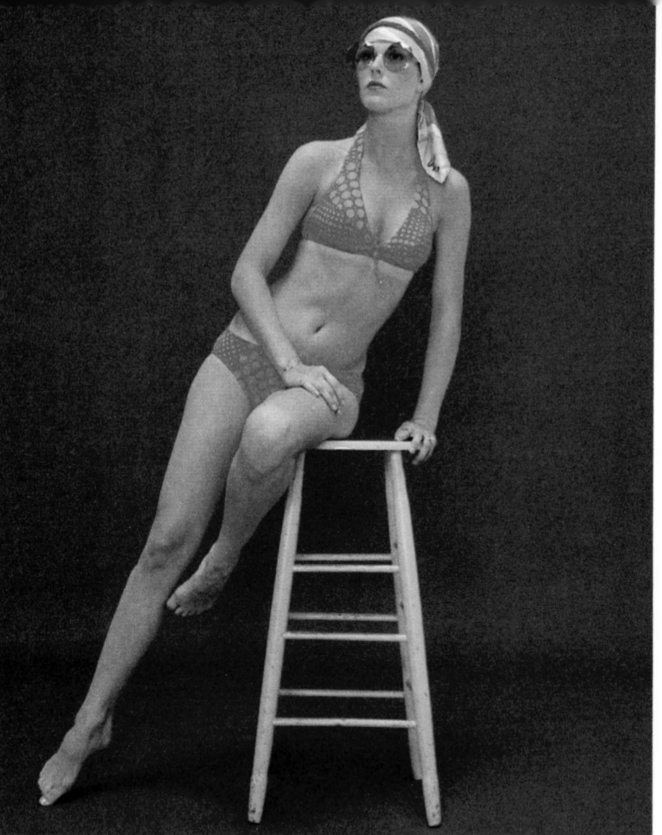

Long rolls of seamless colored paper provide simple, uncluttered backgrounds which are easily changed to complement varying subjects.

quickly dates your work. Probably the most widely used background is a large, flat, unmarked surface. This can be paper (such as a large roll of seamless background paper nine feet wide, suspended from the ceiling), a painted screen, or an actual wall of the studio. To help prevent distracting reflections or color casts, paint with matte rather than glossy paint. By varying the relative amount of illumination on this background, you can easily control the overall tone and introduce variations by throwing a shadow across an area of the background.

You can produce simple backgrounds without difficulty. They can be made of a piece of lightweight muslin stretched on a frame of ample size and painted with flat latex paint. Old tapestries make good backgrounds if used sparingly, as do bookcases and dark-toned plywood or paneled screens, especially for men. Incidentally, a posing platform about eight inches high is an excellent aid in the portrait studio. It helps to elevate the subject to a more convenient working height and to eliminate the background floor line in three-quarter portraits.

Background Color. Give the color of the background careful consideration. Backgrounds having large masses of one bright color are usually not suitable because they have a tendency to overpower the color likeness of the subject. An effective background might employ a soft cloud effect in which the colors are quite subdued. Slightly warm-colored backgrounds are suitable for most subjects, especially for low-key portraits. In general, avoid cold-colored backgrounds because they reflect from the sides of the face, giving a sickly look to the subject. Also, proper visual color balance is more difficult to achieve in printing a color portrait with a cold background because the complementary colors contrasting with warm flesh tones make the flesh appear excessively ruddy.

Painting a Studio Background. With a section of canvas, some paint, and no artistic training what-

Bookcases make excellent portrait backgrounds. Inclusion of several props, such as the model ships here, tell something about the interests of this executive. This scene could be a studio setup, or an actual location.

Seamless white paper under a curved Plexiglas sweep provides a high-key background for this arrangement of strawberries and gears. Backlighting utilizes the reflective surface of the Plexiglas to mirror the forms of the objects. Photo by Fotiades-Falkensteen.

soever, you can create a portrait background that will result in photographs that are personal and distinctive. Because you do the painting yourself, you can alter the colors and densities until you are satisfied that they will harmonize with the subject.

Materials. You will need canvas from any awning store. The size will depend on the studio space. If there's plenty of space, you can find excellent use for a 12′ × 12′ canvas. This is suitable for full-length, large three-quarter, or family-group portraits. An 8′ × 8′ canvas can handle these categories too, though with a group limit of three. For these sizes, mount the canvas on a simple frame of two-by-twos and tack it into place. Add a set of rollers for mobility.

In these sizes, you may find there are seams. However, with the subject standing five or six feet in front of the background, and with the lens of a 4″ × 5″ camera set at *f*/8 to *f*/11, seams don't show. The seam could be a problem in a smaller studio where space does not permit this separation between subject and background—and here a window-shade-size canvas, suitably equipped to let you roll it up for storage, would be preferable.

You will need either water-base or oil-base colors for your background: water-base for a high-key (pale) background, a semimatte oil-base paint for a darker, low-key background. Any reflections can be banished by applying an overcoat of flat varnish or by blending an additive with the paint to remove

A painted backdrop employing a cloud effect and subdued colors is a versatile background. Added props—a chair, a potted plant, a velvet drape—could transform this background into a suitable setting for a formal portrait.

gloss. Or you can tilt the background slightly so that the highlights don't reflect back into the camera.

Your painting instruments are a roller, brush, sponge, and cloth. The roller and brush produce the harder lines and distinct patterns; if you're in a smaller studio, however, you'll want to skip them entirely. Larger studios with room to maneuver the subject can use them to advantage. Sponges and cloths are used to blend the design together, removing harsh contrast and providing a swirling "oil painting" look.

Keep the center of the canvas relatively pale—darkening as you move outward to the frame. This gives the portrait depth and separation, and it cuts down on the burning-in time later. A word of caution: Stay away from the flesh tones while working the center, so you don't camouflage the subject.

For low-key backgrounds, pick the earthen tones—brown hues, with additions of white, green, black, or red as required. Such backgrounds are good settings for adults and for the more formal type of child and teen portraits. The high-key backgrounds are most effective for children in general and for fashion illustrations. Judge the finished background by viewing it through the ground glass with the camera focused *where the subject will be.*

How many backgrounds should you have? Literally, as many as you can manage. The greater the variety of painted portrait settings available, the more versatile your service. You can find the right background for every subject. Three backgrounds—one high-key, two low-key—would be an excellent starting set.

Because it will increase your versatility, enrich your composition, and cut down on printing costs, you'll find the painted background a simple and serviceable addition to your studio.

Background Lighting. For the photograph to retain the same background color as you observe visually, the background must receive the same amount of illumination as the subject's face. For example, if the main light is four feet from the face, a light of equal intensity must be placed four feet from, and turned toward, the background. Position the subject five or six feet from the background in order to reduce the tendency for the spill from the main light to affect the background tone and color saturation. Do not rely on spill light to illuminate the background; *it should be treated as a separate subject. Light it independently.*

Two other excellent reasons for placing the subject at least five or six feet from the background are to prevent the background color from reflecting appreciably onto the subject, and to allow background detail to go out of focus.

• *See also:* BACK PROJECTION; FRONT PROJECTION; REAR PROJECTION.

Further Reading: Adams, Ansel. *Camera and Lens, The Creative Approach.* Boston, MA: Little, Brown and Co., 1976; Editors of Time-Life Books. *The Camera.* New York, NY: Time-Life Books, 1971; Feininger, Andreas. *Total Picture Control.* Garden City, NY: Amphoto, 1970.

Backgrounds, Eliminating

There are a number of situations in which a photograph of a subject with no visible surroundings is required. Many advertising and fashion illustrations use such images. Composite pages, common in catalogs and publicity books for performers and models, are easily made up from background-free photographs. Instruction and maintenance manuals require "exploded" views and pictures of disassembled mechanisms.

It is quite possible to photograph the subject against whatever background is at hand, and to remove the surrounding material by aftertreatment. Several approaches are used:

Painting the negative with opaque material. (*See:* BLOCK OUT; RETOUCHING.)

Painting over or otherwise removing elements from a positive print. (*See:* BLEACHING.)

Cutting out the desired portion during reproduction. (*See:* PHOTOMECHANICAL REPRODUCTION METHODS; SILHOUETTES.)

Selectively assembling the desired elements in a composite final image. (*See:* COMBINATION PRINTING; DYE TRANSFER PROCESS.)

All of these require considerable handwork and, commercially speaking, considerable expense.

There are methods to achieve the desired results directly and economically. This article deals with some ways to obtain backgroundless photographs in the camera.

Black Materials

It would seem a simple matter to display an object in a black setting and photograph it so that the surroundings do not register on the film. However, many "black" materials are in fact only dark gray, and they have surfaces that reflect a significant amount of the light falling on them. Two kinds of

A black velvet drape absorbs light and appears to have no texture of its own. This is particularly important when the subject itself is highly textured, as are these lion cubs and their wicker basket.

material can photograph dead black because they absorb 90 percent or more of the light that falls on them: black velvet, and black "flocked" fabric or paper. Flocking is a process of spraying or coating a surface with tiny fiber particles. Like the fiber ends of velvet, these create millions of "pockets" between them, which are highly efficient light traps. Flocked materials are available at many large art supply stores and window-display supply houses; they are far less expensive than velvet.

It is essential to smooth out the material under and behind the subject; wrinkles or folds can cause highlight ridges that will register a trace of exposure on the film. The subject may be lighted in any way desired because spill light and shadows falling on the black material will not be seen. The only restriction is that a raking light must not fall directly across the material at a close and low angle, otherwise the tiny ends of the fiber particles will be lighted and the surface texture revealed.

White Settings

An object displayed in a white setting will be completely backgroundless if three factors can be controlled: revealing details in the background material itself, the horizon line, and shadows.

Wrinkles and a rough texture are revealing details. White seamless paper is easier to keep free of wrinkles than cloth. Diffuse illumination from the front rather than the side eliminates texture.

(Below) A studio setup using seamless colored paper curved at the floorline eliminates all background detail. (Right) Black seamless paper creates a "backgroundless" picture when not lighted.

Smoothly curved white paper makes a totally "backgroundless" setting. Shadows and reflections are controlled by lighting. When the subject is a small object, placing it on a light box creates a similar effect.

The meeting, or "horizon," line where the floor surface joins the vertical background can be eliminated by curving the material so that it makes the transition smoothly and continuously. Or the object can be displayed on a pedestal covered with material that curves out of camera range while the background is out of focus in the distance. In both cases, the light on the subject must be diffuse, or revealing shadows will be cast on the surface under the subject. The shadows will fall outside camera range if the subject is suspended on a sheet of glass well above the "floor," but reflections from the glass may become a problem. Alternatively, the shadows can be washed out by placing the subject on a light box or on translucent material strongly lighted from below. Either way, the light intensity of the surroundings must be at least two stops greater than that on the subject to expose as a pure white.

Two-Negative Technique

There is a simple in-camera method of eliminating an unwanted background in a product picture. Briefly, the technique is this: Two separate exposures are made of the product setup—one exposure of the product alone made with a continuous-tone film, and one exposure of the background alone made with a high-contrast film. The two negatives are then registered and printed as a single negative.

This technique of eliminating a background offers distinct advantages over the more commonly used hand-blocking and light-box methods. Great labor savings over the hand-blocking method are realized; flare and halation around the edges of the product—a problem with the light-box system—are eliminated.

Setup and Lighting. The setup for the two-negative technique is, in general, much the same as

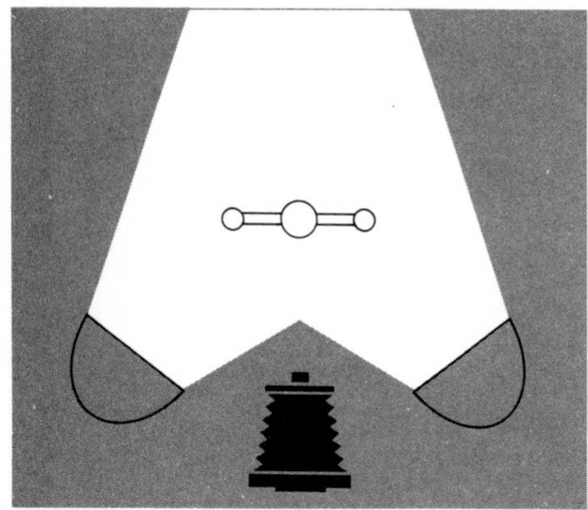

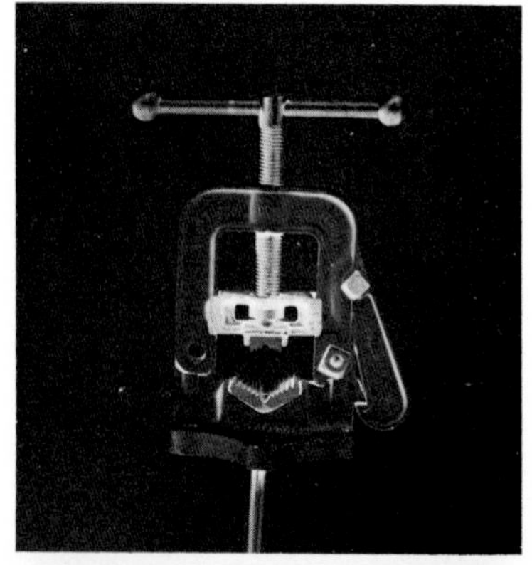

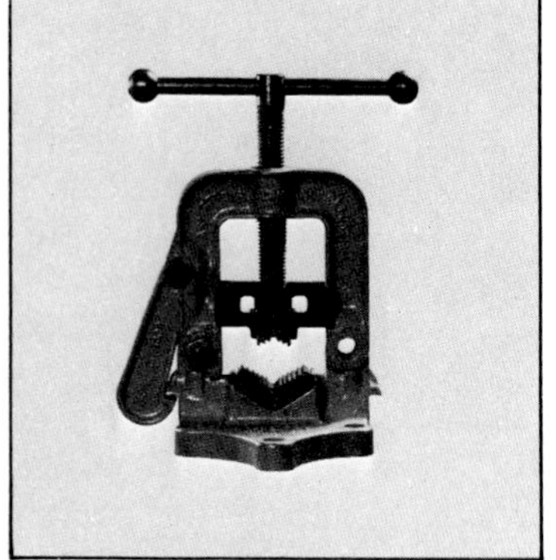

To eliminate a background for a product photograph, the two-negative approach may be used. The lighting should give maximum subject detail. After the two exposures are made, (top) the product alone with a continuous-tone film and (bottom) the white background alone with a high-contrast film, the two negatives are registered and printed as a single negative (right).

you would have for taking a straight product picture. Lighting, however, will be slightly different. The accompanying illustrations show a typical setup for this two-exposure technique. Note the following points:

Subject. Use a support that is steady enough to eliminate the danger of the subject being moved between the two exposures. This support should be as small as possible because you will have to opaque it out on your background negative. You can also use a light table if the subject lends itself to this type of treatment. If a support other than a light table is used, keep the subject far enough from the background so that it will be convenient to light the subject and the background separately.

Lighting. Light the subject to provide maximum detail. You won't need to use any special lighting to give subject-background separation because this separation is provided by the white background. In fact, lighting used to provide separation can often cause a loss of detail around the edges of the subject, particularly if the subject has a high reflectivity. (Note this loss of detail on the upper right edge and on the ends of the handle of the pipe vise in the accompanying illustration.)

Background. Use a piece of white paper large enough to cover the camera field. The lighting on the background must be very even because the high-contrast film used to make the background exposure doesn't have a very wide exposure latitude.

Taking the Picture. The following films and methods may be used for the two-negative approach.

Background Picture. Use Kodalith ortho film. Be sure to use a high-contrast developer, such as Kodak developer D-8 or D-11. This will cut down on pinholes in your negative and will also reduce detail buildup in the subject area.

Subject Picture. Use an Estar-base continuous-tone film. Estar base has great dimensional stability, which is necessary for quick and accurate registering of the two negatives in the printing step. Try using any of a number of Kodak panchromatic sheet films available on Estar thick base.

Exposing the Film. It doesn't matter which exposure you make first, but be certain to observe the following points:

1. Treat each of the two exposures as a separate picture. Only the lights for the exposure being made should be on.
2. Be certain your camera is rock-steady, because it cannot be moved between the two exposures.
3. Set the lens at the same *f*-number for both exposures. Lenses can shift focus at various settings, and you must maintain the same depth of field for the two pictures.
4. When you make the background exposure, be certain that there are no specular reflections bouncing back onto the subject. Sometimes these reflections can be eliminated by keeping the white background only large enough to cover the camera field (using a longer-focal-length lens will also achieve this). If necessary, black tape can be used to cover these reflections, but be careful not to move the subject when applying the tape.
5. Use film holders of the same manufacture. (You can also load opposite sides of one holder with the two films.)

• *See also:* AFTERTREATMENT; AIRBRUSH; BLOCK-OUT; BLEACHING; COMBINATION PRINTING; DYE TRANSFER PROCESS; EXPLODED VIEWS; PHOTO-MECHANICAL REPRODUCTION METHODS; RE-TOUCHING; SILHOUETTES.

Further Reading: Croy, Otto R. *The Complete Art of Printing and Enlarging,* 13th ed. Garden City, NY: Amphoto, 1976;———*Retouching,* 4th ed. Garden City, NY: Amphoto, 1964; Editors of Time-Life Books. *The Print.* New York, NY: Time-Life Books, 1971; Lootens, Joseph Ghislain. *Lootens on Photographic Enlarging and Print Quality,* 8th ed., ed. Lester Bogen. Garden City, NY: Amphoto, 1975; Ruggles, Joanne and Philip. *Darkroom Graphics.* Garden City, NY: Amphoto, 1975; West, Kitty. *Modern Retouching Manual.* Garden City, NY: Amphoto, 1967; Woodland, Harold C. *Creative Photographic Printing Methods.* Garden City, NY: Amphoto, 1975.

Backlight

Illumination falling on the subject from behind or from a direction about 180 degrees opposite the camera position is called backlight. When the main

Backlight creates a bright edge or rim around the subject. In studio portraiture, it is often used behind the head to give a "halo" effect and bring out the lustre of the subject's hair.

light source is in this position, the technique is called "contre jour," or against-the-light photography.

Backlight creates a bright edge or rim around the subject, which serves to separate it from the background. To do this effectively, the backlight must be at least twice the intensity of the brightest frontlight. Outdoors, it is often helpful to position the subject so that the direct sun acts as a backlight. This prevents harsh shadows on the subject, the subject squinting against the glare, and pinpoint-size eye pupils.

For close shots in which the subject fills most of the frame, give an exposure about two stops more than for a subject frontlighted by the sun. For example, if the frontlighted exposure in bright sun should be 1/125 sec. at *f*/11, use *f*/5.6 at 1/125 sec. in the backlighted situation. Or take a meter reading that includes only the shadow area of the subject, excluding any direct backlight, and give about two stops less than the meter reading indicates. When the subject is smaller in the frame, and surrounding detail is desired, give an exposure halfway between that of a highlight reading and that of a shadow reading. An incident-light reading with the meter pointed halfway between the camera and the backlight (that is, at 90 degrees to the camera-subject axis) also will provide a satisfactory exposure.

To reduce overall contrast in relatively close

This wintery forest was cast into a semi-silhouette by taking the photograph directly aimed into the setting sun. Detail in the bark of the trees was preserved by careful choice of exposure. Bracketing exposures provides protection with such subjects.

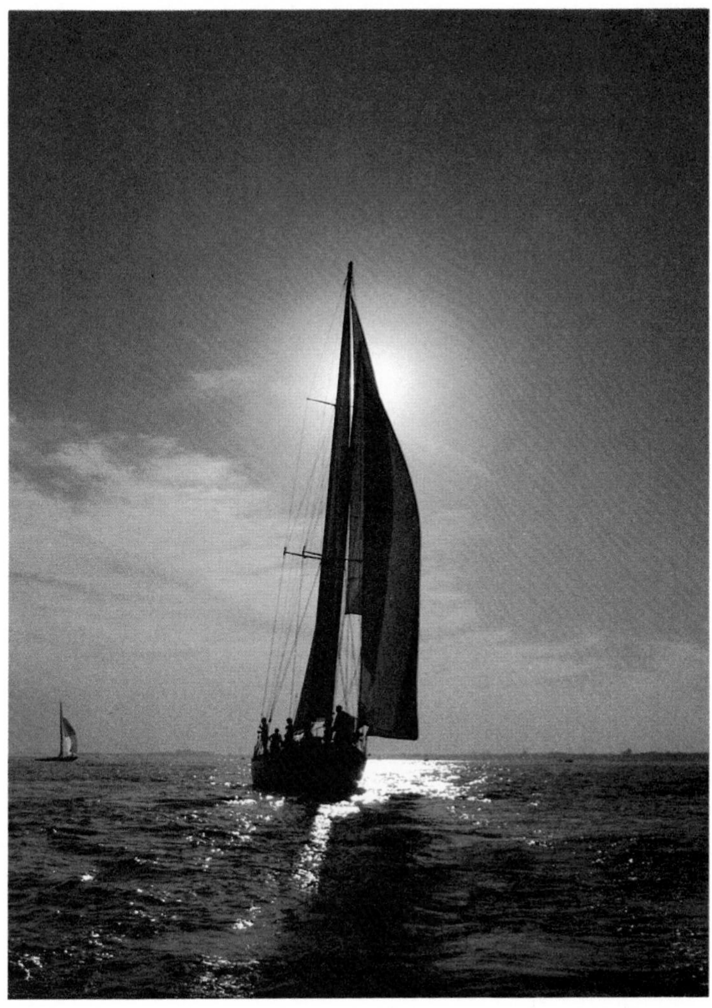

The sun behind this racing sailboat throws a silver halo around the upper mast and sails; light reflected in the water silhouettes the boat itself. Like snow, water is a good reflector—enough backlight is bounced onto the front of the subject to illuminate details.

backlit situations, use a reflector to illuminate the front of the subject, or use fill-in flash.

Determining Flash Exposure

To determine flash exposure, first establish an exposure from an incident-light reading of the backlight itself, or a reflected-light reading of the subject, or a gray card positioned facing the backlight. Note the *f*-stop called for at a shutter speed that permits flash synchronization (1/60 sec. or slower for electronic flash with most cameras with focal-plane shutters). For black-and-white, a 1:3 to 1:4 (fill-in to backlight) ratio is desirable. To find the proper flash-to-subject distance, double the guide number (GN) for the film in use and divide by the *f*-number chosen from the meter reading. For color use a 1:3 ratio, achieved by dividing the *f*-number into GN × 1.6.

For example: GN is 44; incident reading of backlight gives *f*/11 at 1/60 sec. For a 1:4 ratio, place the flash unit (44 × 2) ÷ 11 = *8 feet* from the subject. For a 1:3 ratio, place the flash (44 × 1.6) ÷ 11 = *6.4 feet* from the subject.* Outdoors, the guide number for electronic flash and for bulbs used in deep reflectors will be the same as that normally used inside. For bulbs used in shallow reflectors, a

*Guide numbers calculated in metres will not be the same as guide numbers calculated in feet.

lower guide number is used because there are no ceiling and walls to reflect the light for shallow reflectors. Multiply the usual interior guide number by 0.70 to get the fill-flash guide number.

If a different camera distance is required to achieve the desired framing, remove the flash from the camera for proper positioning, or reduce its intensity with one or more layers of diffusing material. Give the exposure called for by the meter reading (*f*/11 at 1/60 sec. in the example). With flashbulbs, a control over distance can be obtained by using different equivalent exposure settings—for example, *f*/16 at 1/30 sec. or *f*/8 at 1/125 sec. For a silhouette of the subject, do not use fill light; simply give the exposure called for by a meter reading of the backlight.

It is essential to shield the lens from the direct rays of backlight, otherwise contrast-reducing glare, internal reflections and flare, and bright images of the iris diaphragm may be recorded. Use a deep lens hood, shade the lens with your hand or a card, or place the camera in a shadowed location.

• *See also:* LIGHTING.

Back Projection

This is a method of showing a slide or transparency by projecting it onto the rear of a translucent screen; the image is viewed from the other side of the screen. In the studio, back projection is used to provide photographic backgrounds for subjects; in many instances, however, it is being replaced by front projection. Back projection is also used in self-contained display devices; to remove the distraction of the projector from the viewing area; and, in combination with a mirror system, to reduce the projector-to-screen distance required for a given image size.

• *See also:* FRONT, REAR PROJECTION.

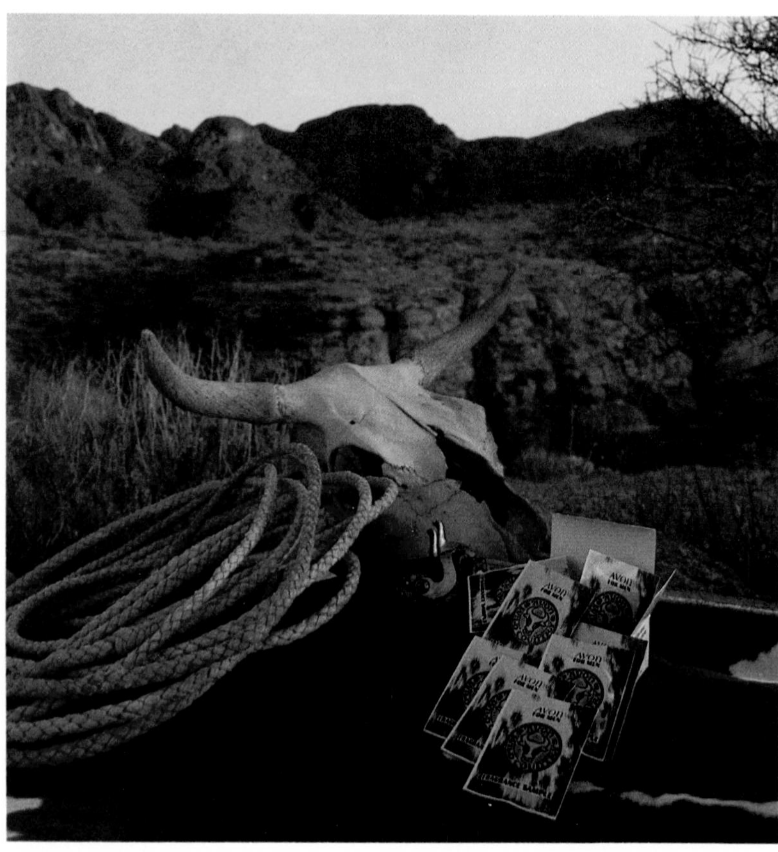

When back projection screens are properly used it should be impossible to tell whether a photograph was taken on location or created in a studio with a background transparency. Realistic props in the foreground help maintain the illusion of a location shot. Photo by Herb and Dorothy McLaughlin.

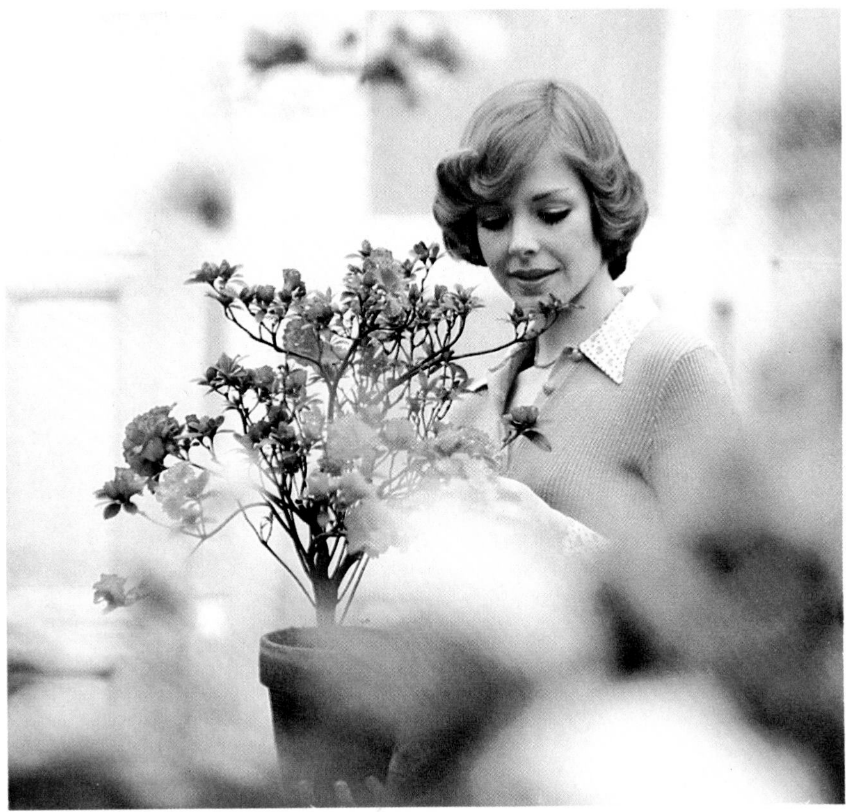

Hazy days that produce diffused light and soft shadows are ideal for taking photographs of people. Flash or reflectors are unnecessary for the elimination of deep shadows, and the natural light is flattering to most subjects.

Bad-Weather Photography

Few good photographers lose pictures because of bad weather. Besides knowing some simple ways of coping with conditions, it's largely a matter of attitude. Picture-taking possibilities are present in most bad-weather situations; you need only look for them. Every change in lighting, atmosphere, or mood demands another shot. The following are some weather situations and what you can do about, and with, them.

Hazy Days

More pictures are taken of people than of any other subject, including landscapes. Fortunately, close-ups of people can be satisfying in practically any type of light; one of the best is hazy-day light.

When the sky becomes milky instead of clear blue, when shadows appear soft at the edges and luminous, and when landscapes begin to lose their "punch," that is the time to take the most flattering pictures of people. On clear days, shadows are harsh and a reflector or flash is essential. But on hazy days, the contrast between highlights and shadows is reduced, and flesh tones are more pleasing because of the softer illumination.

Many excellent nature shots are also taken on hazy days. In the woods, or any area where the light is spotty, the nature photographer often has difficulty on clear days in reducing the contrast sufficiently between highlights and shadows to record detail in both. On hazy days, this contrast difference is much less.

Gray Days

On a completely overcast day, sunlight and skylight are effectively combined into one large diffuse source. The absence of shadows or sunlit highlights gives a flat appearance to pictures, accompanied by low color saturation and a tendency toward bluishness. Skies generally appear overexposed when the foreground is correctly exposed, flesh tones are bluish, and the pictures are frequently underexposed.

Actually, it's quite easy to take excellent pictures under such conditions. For a start, use a skylight filter to correct for excessive bluishness, and concentrate on close-ups. The skylight filter requires no increase in exposure. It does not penetrate atmospheric haze, as often believed, but it does produce a more neutral tone, which gives the appearance of greater visibility. It also helps eliminate bluish flesh tones, particularly evident in close-ups.

Because of the lack of contrasting highlights and shadows, distant landscapes are particularly dreary on gray days. Forget such scenes and look for objects close at hand. When you do try a landscape, remember that skies reproduce poorly on overcast days. Choose an angle to eliminate as much sky as possible, and use foreground objects, such as tree branches, to break up large sky areas.

Be careful about underexposing. There are many degrees of illumination on overcast days, and the exposure level may vary by several stops. On a completely overcast day (not just when a cloud temporarily obscures the sun), you'll need at least three stops more exposure than on a sunny day. You may need another three stops when it's just about to rain. An overall meter reading of the entire subject will be fine in such situations.

To add sparkle, try using flash. You may want to use a reflector in addition to the flash. Two types of lighting are shown in the accompanying diagrams. Flash not only adds contrast but can also be used when photographing people to put desirable catchlights in the eyes.

If you prefer to take close-up pictures of people against a sky background, you can improve the sky tone by using flash to expose your subject. To achieve correct exposure of your subject with the brighter illumination of the flash at close range, use a smaller lens opening (stop down). This means that the sky will receive less exposure and have better color saturation.

Rain

Rainy-day pictures are quite different from those made on overcast days. There are more reflec-

When making close-ups on overcast days, advanced photographers often provide their own "sunlight." You can use flash on camera, although a detachable flash unit positioned high and behind the subject, with a reflector either next to or in front of the subject, usually provides better modeling. Flash will add contrast to the photograph.

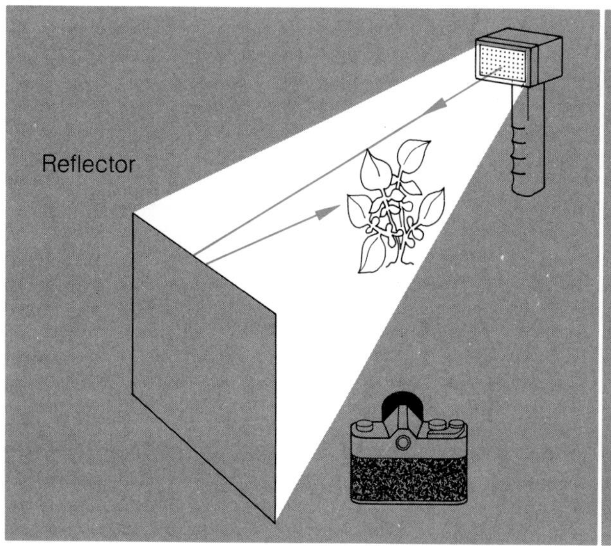

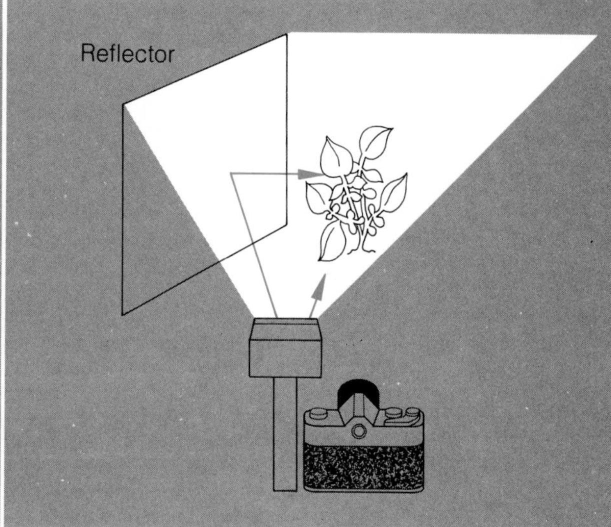

Don't put away your camera on rainy days. Reflections of colored lights produce random and abstract patterns on a rain-wet pavement.

tions, and many objects take on heightened color because of the moisture. For example, fall foliage may appear insipid on overcast days but quite colorful when wet.

The illumination level will vary considerably, depending on the cloud cover. Unless it appears extremely bright, with the sun almost ready to break through, it would be safe to assume during a rainstorm that an exposure increase of at least three to four stops would be needed. Once again, a meter would be helpful.

Protect your camera from the rain. If you can't find an open doorway or other dry spot, an umbrella can be very handy. One drop of rain on the lens can ruin a picture. A deep lens hood is essential for basic protection. Clear glass "Opticap" discs, which fit various lenses just like a filter, are available from the Spiratone Company. They will protect the lens elements from dirt as well as moisture. You can slip a clear plastic bag, mouth downward, over the camera for protection, and reach in from below. Cut a slit in the side for the lens to poke through.

To photograph falling rain, it must be seen against a dark background, and the light must come from one side or from behind the rain (that is, shining toward the camera). Because exposures will be fairly long in the low light level common during rain, you will record streaks of falling water, not individual raindrops.

During an actual rainstorm, a distant landscape may be pretty dreary. The solution is to concentrate more on middle-distance and close-up subjects. Such things as wood and foliage textures, glistening rocks, reflecting puddles, raindrop patterns, and similar rain effects are visually intriguing. In addition, look for colorful umbrellas, kids playing in the rain or mud, wet animals with woebegone expressions, and other human-interest pictures.

Smoke, Fog, Smog, Mist, and Dust

A major factor contributing to the striking beauty of many successful color transparencies is the effective use of atmosphere. Difficult to define, but easy to recognize, atmosphere is employed regularly by the skilled pictorialist to create artistic photographs, in many cases from subject matter not at all out of the ordinary.

Fog and mist establish different planes and give an impression of depth; they also produce a subdued quality that enhances black-and-white photographs. In color, fog, haze, and mist create particularly beautiful effects. The lighting is soft, and colors tend

(Left) Fog, haze, and mist give objects a dreamlike quality that is difficult to obtain under other conditions. These conditions can also conceal unwanted detail, thereby concentrating attention on one aspect of a subject. (Right) Snow on the ground and on branches is easy to photograph and can result in beautiful pictures. Remember to adjust exposure for the additional brightness.

to be grayed, providing a dreamlike quality that is difficult to obtain in clear sunlight.

Another advantage of fog, haze, and mist is that they can conceal unwanted background detail in photographs, thereby concentrating attention on the central subject.

Before you begin calculating exposure for such scenes, it's helpful to know that there are two types of fog: high density, and low density. A high-density fog stays quite close to the ground and limits illumination considerably. An exposure increase of two to three stops is often required. A low-density fog is more dispersed so that little of the sun's effect is lost. In fact, there may be so much scattering of light that the fog acts as a huge reflector, and the illumination may easily exceed that of a clear day by a full stop. This scattering of light makes it extremely difficult to determine exposure without a light meter.

Fog scenes are inherently high-key (have a distinct predominance of lighter tones), and photographs based solely on meter readings, while accurate, are usually too high-key for the average person's taste. Since the conditions that created the scene will probably never again be exactly the same, it's a good idea to make an exposure at the lens setting indicated by your meter and then make two or three more exposures, closing the lens down an additional half stop each time. In this way, you'll have several different effects from which to select the one that pleases you most.

Snow

Snow on the ground is no problem, particularly when the sun is shining. You simply adjust exposure for the additional brightness, and shoot. But snow in the air is another matter. For one thing, it has a nasty habit of clinging to the lens. Regardless of whether it's warm enough to melt, the resultant pictures will be considerably less than masterpieces.

If you use flash when it's snowing, be prepared for plenty of white blobs. Flakes near the camera reflect the light and are always out of focus. You may like the blobs; if you don't, about the only alternative is to stand in a protected area with no snow falling between you and the principal subject. An example: If you're out in the street during heavy snow, shooting a face peering out of a house, chances are that if you use flash, those white spots

will bother you. If you are inside the house, shooting a face peering in, the snow will be behind the subject and you'll have no problem.

Trying to portray a heavy snowstorm is difficult. Too often the day simply looks disappointingly dreary, with little evidence of the falling snow.

For greatest clarity, photograph falling snow against a dark background with light coming from one side. For long, slanting lines, try a slow shutter speed as long as a full second. You'll need a tripod and stationary subjects, of course. You may also need to use a neutral density filter over the lens if you can't stop down far enough.

If you can overlook these minor irritations, you can have fun in the snow. There are mood shots galore—the atmospheric planes of rolling hills, a lone horse with bowed head, brave pedestrians struggling into a gale. Don't forget over-clad children with oversized sleds, or the fragile beauty of branches loaded with wet snow.

Storms

Some of the most spectacular outdoor picture possibilities are of rather commonplace subjects. The lighting is so dramatic that such things as subject matter and composition somehow seem insignificant by comparison. This is particularly true just before or after a storm, when golden shafts of sunlight are contrasted with deep grayish-blue storm clouds.

Street scenes photographed during a snowstorm benefit from touches of bright color, such as the red umbrella here. A slow shutter speed was used to capture the falling snow. Photo by Jan Lukas for Editorial Photocolor Archives.

With rare exceptions, lightning can be photographed only at night, when the shutter can be left open without fear of overexposing the film. After the lightning flashes, the shutter can be closed and the film advanced, or it can be left open so that two or more flashes can be recorded on the same frame. Photo by Michael Fairchild.

Light of this nature is fleeting, and you'll need to work fast. If there's any sun at all (chances are the lighting won't be dramatic if there isn't), exposure will be about the same as on a clear day. Don't let the dark clouds fool you—you *want* them dramatic, and they won't be if you overexpose.

A good rainbow is always impressive. Rainbows record best when slightly underexposed, so give about a half stop less exposure than your meter indicates.

If you're hoping to catch a good lightning flash during a spectacular display, forget it—during the day, that is. The chances of your synchronizing shutter with flash are purely accidental, and very slim. At night, it's a different matter. Then you can leave the shutter open long enough to record one or more flashes.

The size of the lens opening for night lightning photography will be determined by the general illumination, not by the lightning. A lightning flash will record at practically any opening. Select the proper lens opening for an exposure of 10 or 15 seconds during heavy displays, longer if the lightning is infrequent. You'll need a tripod or other firm support.

Further Reading: Editors of Time-Life Books. *Special Problems.* New York, NY: Time-Life Books, 1971; Skoglund, Gosta. *Color in Your Camera,* 6th ed. Garden City, NY: Amphoto, 1975.

A good rainbow always makes an impressive photograph. They record best when underexposed by about half an f-stop.

Baekeland, Leo Hendrik

(1863–1944)
American chemist

Baekeland pioneered plastics research; he invented the first practical phenol-formaldehyde plastic, named "Bakelite" in his honor. In photography, he worked with silver chloride emulsions and, in 1893, introduced the first "developing-out" contact-printing paper, trademarked Velox. This paper was sold for many years by the Nepera Chemical Company of Rochester, New York, which also provided a liquid developer for it called Nepera Solution. Nepera Chemical Company was acquired by Eastman Kodak Company, which continued the manufacture of Nepera Solution for some years and still produces contact-printing paper.

Barium Sulfate

Baryta

Used in the production of photographic print papers and in radiography.
Formula: $BaSO_4$
Molecular Weight: 233.0

White powder; insoluble in water or alcohol.

An intermediate layer of baryta and gelatin between the paper base and the emulsion is used in photographic print papers for three purposes:

1. It promotes adhesion of the emulsion to the supporting material.
2. It covers over the texture of the paper fibers so that the emulsion can be coated evenly. A matte-surface paper may have only a single-coat baryta layer, a glossy paper may have from four to six coatings, which are polished (calendered) by high-pressure rollers before the emulsion layer is added.
3. Most importantly, the baryta layer produces an even, intense white to serve as a visual base for the image that will be formed. Often, fluorescing agents (whiteners or brighteners) are added to increase the visual brilliance of the layer.

Tinted or colored papers are produced by adding pigments to the baryta.

Barium sulfate is opaque to x-rays. It is commonly administered as a solution to patients so that the shape, size, and position of internal organs may be observed and recorded by radiography.

• *See also:* PAPERS, PHOTOGRAPHIC; RADIOGRAPHY.

Barnack, Oskar

(1879–1936)
German engineer and camera designer

Barnack joined the firm of Ernst Leitz, Wetzlar, Germany, in 1911 as a machinist and toolmaker. He is credited with being the inventor of the Leica camera, often erroneously claimed to be intended as a test camera for motion-picture photographers because it used the 35 mm motion-picture film. It has been definitely established that this is not the case; the Leica camera was intended as a still camera from the very beginning. Barnack's Leica prototype was built in 1914; the first commercial model appeared on the market in 1924.

Barn Doors

A lighting accessory consisting of two or four black, opaque, hinged flaps attached to the front of a spot- or floodlight. Flaps are folded inward to obstruct part of light beam, controlling shape and spread.

• *See also:* LIGHTING.

Barn doors may be necessary when only part of the subject is to be illuminated.

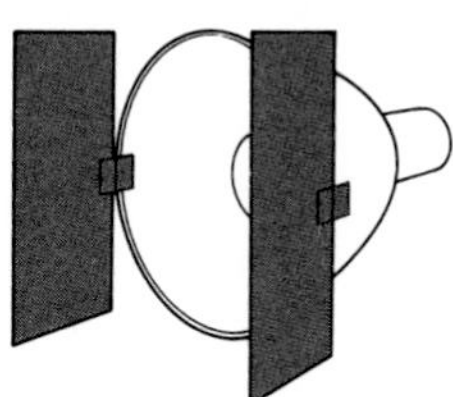

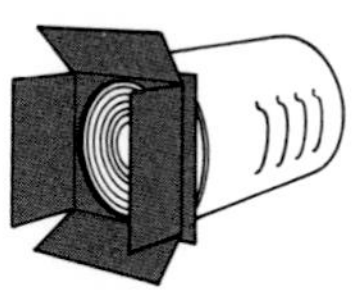

Barrel Distortion

Barrel distortion is a lens aberration in which the magnification of the image is less at the margins of the field than at the center. This causes the image of a square centered in the field to be misshapen, with its sides curved convexly. The image of the subject is smaller out in the field than it would be in a lens without distortion. Barrel distortion is due to excessive refraction of marginal rays, and mathematically, barrel distortion is considered positive, while pincushion distortion is considered negative.

• *See also:* ABERRATION; LENSES; OPTICS; PINCUSHION DISTORTION.

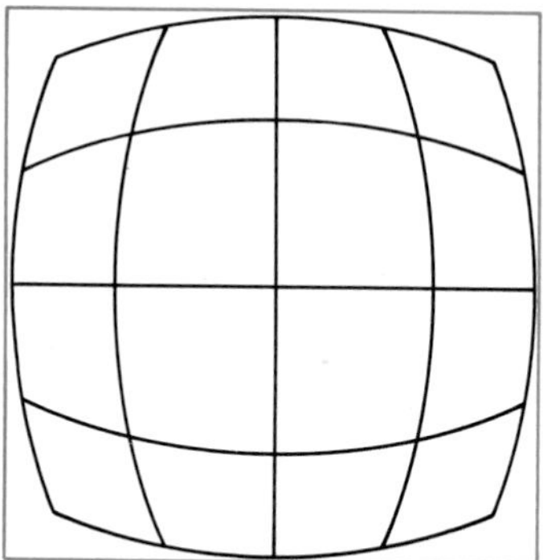

With barrel distortion, lines parallel to a picture edge appear to bend inward near the corners, crowding subject area on a reduced scale.

Base Density

Strictly, base density is the density or light-reducing power of the base material (plastic, glass) of a film or plate, without consideration of the emulsion. Often, however, base density is used to mean base-plus-fog (emulsion) density, also called "gross fog." It is usually meant to indicate the density after processing. While true base density is relatively constant for a given base, because it does not include the density of the emulsion, the base-plus-fog density is a variable dependent on development.

• *See also:* DENSITOMETRY; SENSITOMETRY.

Bas-Relief

Bas-relief is a special effect that gives a pseudo three-dimensional appearance similar to that of low-relief sculpture. It is created by printing from a negative and a positive image of the same subject sandwiched together slightly out of register.

To make a bas-relief, first contact-print a selected negative onto another film to obtain a positive transparency. Subjects with well-defined edges and backgrounds without excessive detail work best. Place the films *emulsion to emulsion* with the negative on top of the film to be exposed. Put a sheet of matte black paper under the films to prevent a fog-

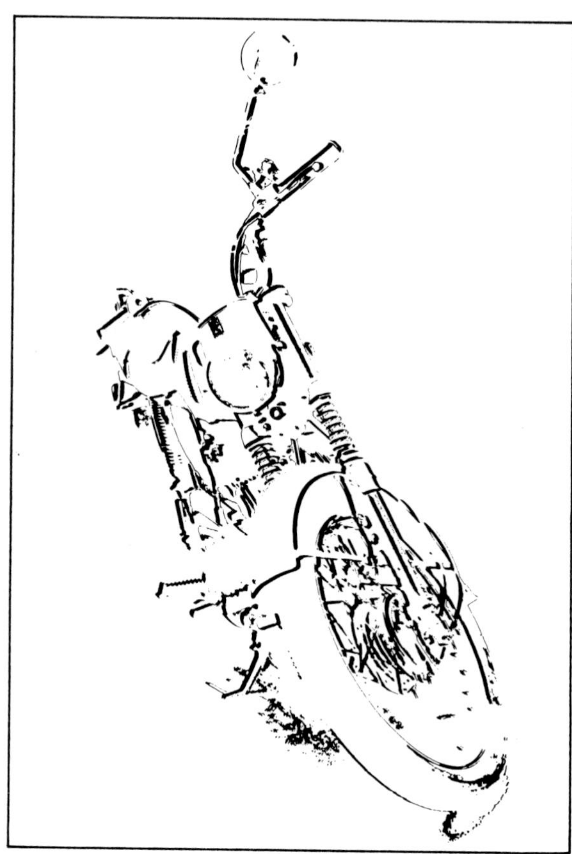

Combination bas-relief and line image with background eliminated using opaque on composite negative. Photo by Joanne B. Ruggles.

This bas-relief was made by contact-printing the transparency onto high-contrast film. The resulting negative was then sandwiched with the transparency and copied to produce this image. Photo by Mike Stringer.

ging exposure from reflected light. Press them firmly in contact with a sheet of glass. All film and glass surfaces must be free of dust. An orthochromatic or blue-sensitive film will allow you to work under a red safelight.

If you use an enlarger as a light source, mask off any light leaks, or improvise a hood between the lens and the easel to prevent fogging from stray light. Calculate trial exposures by taking an incident-light reading (or a reflected-light reading from a gray card) at the easel position. Bracket exposures in half-stop intervals for at least one stop more and less than the meter indication during the first test. Vary the exposure by changing the enlarger lens aperture or the timer-switch setting. Establish conditions and methods that can be duplicated easily in later printing sessions, so you will not have to calculate exposures every time you make a bas-relief.

Process the film normally; a full-range positive image, slightly lower in density and softer in contrast than the negative, will produce good results. If the positive image is denser and more contrasty than the negative, a negative-appearing bas-relief will result. When the positive is dry, tape one edge to a sheet of glass, then place the negative over it. Work over a light box or some surface illuminated from below. Of course, it is easier to observe the effect with medium- or large-format images than with those on 35 mm film. Move the negative image slightly out of register with the positive. The effect varies with the degree of displacement; it is emphasized by moving out of register in the direction of the shadows in the image. Tape the negative along one edge to hold it in the selected position, then place a second sheet of glass on top to press them together. Place this sandwich in the enlarger, or tape the films

(Left) A bas-relief slide. A high-contrast negative sandwiched with the original slide produced black highlights and a dark outline around the subject. (Below) This bas-relief was made from a slide and a high-contrast negative. A color internegative was then made to produce the resulting color print. Photos by Paul D. Yarrows.

to one another for contact-printing. Make a print in the normal manner.

The tonal effects in the print may be reversed by printing from an image created by contact-printing the negative-positive sandwich on another piece of film or by rephotographing it. To rephotograph the sandwich, place it on a light box, or evenly illuminate a white card 12 to 24 inches behind it. Use a mask around the films so that only light passing directly through them can reach the lens.

Bas-relief variations are possible using a very high contrast material such as Kodalith film for the positive image or for both images.

• *See also:* TONE-LINE PROCESS.

Further Reading: Editors of Time-Life Books. *The Print.* New York, NY: Time-Life Books, 1971; Langford, Michael J. *Advanced Photography, A Grammar of Techniques.* London, England; Focal Press, 1972.

Bayard, Hippolyte

(1801–1887)
French government clerk and inventor

Bayard independently invented a photographic process at the same time (1835–1841) as Daguerre and Talbot. He first discovered how to produce negative images on paper, like Talbot. But he went further to devise a way of producing direct positive images on paper during exposure in the camera.

His method was to prepare silver chloride paper (*See:* CALOTYPE.) and expose it to light until it darkened and dried to a deep brown-black. The dark surface was then floated, dipped, or liberally swabbed with a solution of potassium iodide. The paper was drained and exposed in the camera while damp. (An alternate method, introduced about 1841 by Sir William Grove, was to dry the paper after treating it with potassium iodide, and to dampen it just before use with a solution of one part nitric acid in 2½ parts water.)

The action of light liberates iodine, which combines with the blackened silver chloride, bleaching it. The bleaching is in proportion to the strength of the light, thus producing the middle and light tones of the image. Exposure may take from 10 to 40 minutes or longer, depending on the light, the subject, and the speed of the lens. The image is fixed in a standard hypo solution, washed, and dried.

It may be possible to achieve similar results by using modern gelatin-emulsion contact paper rather than preparing chloride paper.

Bayard's process could not compete with the beauty of the daguerreotype or the versatility of the negative-positive calotype process. He also produced positive images on paper by developing them in mercury fumes, in a method similar to the daguerreotype. Although he received little recognition, Bayard was a founding member of the French Photographic Society, and left more than 600 photographs variously produced by his own methods, the daguerreotype, and the albumen and collodion glass-negative processes.

• *See also:* ALBUMEN; CALOTYPE; COLLODION; DAGUERREOTYPE.

BCPS (Beam Candlepower-Second)

BCPS is the unit of measurement of the maximum intensity, taken on the axis of the beam, of a light source in a reflector. It is commonly used to express the output of self-contained electronic flash units. The ECPS (effective candlepower-second) is essentially the same but is computed by averaging values taken over a specified beam angle. Because BCPS/ECPS ratings apply to flashtube-reflector combinations, they are more useful in calculating exposures than watt-second (joule) ratings, which deal with the output of a tube alone.

• *See also:* ECPS; ELECTRONIC FLASH.

Beam Splitter

A beam splitter is a device for dividing a beam of light into two or more individual beams, usually without disturbing the image-forming properties of the beam. (By contrast, devices that create diffraction or dispersion break a beam into separate wavelengths, thereby destroying their image-forming arrangement.)

A beam splitter may be a wedge with two reflecting faces, or a partial-transmission device, such as a half-silvered mirror that reflects part of the beam while allowing the remainder to pass through.

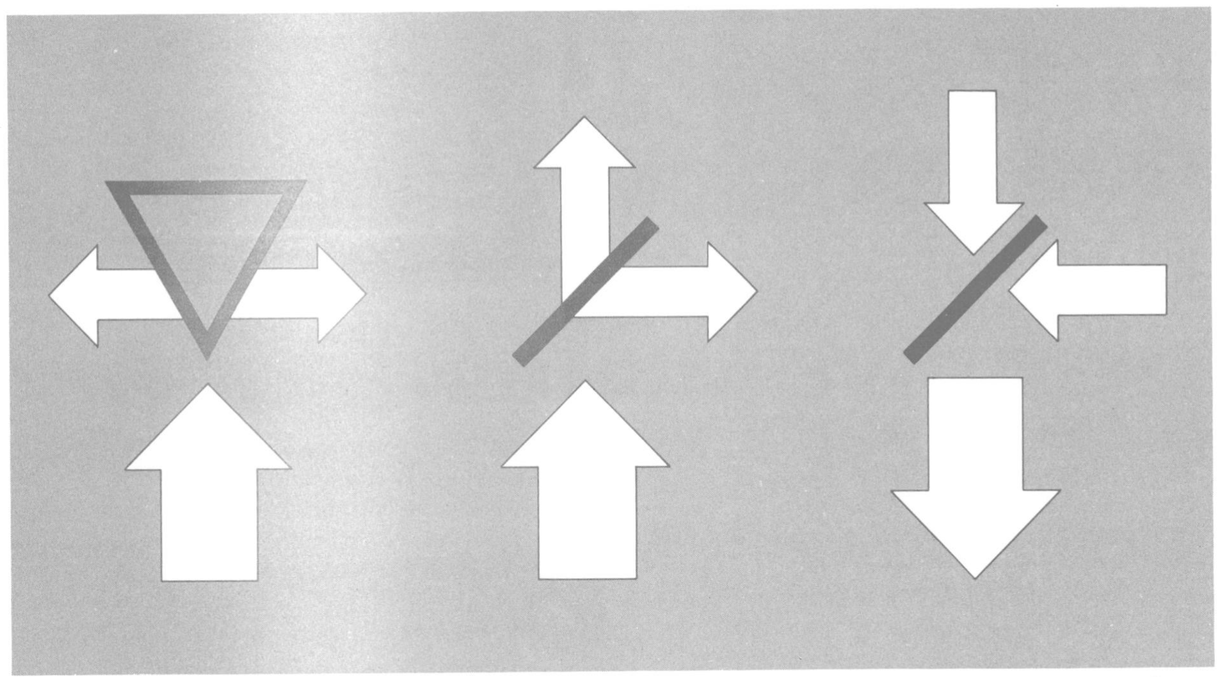

A beam splitter divides a light beam into two or more separate beams, usually without changing the beam's image-forming qualities. (Left) A reflection wedge has two faces that reflect the beam of light in two opposite directions. (Center) This type of partial-transmission beam splitter —a half-silvered mirror is of this type—reflects part of a single beam and allows the remainder of the beam to pass through. (Right) This partial-transmission device—again a half-silvered mirror is of this type—is used in reverse to combine light beams.

Beam splitters are used to project an image directly along the camera lens axis (*See:* FRONT PROJECTION.) or to direct illumination along the lens axis. They are used to divide coherent energy into reference and illuminating beams in making holograms. (*See:* HOLOGRAPHY.) Beam splitters are also used directly or in reverse (that is, to combine, rather than divide, beams) in stereoscopic cameras and projectors, and in rangefinders and some reflex viewing/focusing systems.

An early use was in one-shot color cameras, where the lens image was divided into its red, green, and blue components by beam splitters and filters. The package printers used by school finishers to make multiple, different-size prints from one negative in one exposure utilize multiple beam splitters.

• *See also:* DIFFRACTION GRATING; FRONT PROJECTION; HOLOGRAPHY; PRISMS; RANGEFINDER.

Becquerel, Edmond

(1820–1891)
French physicist

Becquerel carried out many investigations in photography, photoelectric phenomena, and radioactivity. Rays emitted by radioactive substances are known as *Becquerel rays.* In 1840, he showed that an underexposed daguerreotype plate could be intensified by supplementary exposure to red light prior to development. From this is generalized the *Becquerel effect:* A latent image is intensified by exposure to light of a color to which the emulsion is not otherwise sensitive. He noted the visible effect light produced on silver chloride—the foundation of subsequent printing-out papers—about 1847.

Belitzski's Reducer

Belitzski's reducer is a solution of ferric chloride and potassium citrate or oxalate in an acid fixing bath. It removes density from a negative subtractively or with a so-called cutting action; equal densities of silver are removed in all image portions. The effect is to decrease density without affecting contrast.

• *See also:* REDUCTION.

Bellows

A bellows is a flexible, lighttight device of variable length normally used between the lens board and camera back in folding and view cameras, and enlargers. The bellows material is usually folded in accordionlike pleats but may be a kind of soft bag to permit maximum compression (minimum lens-to-film distance) with very short focal-length lenses. It permits changing lens-to-film distance to focus the image sharply. Rigid-body cameras with interchangeable lenses may be fitted with an accessory bellows to accommodate lenses with greater-than-normal back focus or extreme focal length, or to use lenses at the increased distances required to obtain large magnification images in close-up work and photomacrography.

It is important that the interior surface of a bellows be a matte black to minimize internal reflections that lower image contrast. Camera bellows are commonly labeled single, double, or triple extension when their maximum extension is equal to the focal length of a normal lens, or twice or three times the length.

• *See also:* CAMERAS; VIEW CAMERA.

Bellows Extension

In a bellows-equipped camera, the total lens-to-film distance for a given image is sometimes called the bellows extension. (Today, we are swinging toward calling it lens extension because of the other ways it is achieved.) In a camera with an accessory bellows, the extension is the adjusted length of the bellows itself (that is, the distance from the lens to the face of the camera body); the total lens-to-film distance is equal to that extension plus the focal length of the lens in use.

In a bellows-type camera, the available extension affects the choice of a lens. It must be equal to the lens focal length to permit focusing objects at infinity; it must extend more than that to permit

To use this accessory bellows, a camera would be attached to the left end and a lens to the right end. Total lens-to-film distance or bellows extension equals the adjusted length of the bellows plus the focal length of the lens in use. An accessory bellows of this sort is used for extreme close-up photography with rigid-body cameras.

This section of Washington's face on a one-dollar bill was photographed using a bellows at 3:1 magnification. Photo was then enlarged to the size shown here. Photo by Karl Rehm.

focusing objects at closer distances and thus to obtain larger images. This, however, does not apply in folding cameras, where the bellows is single-extension and the lens is front-crown focusing or focuses on a thread. For life-size (1:1) images, bellows extension must be twice the focal length. To determine the total extension required for any image:

$$\text{Total extension} = \text{Focal length} \times (\text{Magnification} + 1)$$

where

Magnification = Image size ÷ Object size

For example, to get a 10 cm (4-inch) image of a 30 cm (12-inch) subject, using a 15 cm (150 mm, or 6-inch) lens, the total extension, or lens-to-film distance, is:

$$15 \times [(10 \div 30) + 1] = 15 \times 1.3 = 19.9 = 20$$

More simply, the additional extension required *beyond the infinity focus position* is equal to Focal length × Magnification.

As a bellows is extended beyond the infinity focus position, the effective value of a marked *f*-stop grows smaller. The effect is significant and begins to require some exposure compensation when the total extension (lens-to-film distance) becomes greater than about 1.3 times the focal length. To find the true, or effective, *f*-number: Effective *f*-number = (Total extension × marked *f*-number) ÷ Focal length. Thus the effective value of *f*/4 with a 15 cm lens used at 30 cm extension is:

$$(30 \times 4 = 120) \div 15 = f/8$$

Since the true value of *f*/4 is two stops smaller, you must open the lens two stops from *f*/4, that is, to *f*/2, in order to obtain an aperture that has a true value of *f*/4. You can check that by substituting *f*/2 for *f*/4:

$$(30 \times 2 = 60) \div 15 = f/4$$

• *See also:* BELLOWS; CLOSE-UP PHOTOGRAPHY; VIEW CAMERA.

Benzene

Benzol; cyclohexatriene

A solvent for oils, fats, waxes, resins, and rubber. It is used as a basis for certain varnishes, retouching fluids, and lacquers.
Formula: C_6H_6
Molecular Weight: 78.05

Benzene is a clear, colorless, and volatile liquid with a characteristic aromatic odor. It dissolves in water to about one part of benzene in 14.3 parts of water; it mixes with alcohol, chloroform, ether, carbon disulfide, carbon tetrachloride, *glacial* acetic acid, acetone, and oils.

CAUTION: Benzol is highly flammable and must not be handled in an area where open flames are in use. Both the liquid and its vapor are toxic; prolonged inhalation of benzene vapor causes anemia and, eventually, respiratory failure.

Benzotriazole

Kodak anti-fog no. 1, Azidobenzene phenylazide

A very powerful restrainer for developers (acting as a density depressant as does potassium bromide), and also an antifoggant for old and stale materials.

Formula: $C_6H_5N_3$

Molecular Weight: 119

Colorless crystals, white powder, or small tablets (Kodak). Benzotriazole is used in prebaths, such as prehardeners, to prevent the formation of fog in subsequent stages. It is also used in the developer bath, in very low concentrations, to suppress fog, and, in the case of paper developers, to improve the tone of the blacks. With developing solutions that utilize phenidone, benzotriazole is often necessary as the antifoggant; potassium bromide is included in such formulas mainly to stabilize the developer against the buildup of bromides from the material being processed.

• *See also:* ANTIFOGGANT; 6-NITROBENZIMIDAZOLE NITRATE.

Berthon, Rodolphe

(Dates unknown)
French optician, astronomer, and engineer

Berthon devised the lenticular-screen film, patented by Keller-Dorian in 1908 and used as a basis for a commercial color movie film called Kodacolor, which was marketed by Eastman Kodak Company about 1928. The process was also marketed by Agfa about 1931 and tried for commercial and theatrical film around 1936. At one time, it was suggested as a medium for color television news photography but was not widely used.

Lenticular films produced their effect by the additive synthesis of color. They had a brief life before being supplanted by modern films that contain dyes in the emulsion and produce color by subtractive synthesis. The system has been revived in self-processing "instant" movie films for amateur use.

• *See also:* COLOR FILMS; COLOR THEORY.

Bichromate

The chromium salts of potassium, ammonium, or sodium are called bichromates (or dichromates). When mixed with an organic colloid, such as gelatin, gum arabic, or albumen, they cause it to harden upon exposure to light. Unexposed portions are not affected and may be washed away in hot water or treated with inks or powdered pigments. These effects form the basis of a number of transfer and pigment processes, including gum bichromate, carbon printing, carbro, bromoil, etched glass, and dye transfer. Bichromated colloids are also used in various photomechanical processes.

NOTE: Bichromate-acid bleaches form free silver ions in solution, which is one of the few constituents of photographic effluents that can be hazardous to human health if taken internally. If such bleaches are used regularly, the free silver ions should be precipitated by the addition of sodium chloride (rock salt) to the effluent, and the effluent should be diluted with water as it enters a sewer system.

• *See also:* entries by individual processes.

Bimat Process

The Kodak Bimat transfer process is a method for rapidly developing and fixing a negative film and simultaneously obtaining a positive copy of the image in the form of a transparency. Two films are used: a negative film and Kodak Bimat transfer film. The transfer film, which is not light-sensitive, but which contains many small particles that serve as nucleating agents, is dampened before use with processing chemicals. After the negative film has been exposed in a camera, it is laminated or pressed emulsion-to-emulsion against the damp transfer film. The chemicals diffuse into the negative to develop and fix the exposed image. At the same time, the unexposed silver diffuses into the transfer film emulsion to form a positive transparency image around the nucleating agents. The process typically takes one to two minutes. Special equipment is required to laminate the films face-to-face for processing. A major use of the Bimat transfer process has been to provide images for immediate inspection in continuous-operation aerial and space photography, and in cathode-ray tube monitoring systems.

• *See also:* DIFFUSION TRANSFER PROCESS.

Binoculars, Taking Pictures Through

A pair of binoculars (or a monocular) can be used in combination with a normal camera lens to achieve telephoto effects. You can photograph the magnified image formed by binoculars and obtain pictures similar to those taken through a telephoto lens.

(Left) A television tower in Stuttgart, Germany, photographed through a 50 mm camera lens. (Above) The same tower photographed from the same point using an 8 × 30 monocular which effectively transforms a 50 mm lens into a 400 mm telephoto lens with an aperture of approximately f/14.

(Top) Photo taken with a 58 mm camera lens. The same scene, photographed from the same position, using a variable focal length monocular mounted directly on the camera body: (center) 350 mm at f/8; (bottom) 650 mm at f/16. Photos by J. D. Cooper.

The optical definition (sharpness, contrast, and distortion) of the image is determined not only by the camera lens, but by the binoculars as well. Because the field of view of most binoculars is smaller than the field of view of most normal camera lenses, the image may be circular with a dark surround and a loss of definition at the edges. Some wide-angle or wide-field binoculars may fill the camera field entirely, thereby overcoming this situation.

Procedures and Equipment

To take pictures, line up the binoculars so that one eyepiece is centered on the camera lens. Place the eyepiece close to the lens but not quite touching it. Allow space for eyepiece movement in focusing. The best way to do this is to use an adapter mount, which will hold both the camera and the binoculars in place and provide a lighttight guard between the two units. Since most binocular-plus-camera combinations achieve effective focal lengths of 300 mm or longer, it is essential to provide firm support for the system, otherwise the slightest camera movement will result in blurred pictures. Some binocular and photo dealers have adapter couplings and tripod mounts especially designed for this kind of photography. Edmund Scientific Company also offers a variety of suitable accessories.

Single-Lens Reflex Cameras. The most practical type of camera for taking pictures through binoculars is the single-lens reflex. The through-the-lens viewing makes it easy to align the camera lens with the eyepiece of the binoculars and to focus. Center the circular image in the viewfinder; then set the distance scale on the camera lens at *its closest distance* and adjust the focus with the binoculars. When the image looks sharp in the camera viewfinder, it will be sharp on the film.

Non-Reflex Cameras. Focusing is more difficult with a non-reflex camera. The rangefinder and viewfinder in this type of camera will not work properly with binoculars. Therefore, you will need to use

These photographs were made at a distance of 20 feet with a single-lens reflex camera coupled to a monocular having a variable focal length of 300 mm–650 mm. Top photo was made with the 50 mm camera lens only. Center photo was made with the monocular at 500 mm focal length. Bottom photo was made with the monocular at 650 mm focal length. Note diminishing depth of field as focal length becomes greater.

both halves of the binoculars—one for taking the picture, the other for both viewing and focusing. It is not practical to use a monocular with a non-reflex camera.

Focusing. First, set the camera lens focusing scale at infinity. Then, adjust focus with the binoculars. For the individual-focusing type, look directly through the eyepiece of the viewing half and adjust it for sharpest focus, then use this same setting for the eyepiece of the taking half. For the center-focusing type, set the adjustable eyepiece at the zero position before adjusting focus with the center wheel. To focus binoculars for picture-taking, look through the non-taking half with one eye while looking at the distant subject directly with your other eye. Adjusting focus in this way helps accommodate your eyes for distance and improves the accuracy of focusing. This is a difficult technique, and you will need some experience to master it. You will probably have to take a series of pictures with a slight change in the eyepiece focus in each picture. The marks on the eyepiece mount will help you calibrate a focusing scale for future use.

Binocular Specifications

The specifications for a pair of binoculars provide two essential pieces of information: the magnifiation power, and the diameter of the objective, or front lens. For example, each half of a 6 × 30 binoculars (or monocular) has a magnifying power of 6× and an objective diameter of 30 mm. A pair of 7 × 50 binoculars each has a 7× power and a 50 mm lens diameter. The power is used to calculate the effective focal length of a camera-lens-binocular combination; the objective diameter is used to calculate the effective *f*-number of the combination.

Determining Effective Focal Length. To determine effective focal length, multiply the focal length of the camera lens by the binocular power. A 6× binocular with a 50 mm lens produces an effective focal length of 300 mm. An 80 mm lens and

7× binocular system has an effective focal length of 560 mm. The power also indicates how many times bigger the image will be using the combination than using only the camera lens. A distant tree will be seven times bigger in an 80 mm plus 7× system than the image produced by the 80 mm lens alone.

Determining Effective *f*-number. The effective *f*-number of a camera-binocular system is determined by the binoculars. Set the camera lens at its largest aperture and adjust exposure by changing the shutter speed. To select the shutter speed that will produce correct exposure, you must know the *f*-number of the system. To find it, multiply the camera lens focal length (in millimetres) by the binocular power; then divide this number by the binocular objective lens diameter (in millimetres):

$$\frac{\text{Camera lens focal length (mm)} \times \text{Binocular power}}{\text{Binocular object lens diameter (mm)}} = f\text{-number}$$

For example, using 6 × 30 binoculars in combination with a 50 mm camera lens:

$$\frac{50 \times 6}{30} = f/10$$

If the effective lens opening of the camera-binocular combination is fairly small (say, *f*/8 or smaller), use a moderately fast or fast film (ASA 125 or faster for black-and-white, ASA 64 or faster for color). This will permit using a high shutter speed, such as 1/250 sec., which will help minimize the effects of camera movement. Using a cable release will eliminate any movement that might be created by pressing a shutter-release button. If the mirror of a single-lens reflex camera can be manually locked in the "up" position before the exposure, this will eliminate another source of vibration.

Exposure Control

Photography with binoculars is not recommended with automatic cameras that do not offer manual control of exposure settings. The electric-eye exposure control in most cameras will not take into consideration the effective lens opening imposed by the binoculars. In any case, bracket exposures by photographing at one speed faster and one speed slower than the chosen shutter speed to get the best results.

• *See also:* TELEPHOTOGRAPHY; TELESCOPES, PHOTOGRAPHING THROUGH.

Further Reading: Cooper, Joseph D. *Photography Through Monoculars, Binoculars and Telescopes,* 3rd ed. Garden City, NY: Amphoto, 1965. Paul, Henry E. *Telescopes for Skygazing.* Garden City, NY: Amphoto, 1976.

Biomedical Photography

Photography of living organisms is undertaken to record and study their birth, growth, life processes, diseases, response to treatment, and causes of death. The pictures may be used for scientific research and

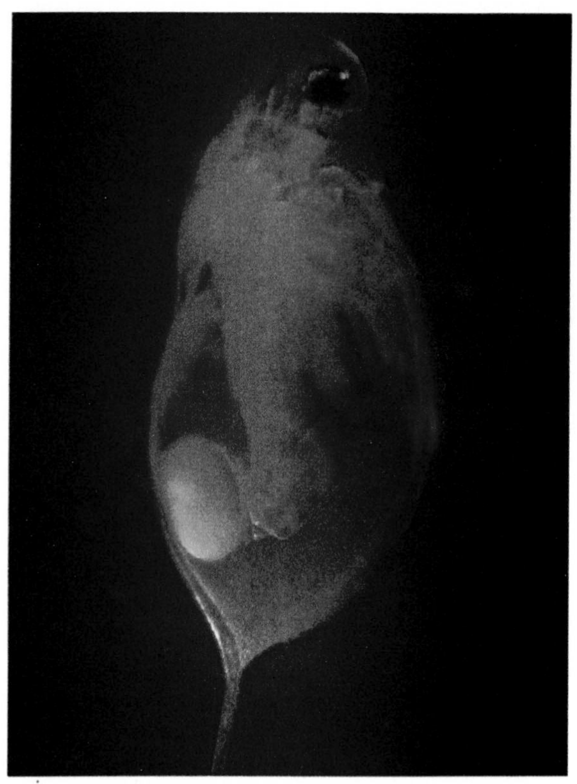

One of the aspects of biomedical photography is photomicrography, photography of microscopic specimens. This water flea, magnified 60 times, was photographed using differential color illumination. Photo © John Delly, 1976.

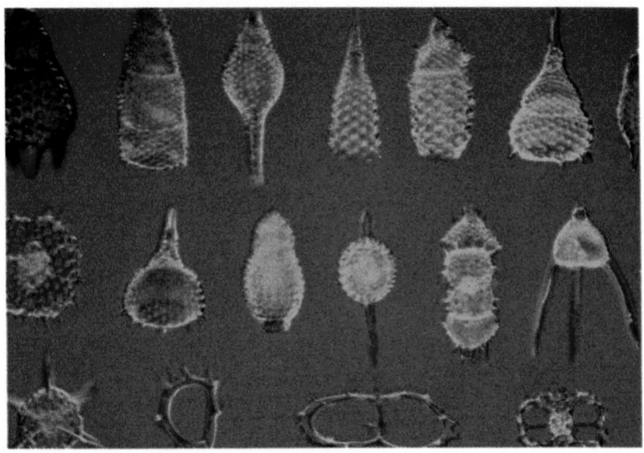

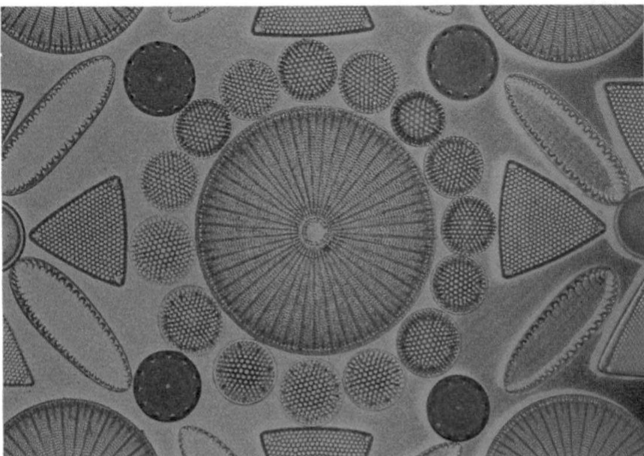

Arrangements of microscopic fauna and flora photographed using differential color illumination. Top photo shows shells of a type of protozoa called radiolaria. Lower photo shows diatoms (microscopic plants). Both specimens are magnified 70 times. Photos © John Delly, 1976.

analysis, or for diagnosis and prognosis of a particular condition. Such biomedical photography may require only a simple camera and flash unit, or it may involve complex scientific equipment and highly specialized materials and techniques. Its subjects range from microscopic forms of life to all animal forms and human beings. It is usually carried out by someone who is primarily a specialist in a particular area—a dentist, an endocrinologist, a veterinarian, or a research scientist, for example—or by a photographer with specialized biological or medical training. The techniques of biomedical photography are covered in a variety of separate articles.

• *See also:* CLINICAL PHOTOGRAPHY; DENTAL PHOTOGRAPHY; ELECTRON MICROGRAPHS; MEDICAL PHOTOGRAPHY; PHOTOMACROGRAPHY; PHOTOMICROGRAPHY; RADIOGRAPHY; STEREO PHOTOGRAPHY; THERMAL PHOTOGRAPHY; ULTRAVIOLET AND FLUORESCENCE PHOTOGRAPHY.

Birds, Photography of

Birds are fascinating creatures of amazing variety. There are thousands of species scattered in almost every area of the world, from tiny hummingbirds with a wingbeat faster than the eye can follow, to flightless creatures, such as the ostrich and penguin. But exotic varieties are not essential for bird photography; you can easily take beautiful pictures of birds by erecting a feeding station or birdhouse within view of one of your windows. Or you can go to a park, botanical garden, or similar habitat in an urban area.

Of course, you can get even more striking, and more valuable, pictures by photographing birds in the field, in their natural ranges. Such pictures are more satisfying too because they represent the culmination of learning about the species that interest you, finding and tracing them, and finally capturing your quarry on film. There is more personal effort involved and a much greater sense of reward when you see your pictures.

Preparation

You must make an effort to know what you are photographing. Study a field guide that will help you identify common birds, and consult other basic bird books at any library. Seek out personal advice from members of a local chapter of the Audubon Society or conservation organizations such as the Sierra Club or Friends of the Earth. Bird-watching groups are in many areas; members of hunting clubs, and biology and science teachers, are knowledgeable.

Before you begin to photograph, study birds directly too. Watch them to see how they perch and move: some constantly hop from twig to twig, others take a perch to remain observing or singing for long periods of time. You can learn the poses, the pauses, the typical attitudes, and the visual details of birds

Nesting birds make fascinating subjects that are sometimes observable from high windows. Care must always be taken, of course, not to approach or disturb the nest in any way. High-speed color film is the preferred medium in bird photography to record swift, abrupt movements and the color differences that are often the only way of differentiating varieties of the same species.

that interest you by watching them through binoculars or a reflex camera equipped with a telephoto lens. The more information you have, the more observation you carry out, the more alert you will be to picture possibilities.

Cameras and Film

By far the most useful equipment for bird photography is a single-lens reflex camera equipped with a telephoto or a telephoto zoom lens, and fast color film. A 35 mm camera offers the greatest freedom of action because of its light weight and convenient size; a roll-film reflex is heavier and a bit slower to operate but has the advantage of a much larger picture area. Motorized film advances are available for cameras of either type; they are a great aid for in-flight or field-action photography, or for remote control setups. At close ranges, other kinds of equipment and shorter-focal-length lenses can be quite suitable, but getting close enough is often a problem.

In order to get a sufficiently large image of most birds from distances that do not disturb the subject, you will need a lens of 200 mm focal length or longer with a 35 mm camera, or at least 300 mm with a 120-size roll-film camera. Long lenses immediately pose problems of picture sharpness inasmuch as they magnify the effects of any camera vibration or movement at the instant the picture was taken. So you must have a camera support—a tripod, a chest or waist support, a monopod, a gunstock mount, or something similar. An independent mirror release or lockup on the camera and a cable release also will do a great deal to reduce vibration effects.

High-speed film permits fast shutter speeds for capturing movement; even perched, many birds have swift, abrupt head and body motions. And fast shutter speeds minimize vibration. Fast films also permit you to use somewhat smaller lens apertures for increased depth of field. Color film is almost universally preferred for bird photography today. In natural light, it provides greater clarity of subject and surroundings than black-and-white, and it records essential color differences that often are the only way of distinguishing varieties of the same species.

Camera Techniques at Home

If you are shooting from your home, choose a window that looks out on an area where birds can congregate naturally and easily; that is, a place without constant movement or loud noises. A children's

In order to get sufficiently large images of most birds from distances that will not disturb them, long-focal-length lenses are essential. This rough-legged hawk was photographed in Ruby Valley, Nevada, with a 200 mm lens. Photo by Michael Fairchild.

play yard is not a good spot. To attract your subjects, put up a feeding station, a bath, or even a birdhouse, but be sure it is away from fences or overhanging branches that would be convenient for cats. A pole-mounted feeder or house should have a guard to keep it free of squirrels and cats and should be located not too far from trees. Birds like to look the situation over at the feeder before making their approach. Find out what heights your birds prefer. Some like to bathe at ground level, others like a bath two or three feet in the air. Some will not feed in the open, others shy away from deep shade and often have similar feelings about the location of their houses or nests.

Put your camera as close to the window as possible to avoid shooting reflections, but make sure there is a curtain that will screen your movements, especially if a feeder is just a few feet away. An amazing series of bird pictures, and a movie, have been made with a three-sided birdhouse. The open,

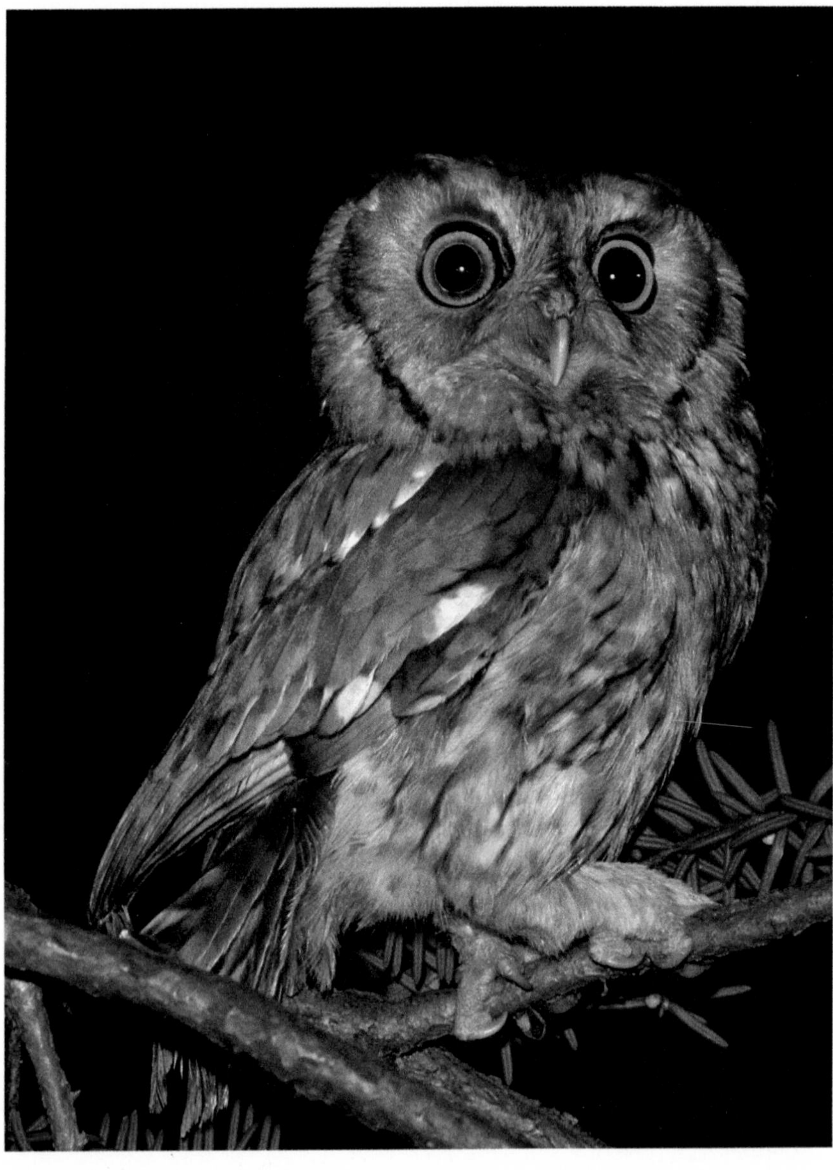

While natural light is generally preferable for photographing birds, it often becomes necessary to use artificial lighting either because of the location of the bird or because of its nocturnal habits. This screech owl was photographed using electronic flash. Photo by Michael Fairchild.

Blue jays generally live in highly populated areas and are not particularly shy birds. Because of this, they are not extremely difficult to photograph, providing the usual precautions are taken against disturbing them. Remember that the background of all bird pictures should be as natural as possible—grass, a tree, the sky—rather than cement or a building, unless, of course, man-made structures are part of the bird's habitat.

fourth side was pressed against a windowpane so the camera could look directly inside. The area around the camera was draped to form a dark tent for the photographer to work in unnoticed. The entrance for the birds, in the opposite side, was about the size of a half-dollar; it admitted ample light for exposures with high-speed film.

Wherever you set up the camera, be aware of the background that will be in the picture. It should be uncluttered and natural—grass, a hedge, or the sky—rather than cement, the side of a garage, or a similar evidence of man—unless, of course, the purpose of the pictures is to show some relationship of the birds to man, such as birds that have nested on a porch, or birds eating at a feeder.

Camera Techniques in the Field

In the field, you must first find the nesting, feeding, or habitual song locations of the birds that interest you. Follow and observe them, then choose your camera position. A hidden location is essential in nest areas; most species will not come near the

nest when unfamiliar things are in the neighborhood, and they may leave eggs unprotected or young unfed long enough so as to be fatal. The common method of hiding is to construct a blind—a temporary structure of natural materials, or a pipe or wooden framework covered with canvas in brown, green, or other colors that fit into the surroundings.

Using a Blind. Birds are visually acute; they notice changes in the environment, especially close to their homes. If you must work at very close range, it is a good idea to erect a blind at a distance of a few hundred metres and move it closer in stages, cutting the distance to the nest in half each time. That would get you from 200 to 12 metres (about 39 feet) from a nest in five days. If your work has serious intent, or your subject is unusual, that is not an unreasonable amount of time and effort to spend in getting ready. And it may be the only way to avoid frightening the bird into abandoning the nest.

The blind itself should be as small as possible, while providing working room inside. The covering must be tied down or pinned to an underlayer of chicken wire stretched between the supports so it will not billow and flap frighteningly with each breeze. Entrance is through a rear flap. Try to move the blind and enter it at a time when the birds are away from the nest. Even so, you are likely to be observed from afar. Many species, seeing something disappear into a blind near their nests, will not approach until they also see something reappear and go away; so you must trick them. Have a companion go to the blind with you, staying close together as you approach, and then leave after a few minutes. That may do it; however, often birds will have learned to distinguish between one and two, or a few. In that case, if two enter the blind, two must leave—your companion and a scarecrow or stuffed-clothing dummy being "walked" alongside—to deceive the bird that the area is clear.

A blind is essential in certain nest areas. (Top) Camera is positioned on tripod inside the blind and allowed to protrude through window cut in cloth. (Center) Blind is camouflaged with foliage appropriate to its surroundings. (Bottom) Photographer awaits an opportunity. Walkie-talkie is for communication with assistant. Photos by Keith Boas. (Right) Nesting American bittern "freezes" in attempt to blend with foliage, rather than leave eggs that are ready to hatch. Photo by Richard D. Robinson.

These photos were taken at a gyrfalcon's nest, 600 miles from the North Pole. They were taken from a sturdy plywood blind fitted with one-way glass windows and braced with wires.

For in-flight photos, a gunstock or another type of shoulder support is needed for a camera with a long-focal-length lens. Camera should be prefocused and panned along with subject; a fast shutter speed is necessary to stop action.

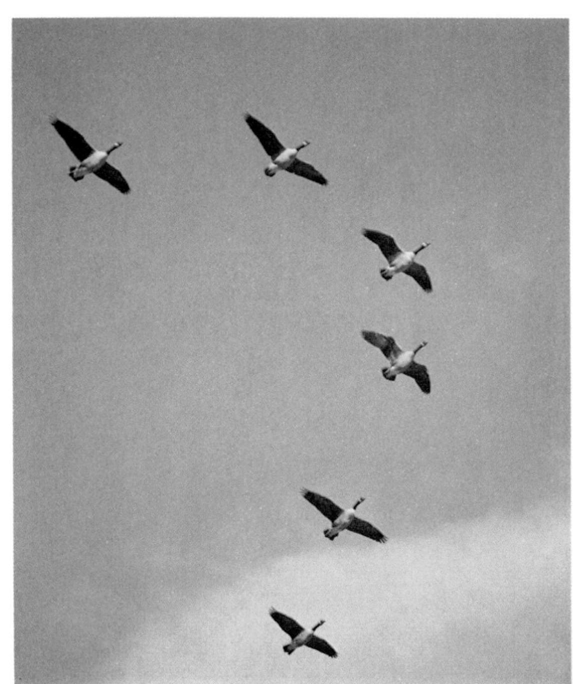

Camera Position. The camera lens should look out through a hole large enough to let you swing the camera to cover some area around the target site. At close range, slide a dull-covered card over the hole before reaching to change camera settings so that a flash of your movement won't alarm your subjects; birds are wary at their nests.

Camera Angle. Nest shots are most revealing when the camera looks down from a somewhat elevated angle. Such an angle is essential to show eggs and newly hatched fledglings, of course. It is easy to achieve with ground-nesting species, but in many cases, your blind will have to be on top of a sturdy A-ladder, or a temporary tower, or up among neighboring limbs.

Conveniences. Inside the blind, you will want a seat (a folding camp stool is convenient), food and drink, warm clothing (or insect repellent, depending on the season), and perhaps a radio with an earplug for very long sessions. Be sure there are temporary pegs or shelves so you can keep equipment off the ground.

Remote-Control Setups. You can get close-up pictures without being close yourself if you can install a camera for remote-control operation. Although it is possible to arrange devices that will trip the shutter when the bird lands on a certain spot or pecks at some planted food, such a setup is usually limited to just one exposure. There is much more flexibility available with an electrically or radio-activated shutter accessory that allows you to make repeated exposures; the camera must also be equipped with a motor wind to advance the film and cock the shutter each time. You can then observe from a good distance, using binoculars, and take a picture whenever you think the moment is good; it takes some experience, but the results can be excellent. A major consideration is to select equipment that does not whir and click too noisily during operation.

Dealing with the Environment. To get a clear view of nest areas, you may have to do some clearing and pruning. It is essential to keep any changes to the environment to a minimum, not only to avoid making the surroundings look unnatural, but so as not to destroy the concealment and protection that the bird has found for its home. Often, you can tie troublesome twigs or branches out of the way and release them as soon as you are finished shooting each time. Above all, *do not touch a nest, eggs, or fledglings;* you may cause them to be abandoned by the adult birds, with tragic results.

Field Action

For in-flight and other action pictures, a gunstock or other shoulder support for a camera equipped with a very long focal-length lens is essential. You must be able to follow movement continuously while providing firm support for the camera. But first you must have knowledge of where your birds range and how they move.

Lighting

For the most part, you will use natural daylight. But nests are often in shaded areas where the light is too dim for convenient shutter speeds with long-focal-length lenses. Electronic flash units are

This osprey approaching its nest was photographed from a location considerably below this peak with a 300 mm lens. Photo by Michael Fairchild.

an excellent solution. You may be able to get close enough to use a camera-mounted unit, but often it will be necessary to set up remote units closer to the subject area ahead of time. The brief flash of light does not seem to disturb most species of birds, but an excessive whine or squeal during recycling may cause trouble. (A big advantage of electronic flash units is that their extremely short flash duration lets you stop birds in flight.)

You will get better pictures by using two units positioned to act as a main and a fill light than by using a single unit, and you will be able to reduce the problems of flat, head-on lighting, especially a lack of dimension or roundness. You may be able to have a long synch cord running directly to the camera, or you can terminate it in an electric-eye trigger switch. That will give you more freedom of movement. The switch is activated by a flash unit on the camera, even though it is too far from the scene to add to the exposure.

Natural light is easiest to use early or late in the day when the sun is at a low angle so it reaches horizontally in among branches or illuminates the underside of birds in flight. At other times, you will essentially be shooting backlighted silhouettes, particularly when aiming upward at your subject. Make exposure readings from a substitute target—your hand, a tree limb, or a dense cluster of leaves; you will seldom have time to measure and set exposure from the subject itself.

Above all, keep at it. There is so much movement and so many variables in the situation that you will have to shoot a great number of pictures to get a few that are outstanding. But the truly good pictures will be well worth all your time and effort.

• *See also:* NATURE PHOTOGRAPHY; TELEPHOTOGRAPHY; ZOO PHOTOGRAPHY.

Further Reading: Hodgson, David. *All About Photographing Animals and Birds.* Levittown, NY: Transatlantic Arts, Inc., 1975; Hosking, Eric and Frank W. Lane. *An Eye for a Bird: The Autobiography of a Bird Photographer.* New York, NY: Paul S. Eriksson, Inc., 1974; Marchington, John and Anthony Clay. *An Introduction to Bird and Wildlife Photography in Still and in Movie.* Levittown, NY: Transatlantic Arts, Inc., 1974; Warham, John. *Technique of Bird Photography,* 3rd ed. Garden City, NY: Amphoto, 1974.

Black-and-White Films

Black-and-white films record subject values primarily in terms of brightness rather than color, so the final positive image is composed only of black, white, and intermediate shades of gray. Most films are intended to record a negative image in which the tonal or brightness relationships are reversed from those of the subject; they are restored to their normal relationships when a positive image is made by printing from the negative. Some films are intended to be processed directly to a black-and-white positive image, and some thin-emulsion negative films may also be processed to produce a positive. All films can be processed to produce a negative image.

This article discusses the characteristics of black-and-white negative films, including how their response is evaluated, and the factors in choosing a film suitable for various photographic purposes. Films that produce color-image records are discussed in a separate article. (*See:* COLOR FILMS.) The structure of films, their manufacture and common basic characteristics, and the considerations in handling and storing films are also covered in separate articles. (*See:* FILMS AND PLATES; STORAGE OF SENSITIZED MATERIALS AND PROCESSING SOLUTIONS.) Many of the topics touched on in this article are discussed in greater detail under separate entries; see the list of cross-references at the end of this article.

Spectral Sensitivity

Spectral sensitivity means *color sensitivity.* Most commonly used films are *panchromatic* films —films that are sensitive to all colors of light.

In the accompanying illustration, the various wavelengths of light are diagramed. Energy whose wavelengths are just shorter than 400 nanometres is called ultraviolet radiation; man cannot see by this type of energy—it is not called light—but nearly all films are sensitive to ultraviolet radiation. A camera lens glass absorbs ultraviolet radiation whose wavelengths are shorter than about 350 nanometres, so that even though films may be sensitive to radiation with these shorter wavelengths, you cannot take pictures with regular lenses. In addition, most panchromatic films are sensitive to blue, green, yellow, orange, and red light.

Gray-Tone Rendering of Colored Objects. While the term *panchromatic* applied to a film means that it is sensitive to all colors of light, it does not mean that such a film is *equally* sensitive to all colors. A photograph made of the spectrum would show a light tone in the near ultraviolet region,

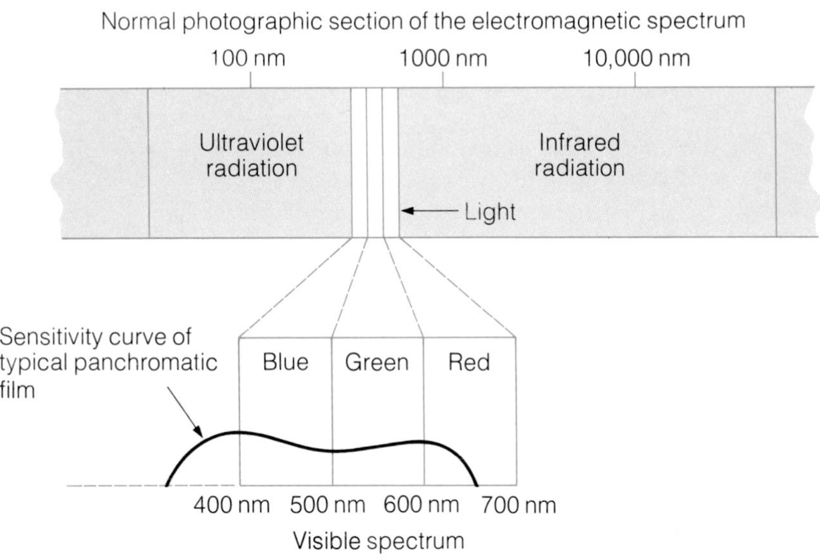

Not all energy wavelengths may be called light. Although energy with wavelengths shorter than 400 nanometres is not light, and cannot be seen by the eye, most films are sensitive to this energy. The curve in this diagram shows the energy sensitivity of a typical panchromatic film.

where the human eye sees darkness, and lighter tones in the blue region of the spectrum than in the green, yellow, orange, and red regions. This is because the film is less sensitive to these other colors than it is to ultraviolet radiation and to blue light.

To obtain a gray-tone rendering of colors that approximates their visual brightnesses, a Kodak Wratten filter No. 8 should be used in daylight with panchromatic film, while a No. 11 filter should be used for the same purpose with artificial light.

Color Sensitivity Classes. Black-and-white films are generally divided into four color sensitivity classes:

Blue-Sensitive, or Ordinary. Films in this class are sensitive only to ultraviolet radiation and blue light. Although in the past, blue-sensitive films with normal contrast were available, the only films with this sensitization now available are higher-than-normal contrast films usually used for copying or black-and-white transparency work. A big advantage of blue-sensitive films is that they can be handled and processed in the darkroom with a safelight.

Orthochromatic. This class of films is sensitive to ultraviolet radiation, and blue *and green* light. Ortho films can also be processed with safelights (usually red in color). Some copy films are ortho in sensitization. There is one Kodak normal-contrast ortho film, Kodak Tri-X ortho film, which is quite popular for portraits of men. (The darker, gray-tone rendering of reds is thought to add a more masculine look.) Used with a yellow filter (No. 8) outdoors, the results are similar to those on pan film when a green or a yellow-green filter is used. This effect includes lightened foliage, with added detail and darkened sky.

Panchromatic. Since panchromatic films are sensitive to all colors of light as well as to ultraviolet radiation, they are used more extensively in professional photography than any other kind of black-and-white negative material. In addition to their ability to give gray-tone renderings of subject colors approximating their visual brightnesses, and to give a variety of gray-tone renderings by the use of filters, panchromatic films are available in the widest range of speeds, resolving powers, graininess levels, and enlargeability ratings.

Infrared. Like other silver halide films, infrared films are sensitive to ultraviolet radiation and blue light of some wavelengths. Unlike panchromatic film, however, infrared is not sensitive to green light but is sensitive to the longest wavelengths of red light and to the near-invisible wavelengths of infrared radiation. It is usually exposed through a deep yellow or red filter that absorbs the ultraviolet radiation and blue light, and it records only the infrared image.

While infrared films are used primarily in technical fields (scientific, aerial, medical, photomicrography, and the like), they have two important uses for the pictorial photographer. When they are used with a red filter, the effects of haze are lessened, and distant objects are recorded with greater clarity. Further, since plant foliage reflects large percentages of the incident infrared radiation, foliage photographs as a very light gray or white, which gives an unusual effect. This is especially true against the black sky rendered by infrared film when the sky is blue.

When relatively large filter factors result in exposure times greater than about one-half second, correction should be made for the reciprocity effect.

Blue-Sensitive Films

Spectrogram to Tungsten Light

Orthochromatic-Sensitive Films

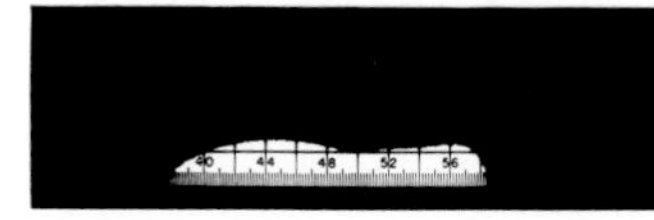

Spectrogram to Tungsten Light

Panchromatic-Sensitive Films

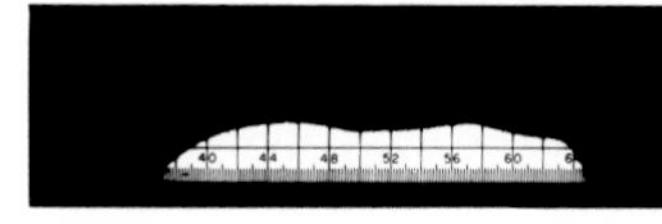

Spectrogram to Daylight

Infrared-Sensitive Film

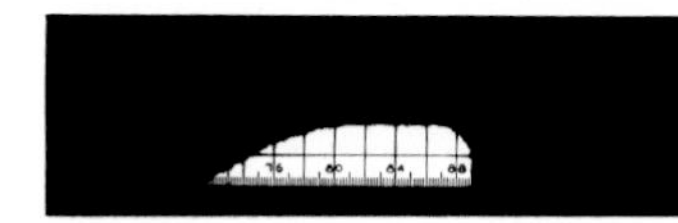

Spectrogram to Tungsten Light

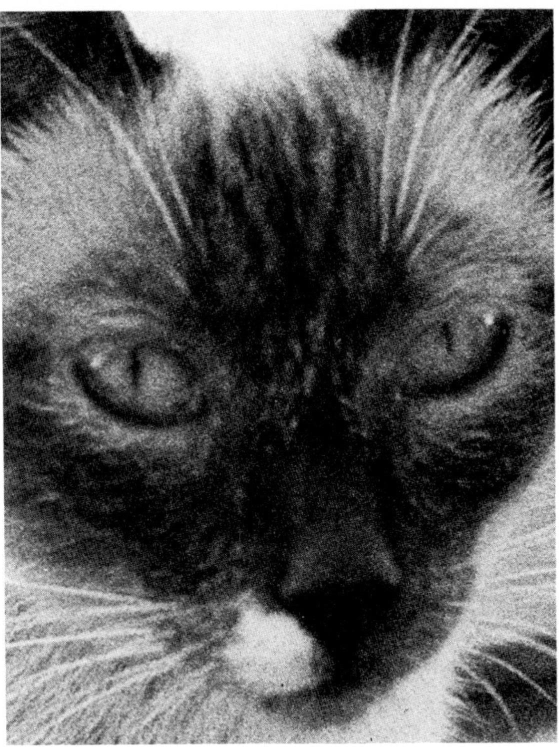

Too much graininess in a film may affect photographic quality. Sharp definition of the Siamese cat's markings (left) is greatly diminished in enlargement (above) because of film's excessive granularity. Photos by Karl Rehm.

Spectrograms

The spectrograms on the opposite page show color sensitivity of the types of films discussed here. The number scale represents the color of light or the wavelengths (multiply the scale number by ten to get the wavelength in nanometres). The height of the graphical image at any point indicates the film's relative sensitivity to that particular wavelength of light but does not indicate film speed.

Image Structure Characteristics

If all negatives were contact-printed, negative images would appear as perfectly smooth in texture and absolutely sharp in definition. Nearly all negatives get enlarged, however, and when a photographic image is enlarged enough, it becomes apparent that there is a random pattern in the images of uniform areas caused by the negative emulsion structure, and that all edges and detail are not perfectly sharp, even in the plane of best focus. These limitations are due to the physical structure of the negative image.

The visual effect of unevenness in areas that should be uniform is called *graininess.* A particular measure of graininess is called granularity.

The ability of a film to record fine detail is called *definition,* and definition is a composite effect of graininess, resolving power, and sharpness. However, the measure usually made of this film characteristic, using resolution test targets, is called resolving power or resolution.

Graininess. The densities in a black-and-white negative are composed of microscopic grains of black metallic silver. By their random placement in the gelatin of the emulsion, there is a statistical clumping of the grains that forms the familiar granular pattern which becomes visible when a negative is enlarged enough. As a rule, the faster the film is, the greater is its tendency toward graininess. Advances in film-making technology have gradually improved the graininess in films so that films today have a finer grain than previous films of the same speed.

Graininess is measured by a method that results in a number designation called granularity. From these numbers, a rating of the graininess is made with the following designations:

Micro Fine	Medium
Extremely Fine	Moderately Coarse
Very Fine	Coarse
Fine	

In addition to the inherent graininess characteristics of the film emulsion, other factors also affect the actual graininess of the finished negative.

The type of developer has an effect. A fine-grain developer decreases the graininess, usually with some loss in film speed. Overdevelopment increases the graininess, whether by extended development time, increased temperature, or by the use of an energetic developer formula. High density in a negative also increases graininess; this is one of the most unfortunate results of overexposure. Correct exposure and development almost always results in an optimum graininess condition. Large, eventoned areas in a picture will appear more grainy than areas with considerable fine detail. Temperature or pH shock during processing also can increase the appearance of graininess, although temperature shock usually causes fine reticulation that shows up as graininess.

Resolving Power. The resolving power of a film emulsion refers to its ability to distinguish fine detail. It is measured by photographing resolution charts or targets under exacting test conditions.

The resolving power value depends on the contrast of the test target, the exposure, and, to a lesser extent, on the development of the film.

Resolution falls off greatly at high- and low-exposure values, reaching a maximum at some intermediate value; it is for this exposure that the resolving-power classification is given in film data sheets.

Resolution is dependent on the contrast of the image, hence the contrast of the target. The following list gives descriptive terms for high-contrast resolving-power values.

Low—50 lines/mm or below
Medium—63, 80 lines/mm
High—100, 125 lines/mm
Very High—160, 200 lines/mm
Extremely High—250, 320, 400, 500 lines/mm
Ultra High—630 lines/mm or above

Film Speeds

The function of a black-and-white film is to build up silver density to form an image. A certain minimum amount of exposure is required to build up enough density to be visibly different from the unexposed portions of the film. How much exposure is required differs according to the emulsion design. For example, panchromatic film *A* may require only one unit of exposure to produce the first visible or printable density, usually considered to be a density of 0.10 greater than the base density of the developed film, while film *B* requires two units, and film *C* four units. Thus *A* has twice the speed of *B* and four times that of *C*.

In the United States, the speed number assigned to each film is for use with meters and other exposure computing devices that are marked for ASA speeds. These speed numbers are determined by a sensitometric procedure specified in ANSI Standard Method for Determining Speed of Photographic Negative Materials (Monochrome, Continuous-Tone), PH2.5. This standard method is based on the statistical average of a large number of scene-luminance measurements. The film-speed numbers are arithmetic, thus they indicate directly the relative sensitivity of the various films to light. For example, if all other factors in a system are equal, a film with a speed of 200 requires twice as much exposure as one with a speed of 400.

Use of film-speed numbers generally leads to the minimum exposure needed to yield good-quality negatives. However, the *effective* speed of a film may be altered by conditions of exposure and development that differ appreciably from those used to determine the film speed. Consequently, a higher or lower speed number, or exposure index, may produce correct exposure in particular conditions. Films used for copying or technical applications in which the material is generally exposed to artificial light are given an exposure index. Because conditions in such applications vary greatly, exposure indexes are intended mainly as a guide or starting point for making trial exposures.

In data for Kodak panchromatic films, only one speed number is given for all light sources. For orthochromatic films, two numbers are given: one for daylight, and one for tungsten light. Since blue-sensitive films are not generally exposed to daylight, an exposure index for white-flame arc is given in addition to the index for pulsed-xenon, tungsten, and quartz-iodine illumination.

Film speeds for infrared-sensitive films can only be suggested starting indexes because while exposure meters are calibrated for visible radiation, infrared pictures are exposed with invisible radiation. Moreover, similar light levels may be very different in the amount of infrared radiation they contain. When possible, trial exposures should be made to determine the proper exposure for any particular set of circumstances.

Contrast

Films of a given sensitivity class may differ in contrast as well as in definition and speed. In a positive image, contrast is the degree of difference between the various shades of gray, from black to white. In a negative, contrast is the difference between the developed silver deposits, called *densities,* resulting from various exposures. In practical photographic situations, the exposures are produced by the different subject brightnesses. In tests to determine the inherent contrast of a film, exposure is usually made through a step tablet—essentially a specially graduated neutral density filter—to produce exposures that increase in precisely equal amounts.

The inherent contrast of a film is approximately determined by its emulsion design. When film *A* is processed in a particular way, the silver density may increase by 25 percent for each doubling (one-stop increase) of exposure, while film *B*, processed in a particular way, may increase density by 40 percent each time the exposure is doubled. Thus *B* takes fewer steps of exposure than *A* to go from a minimum to a maximum density (that is, from black-printing to white-printing density). And the amount of density increase from step to step is greater in *B* than in *A*. In descriptive terms, *B* has greater contrast than *A*.

Contrast is measured by using a densitometer to read the light-stopping power of the various densities; the results are graphed in relation to the exposures that produced them. Negative contrast is always measured in terms of a stated development because contrast increases in most films as development increases.

Characteristic Curve

The graph of a film's response to controlled exposure increases, given specified development, is called its characteristic curve. Other names sometimes used for this curve are H & D curve, after Hurter and Driffield who started the study of film exposure in the 1880s, and D-Log E curve, for the coordinates plotted. Because of its shape, the characteristic curve is generally divided into three distinct regions: the toe, the straight line, and the shoulder. The shape of the characteristic curve varies with different emulsions.

Measuring Contrast

The slope, or upward slant, of a characteristic curve varies with contrast; it is a steep rise with high-contrast material, a low, gentle slope with low-contrast material. The slope of the curve for most

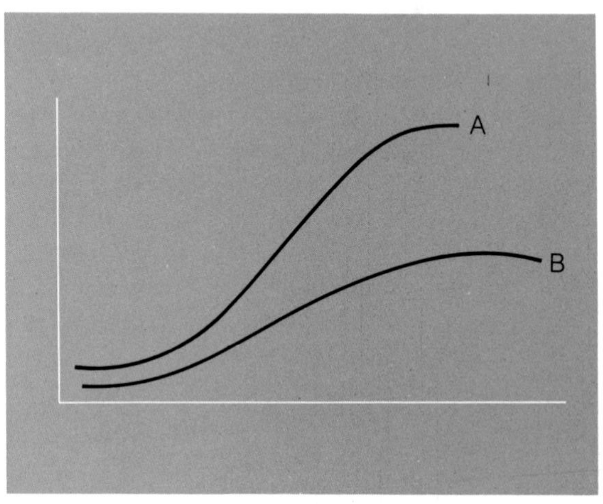

Typical characteristic curves of two different film emulsions. A *has greater inherent contrast than* B.

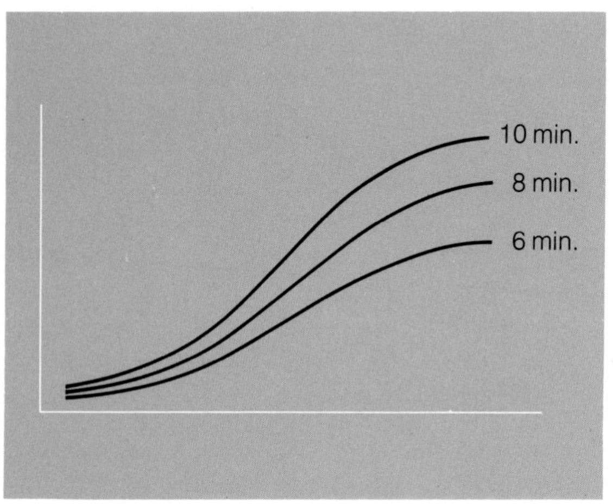

The increasing slope of these characteristic curves shows how the contrast of a single emulsion increases as the development increases.

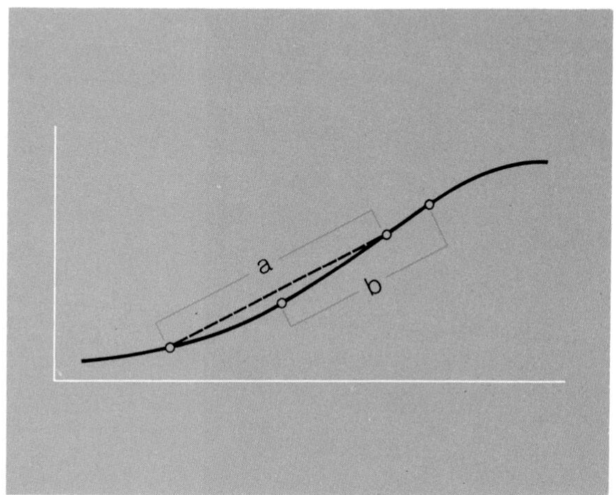

Gamma (b) is the slope of the straight-line portion of the curve. Contrast index (a) is the slope of a line joining points that are the limits of the printable densities.

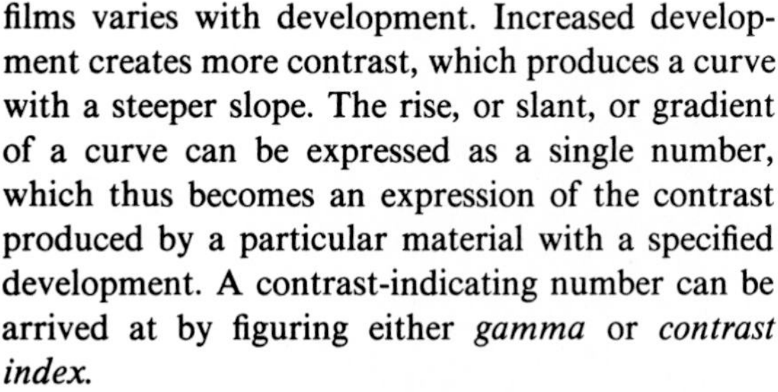

films varies with development. Increased development creates more contrast, which produces a curve with a steeper slope. The rise, or slant, or gradient of a curve can be expressed as a single number, which thus becomes an expression of the contrast produced by a particular material with a specified development. A contrast-indicating number can be arrived at by figuring either *gamma* or *contrast index.*

Gamma. Gamma is the tangent of the angle that the straight-line part of the characteristic curve makes with the horizontal. Because the shape of the toe and the length of the straight line of the curve vary with different emulsions, gamma does not always yield consistent results in measuring development contrast. For this reason, the development times recommended for Kodak continuous-tone films are now based on a value of contrast index.

Contrast Index. Contrast index is the gradient of a straight line drawn between two points on the characteristic curve. These points represent the highest and the lowest useful densities in a normal negative. Again, the value of contrast index is the tangent of the angle that this straight line makes with the horizontal. Negatives developed to a given contrast index—0.56 to 0.60 for normal continuous-tone work—will have similar density ranges.

Choosing a Film

There are a number of factors that determine the choice of a black-and-white film:

1. Availability in format to fit camera
2. Contrast
3. Color sensitivity
4. Speed
5. Characteristic curve shape
6. Other emulsion characteristics
   a. Graininess
   b. Resolving power
   c. Degree of enlargement

Points 2 to 6 have already been discussed in general. Points 1 and 2 are covered here in terms of specific films.

Format Availability and Film Usage

Some subjects can be photographed with nearly any type of camera and with any of a number of films. Other subjects may require a certain type of camera for which a limited number of films are available.

Sheet Films. The widest variety of film emulsion types is available in sheet film. Because sheet-film cameras are generally first choice for copying, ar-

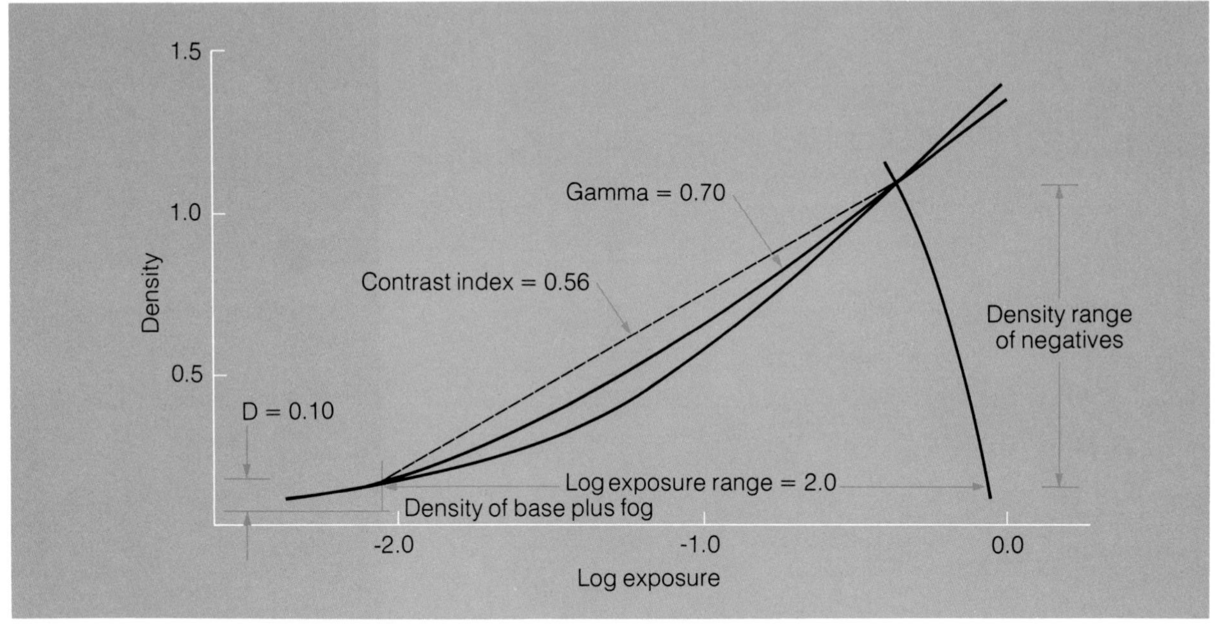

These two films have been developed to the same contrast index. Despite the difference in gamma, the density range is the same for both films; they can be printed on the same paper grade.

FILM USE	*KODAK* FILMS, SHEETS
Line copy—extreme contrast	*Kodalith* ortho *Kodalith* pan
Line copy—very high contrast	Contrast process pan Contrast process ortho
Continuous-tone copy	Commercial films Professional copy
Direct duplicate negatives	Professional direct duplicating
Positive transparencies	*Translite* Commercial films Fine-grain positive
Continuous tone—medium speed	*Ektapan* *Plus-X* pan professional
Continuous tone—high speed	*Super-XX* pan *Tri-X* pan professional *Tri-X* ortho *Royal* pan
Continuous tone—extremely high speed	*Royal-X* pan
Special sensitivity—aerial	High-speed infrared

chitectural photography, and photography where large film-format size is required for maximum image definition, films for a wide variety of uses are made in sheet form. Some suggestions for various purposes are listed in the accompanying table.

In addition to these sheet films used commonly by professional photographers, there are more specialized sheet films available, which are used in fields such as graphic arts, radiography, and engineering drawing reproduction.

FILM USE	*KODAK* FILMS, ROLLS AND/OR 35 mm
Line copy—high contrast	High-contrast copy
Continuous tone—low speed	*Panatomic-X*
	Panatomic-X professional
Continuous tone—medium speed	*Plus-X* pan
	Plus-X pan professional
	Verichrome pan
Continuous tone—high speed	*Tri-X* pan
	Tri-X pan professional
	Royal-X pan
Continuous tone—extremely high speed	Recording film

FILM USE	*KODAK* FILMS, LONG ROLLS
Line copy—extreme contrast	*Kodalith* ortho
Line copy—very high contrast	High-contrast copy
Continuous-tone copy	Ortho copy
Direct camera positives	Direct positive panchromatic
Transparency prints from negatives	*Eastman* fine-grain release positive
Continuous tone—slow speed	*Panatomic-X*
Continuous tone—medium speed	*Plus-X* pan
	Plus-X pan professional
	Plus-X portrait
	Ektapan
Continuous tone—high speed	*Tri-X* pan
	Tri-X pan professional
	Royal pan
Continuous tone—extremely high speed	Recording film

Roll Films. For many years, roll films, including 35 mm magazines, were considered amateur products. In recent times, with improvement in film emulsions and in cameras, roll films have been increasingly used by professional photographers. The accompanying table suggests some uses of roll films.

Long-Roll Films. Where the type of photography involves many similar exposures, and where other factors permit, cameras that use long rolls of film are often used. Some types of portraiture, school photography, mass-production copying and duplicating, and some types of 35 mm sports photography are examples. While the long rolls are designed to fit long-roll cameras or camera backs, some types are cut into shorter lengths and loaded into magazines or cassettes. See the accompanying table for various types and uses of long-roll films.

Characteristics of *Kodak* Black-and-White Films

A major factor to be considered in choosing a film for black-and-white photography is the film emulsion contrast. Extremely high-contrast, very high-contrast, and high-contrast films are nearly always used for special-purpose photography. For most picture-taking, either outdoors or in the studio, the photographer requires a medium-contrast film, and choice is based on such factors as availability, speed, graininess, characteristic curve shape, spectral sensitivity, and resolving power. In the following paragraphs, the characteristics of various films are discussed.

Extremely High-Contrast Films. When you must copy a line drawing, printed text material, or other high-contrast subject, extremely high-contrast films, such as Kodalith ortho film, might well be your first choice. Developed in Kodalith developer (or one of the other developers for Kodalith films), they essentially produce two tones: an extremely high density black, and a low-density base-plus-fog clear tone. While exposure of extremely high-contrast films is critical to avoid the low background densities that result from underexposure, or the filling in of copy that occurs with overexposure, some development latitude is obtained when the film is developed by inspection. Kodalith ortho film can be developed under a red safelight. Because the film speed changes with development time with little change in contrast, development can be stopped when the right balance between black and white has been achieved.

Where extremely high-contrast copies of colored originals are needed, Kodalith pan film can be used. Filters can be used to control the colors to be left in (held) or dropped out—reproduced as black or white in the final reproduction. These extremely high-contrast films can also be used for contact-printing and enlarging to make high-contrast transparencies.

Kodalith ortho and Kodalith pan films can also be used to make block-out masks in a camera, by contact with the negative or on a pin-registration easel with an enlarger. Photographic derivation processes, such as tone-line, posterization, and block-effect, nearly always make use of extremely high contrast films.

Very High-Contrast Films. Kodak high-contrast copy film, while it does not have as high an emulsion contrast as the Kodalith films, is also used primarily to copy text materials. There is a difference, however, because Kodak high-contrast copy film has extremely fine graininess and ultra-high resolving power. Because of this, it can be used to make greatly reduced size copies of originals. Developed in Kodak developer D-19, it produces microimages that can be read (with magnification) in negative form, or enlarged to make duplicate copies. Its speed is greater than that of the Kodalith films, which makes it suitable for the rapid photography of multiple documents. The emulsion is panchromatic so that it reproduces subject colors in a reasonable gray-tone rendering, and it can be used with filters to lighten or darken subject hues.

High-Contrast Films. Copying photographic prints and making positive transparencies from negatives require a high-contrast film. For years, Kodak commercial films have served these purposes as well as others where a high-contrast film is re-

While orthochromatic film is not specifically designed for general photographic purposes, it may be used for creation of special effects. In this photograph, what might have been a conventional landscape has been rendered instead as a dramatic silhouette by the use of a high-contrast film which eliminated the gray tones. Photo by Karl Rehm.

quired. Both are blue-sensitive films and can be developed under relatively bright safelight conditions.

Where somewhat more contrast is needed, and where ortho- and pan-sensitization is of value, Kodak contrast process ortho film and Kodak contrast process pan film are available. The panchromatic version is particularly useful in copying photographs with colored stains through filters, which eliminates or minimizes the stain on the copy.

Kodak professional copy film is designed for the exact purpose of copying black-and-white photographic prints. It has a special curve shape that enhances highlight separation. A long-roll version is Kodak ortho copy film.

Kodak fine-grain positive film is another film useful for making positive transparencies from negatives. For 35 mm positive transparencies, Eastman fine-grain release positive film is available.

Kodak direct positive panchromatic film is designed to make copy positives directly from prints. It is processed by reversal. It can also be used to make transparencies of normal subjects under daylight or tungsten illumination.

Duplicate negatives are often made by using commercial film. An intermediate positive is made first, and the duplicate negative printed from the positive. This extra step is eliminated when Kodak professional direct duplicating film is used. This film does not require reversal processing. A 35 mm version of this film, with a slightly bluer color, is Kodak rapid processing copy film.

Medium-Contrast Films. There is a wide range of speeds available in different medium-contrast film emulsions, and one of the major factors in the choice of a medium-contrast film is speed. The decision cannot be made on the basis of speed alone, because there is an inverse ratio of speed to graininess that often requires a compromise. It is almost invariably true that the faster the film, the grainier it is, and vice versa. The usual choice made is that the slowest film, hence the finest grain, will be used, which will permit adequately short exposure times and small enough apertures for the lighting conditions that prevail.

Kodak Panatomic-X film and Panatomic-X professional film are the slowest, finest-grain Kodak films available with medium-contrast characteristics for general-purpose photography. They are generally chosen for outdoor work where fast subject motion is not involved, and when a high degree of enlargement is anticipated. They are also used in studio work where subjects at relatively close distances are to be illuminated with flash.

The medium-speed films are chosen for general-purpose photography outdoors and for much studio work where a reasonable lighting level can be maintained by either incandescent lights or electronic flash. Kodak Plus-X pan, Plus-X portrait, and Plus-X pan professional films have very similar emulsion characteristics. While the graininess is in the same category as that of the Panatomic-X films, the resolving power and degree of enlargement are one category less. These films have short toe and long straight-line characteristics, making their use ideal in high-flare conditions such as are usually encountered outdoors, as well as giving them unusually good tone reproduction characteristics.

Medium-contrast films pick up the varying shades of black-gray-white which are generally desirable for the production of high-quality black-and-white photographs. The photograph at left demonstrates the considerable range of tone exhibited by such films. Photo by Harald Krauth.

(Left) Short-toed films are ideal for high-flare conditions usually encountered outdoors; such films also possess especially good tone reproduction characteristics. (Right) For low-flare studio conditions, long-toed films are suitable. Note exceptionally good highlight separation produced by this long-toed film.

Kodak Plus-X pan professional films have emulsion characteristics different from those of the films listed above. Even though the grain is not as fine as in the other Plus-X films, the degree of enlargement is listed in the same category. The characteristic curve shape of Kodak Plus-X pan professional film can be described as "all toe" in the exposure range normally used. This makes these films suitable for low-flare (studio) conditions and provides unusually good highlight tone separation.

Kodak Verichrome pan film is often considered a film for amateur use only, but it is sometimes used by professional photographers. It has emulsion characteristics similar to those of Kodak Plus-X pan film. It could be considered as an alternative to Kodak Plus-X pan professional film, without the retouching surface, and it is the only Kodak black-and-white film available in some roll-film sizes. It is capable of recording very professional pictures.

Kodak Ektapan film is made the same speed as Kodak Vericolor professional film so the photographer can use the two films interchangeably without having to change exposure. It is often used as a test film for professional color exposures; when the quickly processed Ektapan film negative shows proper exposure, light balance, and subject arrangement, the photographer can expose his color negative film with more assurance that he will get a good negative. With its long toe and retouching characteristics, Ektapan film is used frequently to make portraits with electronic flash.

The speed of Kodak Super-XX pan film places it midway between medium- and high-speed films. Because of its short toe and long straight-line curve characteristics, Super-XX film has long been used in such special applications as making separation negatives from still setups or from transparencies when dye transfer prints are to be made. Because of its moderately high speed and fine curve shape, it also serves well as a general-purpose sheet film for both outdoor and studio usage. Both surfaces are suitable for retouching.

Both Tri-X pan professional film (rolls) and Tri-X pan professional film (sheets) are fast films, permitting a moderate degree of enlargement. Both have extended toe curve characteristics that make them especially suitable for low-flare-level studio use, with the expected gain in highlight separation so useful for commercial and professional photographic subjects. These desirable characteristics, combined with two-side retouching surfaces, make these films popular for outdoor informal portraiture under the low-contrast and backlit lighting conditions usually used for this type of photography.

Kodak Tri-X pan film is a different type of film from the Tri-X pan professional films just discussed. Its speed is higher, its surfaces are not specially treated for retouching, and its characteristic curve is shaped differently. It is used widely as a general-purpose film—it is fast enough so that it can be used for much available-light photography yet slow enough that it can be exposed in daylight with most cameras. Its special curve shape gives Kodak Tri-X pan film a wider exposure latitude than almost any other film. Its high speed permits reasonable exposure times with filters having relatively large filter factors.

Another fast sheet film primarily for studio use is Kodak Royal pan film. Its speed, its long toe curve characteristics, and its two-side retouching feature make it widely used for interior commercial, industrial, and professional purposes. Its high speed permits the small apertures often required for industrial and commercial pictures without excessively long exposure times. Kodak Royal pan film is the favorite studio view-camera film of the Kodak professional photographers.

Kodak Tri-X ortho film is a fast ortho film used when red sensitivity is not a requirement. Some photographers prefer the tonal rendition of landscapes made with an ortho film and a yellow filter. The lack of red sensitivity in ortho film records the warm shadows in portraits as darker than they appear visually, thus accentuating facial wrinkles. Hence ortho film adds "character" or "ruggedness' that can be effective in portraits of elderly men, outdoorsmen, or athletes. Both sides of this film are suitable for retouching.

When an extremely fast film is required, as for low light level or fast-action photography, Kodak Royal-X pan films are strongly recommended. With these films, the degree of enlargement is moderately low due to medium graininess and medium resolving power; however, when the extra film speed means the difference between usable pictures or no pictures at all, the choice is obvious. These two films have the short toe, long straight-line characteristic curve that results in excellent tone reproduction. Their exposure latitude is excellent, a desirable feature in available-light photography.

Another extremely fast film for 35 mm photography is Kodak recording film. With faster lenses available on 35 mm cameras than on larger cameras, the use of Recording film with an ultra-fast lens on a 35 mm camera gives the fastest combination for extremely low-light-level photography currently available.

• *See also:* CHARACTERISTIC CURVE; CONTRAST INDEX; FILMS AND PLATES; NOTCH CODES; STORAGE OF SENSITIZED MATERIALS AND PROCESSING SOLUTIONS.

Further Reading: Carroll, John S. *Photographic Lab Handbook,* 4th ed. Garden City, NY: Amphoto, 1977; Pittaro, E. M., ed. *Photo Lab Index.* Hastings-on-the Hudson, NY: Morgan and Morgan, Inc., 1977. Eastman Kodak Co. *Kodak Films for the Amateur,* rev. ed. Rochester, NY: Eastman Kodak Co., 1975.

Black-and-White Printing

The final step in black-and-white printing is to make a print that restores the tones of the subject to a positive-appearing image. The procedures are simple. Photographic paper is exposed either in contact with a selected negative, or to the negative image projected by an enlarger. The exposure may be shortened or lengthened locally by dodging or burning-in portions of the image. The positive image becomes visible upon development. Its strength and coloration are the result of the interaction of negative characteristics, paper coloration and contrast grade, developer characteristics, and the degree of development. The image may be altered by special treatment such as re-exposure after partial development (Sabattier effect), local or overall reduction (bleaching), intensification, and toning. It becomes permanent upon proper fixing and washing. The details of these procedures are discussed separately under the headings listed at the end of this article.

The fundamental task of black-and-white printing is to provide tone reproduction that is technically excellent and suitably expressive of the subject.

Excellent tonal reproduction involves a number of factors: delicate gradation in the highlights, with diffuse highlights separated tonally from specular highlights, which are reproduced as white paper; good separation throughout the middle tones; a range of shadow tones that provides enough detail but still has some areas of deepest black to provide a tonal foundation. The contrast and key must be appropriate to the subject, as must sharpness and degree of graininess. "Key" describes the predominant tonal range of the print; it may be light (high key), or dark (low key), or normal.

Photographic technical quality comes from every step in the photographic process. It comes from selection of the film, lighting of the subject,

Good technical printing quality makes the difference between a drab photograph and one that lives. This means excellent tonal reproduction in highlights, middle tones, and shadow tones, and appropriate contrast, key, sharpness, and granularity.

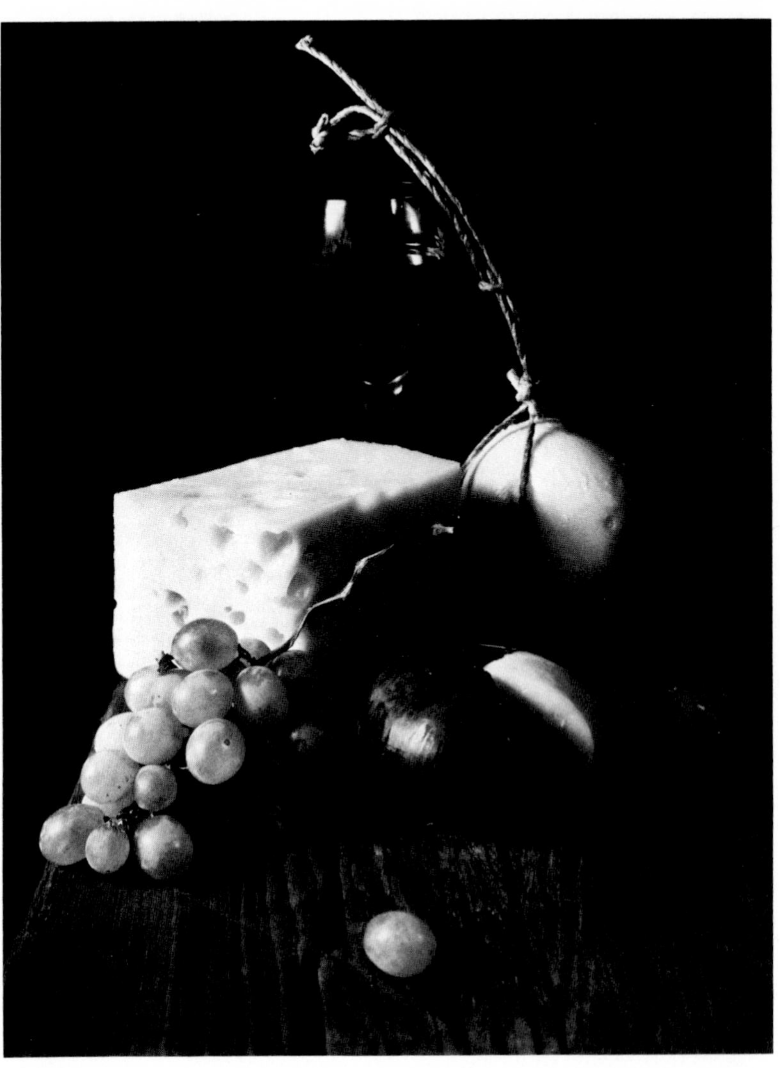

Even in low-key (predominantly dark-toned) photographs, good reproduction of highlights should be an important consideration. In this print, highlights appear muddy and the photograph lacks sparkle.

careful handling of the camera, accurate exposure and processing of the film, selection of the photographic paper, and from correct exposure, processing, and finishing of the print. All these steps in the photographic process work together to produce the quality of the photographic print. The factors that directly affect or control the printing process are discussed here.

First Considerations

In making black-and-white prints, two of the most important considerations are choosing a paper with a contrast that suits the negative and obtaining correct exposure.

Factors that Affect Print Contrast. The contrast of a paper can be chosen by matching the density range of the negative to the log-exposure range of the paper. In practice, however, this method is only an approximation. The actual contrast obtained in a print from a given negative is affected by a variety of factors. Together, they influence the choice of paper contrast that must be used to obtain a good print. The inherent contrast of the paper does not change, of course, but the effective printing contrast of the negative varies according to the type of illumination used in the enlarger, the color quality of the exposing light source, and the quality or condition of the enlarger lens. In contact printing, con-

Printing the same picture on a paper of higher contrast restores brightness to the highlights and gives the photograph the desired effect of brilliance.

trast is uniform with most equipment, but when a small light source is used at a considerable distance from the negative, contrast is slightly higher than it is with a diffused light used close to the negative. Most diffuse-light enlargers yield a contrast similar to a diffuse-light contact printer. Modern condenser enlargers are usually of a type known as semi-specular. They yield contrast about one grade of paper higher than the diffuse-light type.

Color Quality of Light Sources. The color quality of the printing light source is not very important in using ordinary papers, but a bluish light, such as mercury vapor or a fluorescent tube, reduces contrast slightly. The reverse is true of Kodak selective-contrast papers; a bluish light tends to increase contrast, whereas a yellowish one reduces it. These papers are designed for exposure to tungsten illumination (3200 K).

Contrast of Negatives. The contrast, or density range, of a negative is sometimes greater than a paper can reproduce without loss of detail in either shadows or highlights. A good-quality negative can be defined as one that will make a high-quality print when printed on the paper you choose with your enlarger or contact printer.

Shadow densities, determined primarily by exposure, are great enough to reproduce

(Left) Tone reproduction, the process of converting the neutral and colored tones of the original subject into the whites, grays, and blacks of the print, is one of the most important factors in technical print quality. The actual quality of this fine print was not reproduced with complete accuracy because of the limitation of the printing process used for this book; nevertheless, note the wide range of tone variation as represented in the tone-bar below the picture. (Opposite page) While it is generally considered appropriate to print for as much detail as possible, in certain cases, a more effective print may be created by increasing exposure in dark areas so that they will reproduce as solid blacks in the final print.

tones just lighter than black (0.10 to 0.15 above base-plus-fog density).

The density range of the negative, as achieved by development, matches the scale of the paper when exposed by printing equipment, or is made to match by dodging (holding back or burning-in).

It is generally preferable to make negatives that suit a particular paper, rather than to produce negatives and then find a paper that suits them.

Tone Reproduction

Tone reproduction is one of the most important factors in technical print quality. The black-and-white photographic process converts the neutral and colored tones of the subject into whites, grays, and blacks in the print. How well these tones represent the visual aspects of the subject is a prime measure of the photographic quality.

The brightness range (technically, the luminance ratio) of the typical outdoor, 45° front-lighted subject greatly exceeds 1000-to-1 if you include the deepest shadow and the specular highlights. The black-and-white paper can reproduce a brightness range of only slightly over 100-to-1, at best (glossy paper). You must do two things to fit the subject range to the paper range:

1. Compress the tonal scale.
2. Let all specular highlights print as white, and let all the deepest tones print as black. The deepest tones are usually dark subjects in shadow and relatively unimportant to the picture.

When you eliminate the specular highlights and deepest blacks from the subject tonal range, you are left with about a 160-to-1 brightness range from the *diffuse* highlight tone to the dark tone to be reproduced just lighter than black in the print. The print range from the diffuse highlight tones, which are printed with a density of about 0.04 greater than that of the paper base, to the dark tones, just lighter than black, which are printed about 0.90× the maximum obtainable density is about 60-to-1 for glossy paper. This means that the subject range is compressed to make the tonal range fit the scale of the paper.

The film, however, compresses the tonal range even more than this—so that the tonal range is actually expanded when the negative is printed.

While this compression and expansion of the brightness ratio is occurring in the typical black-and-white photographic process, all parts of the tonal scale are not compressed and expanded evenly. The darkest tones in the shadow areas are dropped from the reproduction—they are reproduced as black with no detail. The tones just lighter than black are compressed considerably. Dark tones are compressed somewhat. The middle tones are usually reproduced in the print with no compression at all. This means that the brightness ratio between adjacent tones in the middle of the tonal scale is nearly the same in the print as it is in the subject. In the highlight region, the tones are compressed, but not as much as they are in the shadows. This occurs because in properly exposed and developed negatives there is the same compression in the highlight region as in the midtones, while the shadow region is *compressed* in the negatives by being recorded in the toe of the characteristic curve. This type of tone reproduction, with relative values, is shown in the accompanying series of diagrams.

The quality negative, then, is one that will make a high-quality print on your printing equipment, and a high-quality print will have the type of tonal reproduction just described.

The subjects in some pictures do not have specular highlights. It is then usually advisable to print the diffuse highlights light enough to show some effect of brilliance, while maintaining just enough tone to suggest detail.

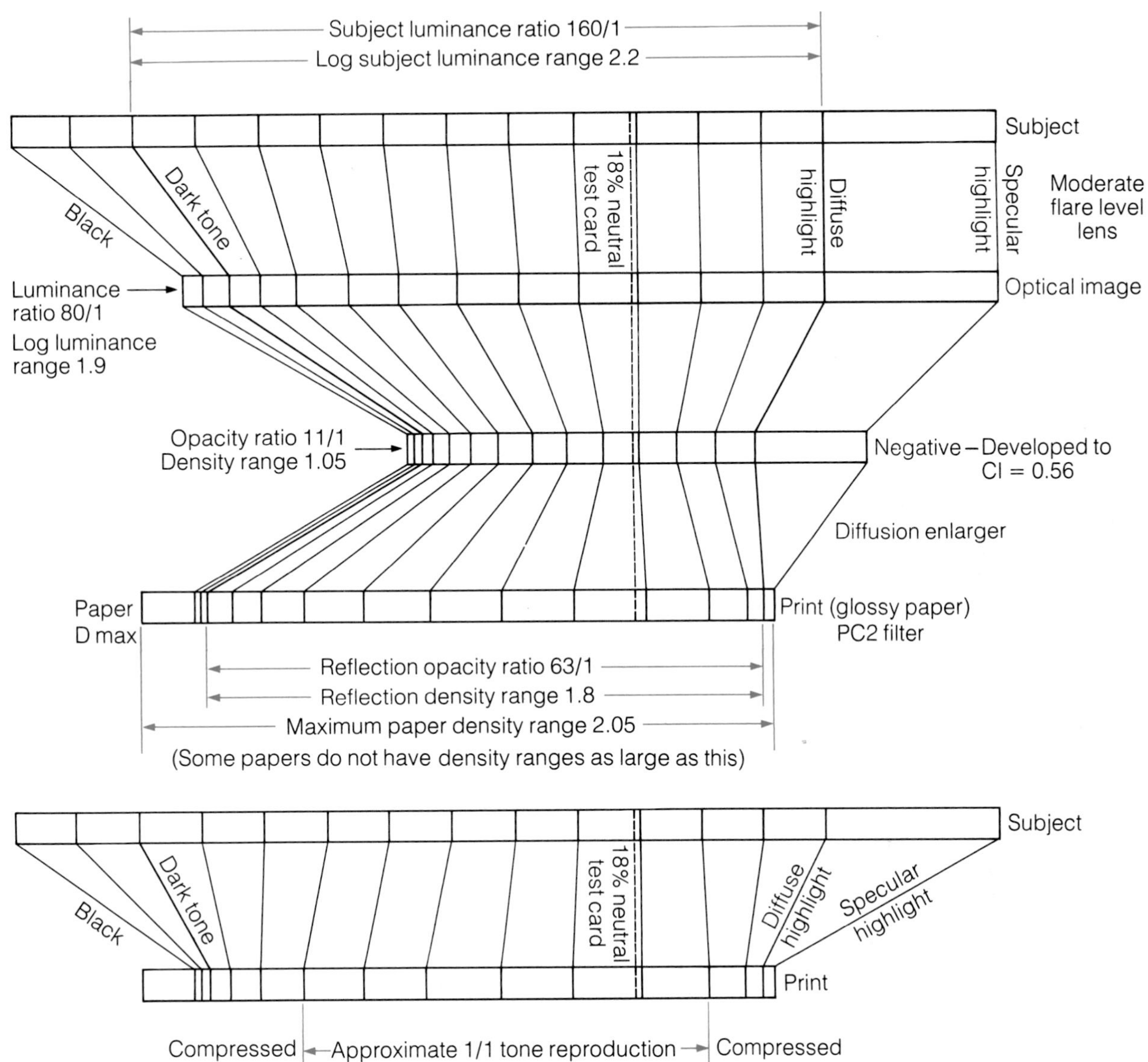

The graphic representation of typical photographic tone reproduction with relative values.

Judging Negative Quality Visually

Not all photographers have equipment to measure negative densities, but experienced photographers can usually tell by a visual examination whether or not a negative has the quality suitable for a particular purpose. Those with less experience may have some difficulty in choosing the best negative from among several. One method is to place the negative, emulsion side down, on a sheet of good black-and-white printed matter. See the accompanying illustrations on the next two pages.

If the negative is to be printed on a diffusion-type enlarger, it should be just possible to read the large type through the diffuse highlight areas of the negative. The deepest shadow areas should be clear,

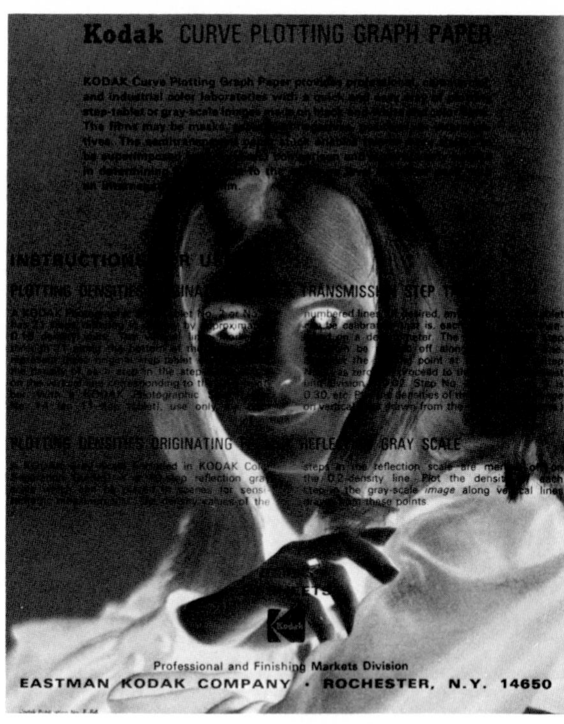

(Left) A negative to be printed on a diffusion-type enlarger should appear clear in deepest shadow areas, while detailed shadow areas should show varying densities. (Center) A negative to be printed on a condenser enlarger should have similar characteristics in shadow areas, but less density in diffuse highlight areas. (Far right) Resulting print will give no indication of negative quality or type of enlarger on which it was printed.

while detailed shadow areas (lighter tones in shade) should show varying light densities. A negative that passes this test should print well on a medium grade of paper on a diffusion enlarger.

A negative to be printed on a condenser enlarger will have similar characteristics in the shadow areas, but the diffuse highlight areas will be less dense, and the printing should also be readily distinguishable through these areas.

Other characteristics of a good-quality negative are usually:

Every part of the negative that is intended to be sharp should be sharp when viewed with a magnifying glass.

The overall density should allow reasonably short printing exposures.

The density range of the negative should be such that the negatives will print on grade 2 or medium-grade paper on your printing equipment to give good highlight and shadow reproduction.

The deepest shadow areas should be clear in the negatives, while the shadowed light tones should show adequate detail in the negative.

The diffuse highlights should have gradation and should have noticeably less density than the specular highlights.

The image should not print with more effective graininess than can be expected from the type of film emulsion at the magnification used.

The negative should be free from physical imperfections: scratches, static markings, scum, water spots or water marks,

pinholes caused by dust or improper film developer, or dried-on dust particles.

The negative should be free from mottle or uneven densities caused by improper agitation during development or a very short development time.

Photometry in Black-and-White Printing

Experienced photographic printers can estimate exposure and select a suitable contrast of paper with reasonable accuracy. Beginners, or those who print only rarely, may have difficulty in making good prints without a good deal of trial and error, and a consequent waste of material. In these circumstances, on-easel photometry can be used to estimate exposure and to match the density range of the negative to a suitable contrast of paper. For this purpose, an electronic densitometer equipped with a probe is the most suitable instrument.

As stated earlier, when the density range of the negative approximately matches the log-exposure range of the paper, the resulting print will, in many cases, have acceptable contrast. To find the density range of a negative, read and record a shadow area and a diffuse highlight area in the negative in which you expect detail to show in the print. The difference between the two readings is the density range. If a subject has a normal brightness ratio of 160-to-1 the density difference (negative density range) should be about 1.05 for negatives to be printed with diffusion enlargers or 0.80 for negatives made for condenser enlarger printing. For example:

	Diffusion Enlarger	*Condenser Enlarger*
Lightest Diffuse Highlight Density. . .	1.20	0.90
Detailed Shadow Density.	−0.15	−0.10
Density Range.	1.05	0.80

In reading the densities to determine density range, disregard specular highlights on polished metal, glass, and similar glossy surfaces. They contain no detail and so would give a false estimate of density range. In portrait negatives, select a skin tone in which some detail will appear in the print. Likewise, avoid selecting shadow areas where there is no apparent density greater than the film base.

The aim density ranges of 0.80 for condenser enlargers and 1.05 for diffusion enlargers are average figures derived from measurements made on a number of modern enlargers with clean lenses. Your enlarger may be slightly different—prints made on grade 2 or medium-grade paper (or on a selective-contrast paper with a Kodak Polycontrast filter PC2) may consistently have too little or too much contrast. When the contrast is too low, increase the developing time and find a higher density difference that produces the contrast you want on grade 2 paper with your enlarger. If the contrast is too high, reduce the development time and find a lower density range figure that gives the contrast you want. According to the log-exposure ranges given for Kodak papers, a negative with a density range of about 1.05 will print satisfactorily on grade 2 paper or on a Kodak selective-contrast paper with a Polycontrast filter PC2 with a diffusion enlarger.

The actual density difference of many negatives will be higher or lower than your aim, due to subject contrast variation. Various paper grades are available to compensate for these differences.

Since contrast in a black-and-white print is partly subjective, the above method will not always yield the ideal contrast of paper; however, it provides a useful starting point.

Basically, all electronic densitometers work on the same principle, but they vary greatly in detail according to the application and the manufacturer's design. Consequently, you should follow the manufacturer's instructions in operating any particular instrument.

In black-and-white printing, photometry is complicated by the use of papers with widely differing speed, and by the subjective nature of density and contrast in monochrome prints. Consequently, you must often override the exposure indicated by the instrument to obtain a desired result.

Setting Up a Densitometer. To set up a densitometer for black-and-white printing, first calibrate the instrument for the speed of the paper you are using, and then select a highlight density in the projected image; this density should be one that will contain some detail in the print. Place the aperture of the probe on the density you have chosen and then adjust the instrument until the needle or pointer reads at a midpoint on the meter scale. By trial and error, adjust the densitometer until correct exposure is obtained with a negative of normal contrast and density at an exposure of about five seconds. As far as possible, adjust exposure by altering the lens aperture to bring the pointer to a predetermined value on the scale. In effect, you are then reading the same light intensity for every negative. Since most modern densitometers are equipped with cells that are sensitive to the safelight, do not allow the safelight illumination to fall directly on the densitometer probe. Also, avoid letting stray white light from the enlarger head be reflected onto the easel.

Integrated-Light Reading. The above procedure makes use of what is known as spot reading. Another method is to integrate the light transmitted by the lens to obtain a mean value for all the densities in the negative. The light is integrated with an integrating cone on the probe of the densitometer or by placing a sheet of diffusing material over the lens. This method is simpler than spot reading, but it is prone to failure with negatives of unusual subject matter or to abnormal negative quality. For example, a print from a negative having a large amount of shadow area will often be underexposed, whereas a large amount of highlight area, such as the sky, will cause the instrument to indicate more exposure than necessary.

Print Quality

Making a high-quality negative is the first vital step toward making a quality print. The print is the place where quality shows—where all your work in lighting, composing, posing, and all the care in photographic technique come together.

Just as care in making the negative is important, care in making the print is equally necessary if the highest quality is your aim.

Two types of factors enter into a definition of print quality. One is *subjective*—it has to do with the photographer's interpretation of the subject. Two people could make prints from the same negative that would look considerably different—and yet both might be high-quality prints. The other is *objective* and has to do with technical quality, which involves the following factors:

Choice of a paper appropriate for the subject and use of the picture.
Specular highlights printed as white (paper base white), with diffuse highlights printed as delicate grays.
Dark subject tones in the shadows reproduced as *black* (maximum density) in the print.
Mid-to-light subject tones in the shadows reproduced as dark, but *lighter-than-black* tones in the print.
Adequate tonal separation throughout the midtone range of the print.
Lack of graininess, unless grain is used for a special effect.
Adequate sharpness throughout, except where the degree of unsharpness makes it clear that the photographer's *intent* was lack of sharpness (selective focusing, unsharp streaks to show motion, zoom effect, etc).
Imperfections such as dust specks, stains, etc. completely *removed.*
No retouching visible.

There are two treatment approaches in the making of photographs.

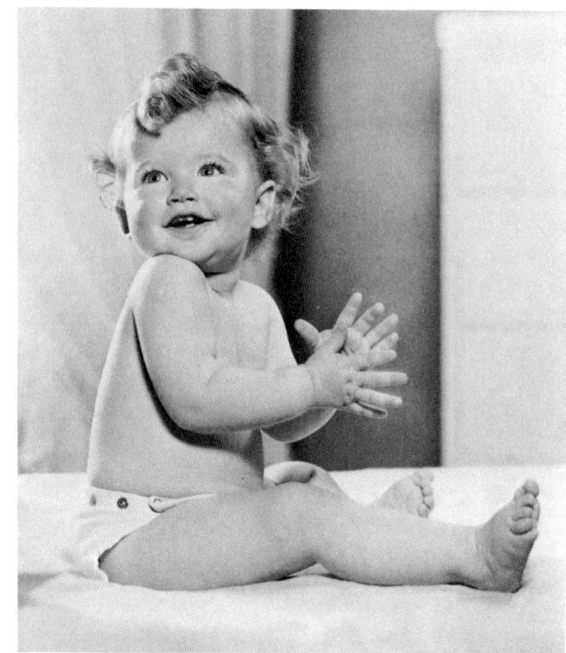

(Left) In printing high-key (predominantly light-toned) photographs, the tendency is often to eliminate darker tones altogether. This is often a mistake. (Right) Note how darker tones add life and a quality of brightness to the picture.

1. The print is intended to be a medium that will visually communicate the subject to the viewer as clearly as possible. The print itself is inconspicuous—the viewer should be aware of the subject, not the print.
2. The print itself becomes an object of the viewer's attention along with the subject. As in other plastic art forms, the technique is permitted to show and becomes a partner with the subject in transmitting the visual message. Usually, at least a part of the intent of this photographic approach is to give aesthetic pleasure.

In the first approach, smooth paper surfaces are chosen. The subject is reproduced as clearly and as close to a visual approximation of the original subject tones as the process will permit. The print becomes a "window" through which the viewer sees the subject.

In the second approach, there is considerably more variation in type of photographic quality. Grain or a pattern provided by the print surface or by a texture screen may be evident. The tonal range of the print may be altered to create any of a number of tonal effects. The image may be softened by diffusers. The final negative(s) from which the print is made may have been "derived" from the original negative by one of the many derivation processes such as bas-relief, line-tone, posterization, or use of the Sabattier effect. In some of these processes the gradation of tone that is an intrinsic part of the normal process is purposely destroyed. Even when these processes are used, however, the clean whites and deep blacks referred to earlier as part of photographic quality are necessary.

Print Contrast and Density. These are both subjective and technical effects over which the photographic printmaker has control. They must be controlled in such a way that the print has a tonal rendition suitable to the subject. Print contrast, once the negative is made and the enlarger chosen, is

(Top) "Hot spots" occurring from overexposure to the safelight may result in loss of detail or in fog that adds a gray tone to the highlights in the print. (Bottom) Precautions against overexposure will result in improved quality.

controlled by choice of the paper grade and the developer. Print density is controlled primarily by paper exposure. It is probable that more poor-quality prints result from attempting to correct for wrong print exposure by increasing or decreasing development time than from any other cause.

The surface sheen of the paper has an effect on the visual scale of the print. Papers with glossy and high-lustre surfaces have longer visual scales than papers with lustre and matte surfaces. Better visual tone separation will be achieved in prints of full-scale subjects when they are printed on glossy or high-lustre papers.

Above all, keep the following rules in mind:

Select the paper grade to match the negative, type of enlarger, and print developer.

Expose so that the print density is just right when it has received the full development time.

Printing Technique in Black-and-White

You can achieve good technical print quality by carefully carrying out the procedures given above, and by taking into consideration the following printing factors as well.

Safelights. Always use the safelight filter recommended for the paper you are using, and observe the working distance as well as the correct bulb wattage. Even then, a safelight is safe only for a limited time. Excessive exposure to the safelight results in fog that adds a gray tone to the highlights in the print. This effect is insidious because the fog cannot be seen on the white borders or other unexposed parts of the paper. In many cases the safelight exposure is not sufficient to make the silver grains developable, but when it is added to the printing exposure it is sufficient to degrade the highlights. There are methods for testing safelighting. (*See:* TESTING.) Be sure to test safelights at least twice a year.

Fog. The remarks about safelight fog also apply to leakage of light from the enlarger lamphouse, a badly fitting pass-through lid, or an unsafe light trap at the entrance to the darkroom. Any leakage of light, whatever the source, should be eliminated. Painting the wall area behind the enlarger, and the ceiling area above the enlarger, black will help reduce the effects of stray light escaping from the enlarger.

Print Exposure. To get the best possible prints from negatives, it is especially important to expose prints so that they reach the correct density in the full, normal developing time.

To be realistic, this method involves remakes. If the pressure of work makes it necessary to aim at adequate rather than top quality, and thereby cut the number of remakes, look for a photographic paper that has good developing latitude. Such a paper will allow you to get acceptable prints by varying development time to compensate for variations among negatives.

Improved prints can be achieved by dodging or burning-in during the printing exposure. Some tonal areas can be lightened by holding-back, other areas can be darkened by printing-in. Just don't overdo it so that the technique shows.

Another contribution that total exposure control can make to print quality is to give improved tonal separation. Normally the paper contrast grade is matched to the negative contrast, but with some subjects this can result in insufficient tonal separation, especially in the middle tones. When this happens, choose a higher grade of paper, and make the contrast fit by burning in the highlight areas and holding back the shadow areas.

Developing Prints. The best quality is achieved when you expose prints so that the print develops to the correct density at the full normal development time. The farther away from the recommended development time a print gets, the poorer the print quality is likely to be.

Considerable print underdevelopment causes muddy, and perhaps uneven, image tones that may have an unpleasant brownish image color. Overdevelopment results in a lack of highlight detail, fog, stain, or all three at the same time. Remake each poor print as you go along. Don't wait until the prints have been dried before discovering that their quality is poor. Print developing times are based on continuous agitation. Rock the tray or move the print around in the solution if you're developing only one print. Use interleaving agitation if you are developing more than one print at a time.

If you are interested in print quality, *do not* try to evaluate tonality, contrast, or other quality factors while the print is in the developing tray. Although you may use this kind of visual inspection when doing volume work that requires only adequate prints, it is not suitable for high-quality results. The reduced intensity and the color of safelight illumination will distort your judgment. Instead, wait until the print has been in the fixing bath for at least a full minute, with constant agitation. Then lift it out, drain it, and put it on an inspection surface—a sheet of plastic or thick glass standing at a slant in the sink, just behind the fixer tray, is convenient. Turn on a white light; if the print has any yellowish coloration, the paper has not cleared completely. Turn off the light immediately and return the print to the fixer for at least another minute. Otherwise, examine the print carefully. If all factors seem satisfactory, turn out the light and complete fixing the print for the full time required. If anything is not right, discard the print and make another that corrects the fault. Fixing poor prints is a waste of time and chemicals. Do not be tempted to save a print in the hope that it will turn out to be "good enough"—this is a standard of mediocrity

that has no place in high-quality black-and-white printing.

Dry-Down in Density and Contrast. Learn to judge wet-print density in the inspection light against final dry-print density. Prints nearly always look darker and seem to have less contrast dry than wet. Experience will teach you just how much lighter a wet print should look than a dry print with just the right density. You will also learn that if the print looks even slightly flat wet, it will look even flatter when dry. Learn to judge how the print should look under the inspection illumination, so that it will have the quality you want in white light when it is dry. It may take some experimentation to match this light to the intensity under which your prints will normally be seen. If a print will dry to the wrong contrast, it's faster and easier to make it over on higher contrast paper right then, while the negative is still in the enlarger, than to wait until the print is dry. Prints made on matte and lustre papers show more dry-down change than those made on high-lustre or glossy papers.

Developer Temperatures. Always develop prints at the same temperature. It's difficult enough in

A generally well-exposed photograph (left) may contain certain areas that are underexposed and therefore deficient in important detail (center). Improved detail in areas of dark shadow can be obtained by dodging, or holding back, during the printing exposure (right). Care must be taken when areas are dodged so that the adjoining areas are not affected by the process.

printing to hit the right exposure for a variety of negatives; it's doubly difficult if you also have to compensate for changing developer temperature. A great amount of waste and many poor prints result from this situation.

Developer Contamination. The activity of the developer and the image tone of the print can be changed by contamination with small amounts of fixer or stop bath. Again, exposure assessment is more difficult than it need be, and with some paper and developer combinations, the change in print quality is drastic. Generally, contamination of developer is caused by splashes and by failure to rinse the hands thoroughly after handling other chemicals.

Processing Solutions. You make the best prints with fresh processing solutions. Keep the developer, acid stop bath, and fixer fresh to avoid stains, poor image tone, and the formation of scum on the surface of the print.

Washing Prints. Prints made on conventional papers must be washed well for an hour at a temperature of 18 to 24 C (65 to 75 F) to be permanent. Use of Kodak hypo clearing agent, or the equivalent, shortens this time by two-thirds and lowers water

Usually, paper contrast is matched to negative density range. However, this may result in inadequate midtone separation (left). Using a higher grade of contrast and dodging during enlarging can improve midtone separation and maintain highlight and shadow tone reproduction (right).

consumption. Papers with a water-resistant base need only a 4-minute wash—*do not overwash.* Kodak hypo clearing agent need not be used with these papers. It offers little advantage and is not recommended.

Drying Prints. Excessive drying temperatures can change the image tone of toned prints and of some warm-tone papers. Do not heat-dry papers with a water-resistant base.

Storage of Photographic Paper. Although black-and-white papers are relatively stable materials, the shelf life of their high-quality characteristics will be extended by storage at correct temperatures and in conditions of correct relative humidity. Store paper in a cool, dry place—normally less than 21 C (70 F) for working stock and between 4 and 10 C (40 and 50 F) for prolonged storage. A relative humidity of about 40 percent is suitable.

Permanence. This is yet another aspect of print quality. It's largely a question of careful processing. (*See:* ARCHIVAL PROCESSING.)

Photographic Materials

The materials you use in photography also play a part in the quality of the final result. In buying photographic materials, the aim is best served by using high-quality materials. Choosing the best quality and most suitable films, papers, and chemicals will do justice to your professional skill and will generally result in true economy in the long run.

There is a great deal of variety in black-and-white film and paper products. It's therefore important to choose those that give the results you are seeking. Although many films and papers are versatile, generally one or two of them will be particularly suited to a given application.

• *See also:* ARCHIVAL PROCESSING; BURNING-IN; CONTACT PRINTING; CONTRAST; CONTRAST INDEX; DENSITOMETRY; DEVELOPERS AND DEVELOPING; DODGING; ENLARGERS AND ENLARGING; NEGATIVES; PAPERS, PHOTOGRAPHIC; SAFELIGHTS; TESTING; VARIABLE CONTRAST.

Further Reading: Carroll, John S. *Amphoto Home Darkroom Course: Elementary Black and White.* Garden City, NY: Amphoto, 1976;——*Amphoto Darkroom Course: Advanced Black and White.* Garden City, NY: Amphoto, 1977; Pittaro, E. M., ed. *Photo Lab Index.* Hastings-on-the Hudson, NY: Morgan and Morgan, Inc., 1977; Croy, Otto R. *The Complete Art of Printing and Enlarging.* Garden City, NY: Amphoto, 1976; Jonas, Paul. *Manual of Darkroom Procedures and Techniques.* Garden City, NY: Amphoto, 1972; Lootens, Joseph Ghislain. *Lootens on Photographic Enlarging and Print Quality,* 8th ed., ed. Lester Bogen. Garden City, NY: Amphoto, 1975; Picker, Fred. *The Fine Print.* Garden City, NY: Amphoto, 1975; Vestal, David. *The Craft of Photography.* New York, NY: Harper and Row, 1975; Woodhead, Harold C. *Creative Photographic Printing Methods.* Garden City, NY: Amphoto, 1975.

Black-and-White Prints from Color Films

You can make high-quality black-and-white prints from color negatives and color transparencies. To make a print from a color negative, print directly on Kodak Panalure paper in much the same way as you print a black-and-white negative on ordinary photographic paper. To make a black-and-white print from a color transparency, first make a black-and-white negative from the transparency, then print in the normal way. Both methods are explained here.

Prints from Color Negatives

Conventional Papers. When color negatives are printed on regular black-and-white enlarging

Compare prints made from color negative film. (Below left) Print made on blue-sensitive Kodabromide paper; reds and yellows are too dark, blue is too light. (Below right) Kodak Panalure paper, containing a panchromatic emulsion, records all tonal values correctly.

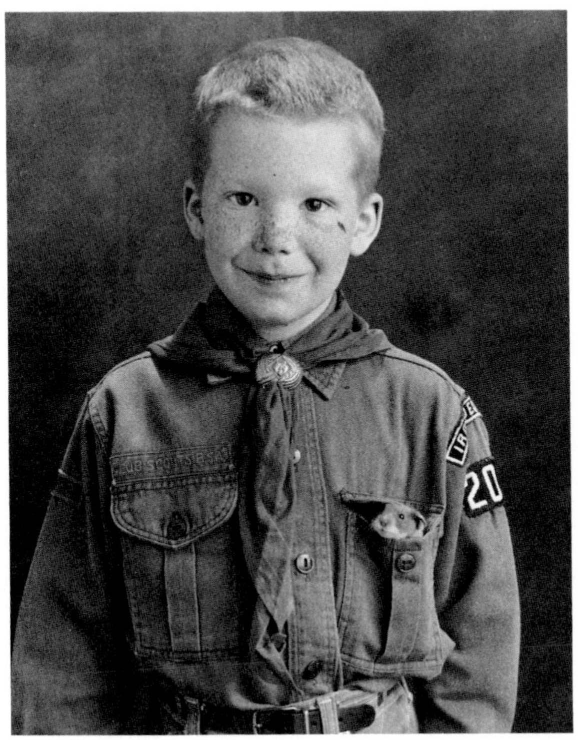

paper, the increase in apparent grain and the balance of tones in the monochrome print are often unsatisfactory. This is because regular printing papers are sensitive mainly to blue light. In other words, these materials *see* a color negative as though it had a blue filter over it. As a result, objects that were red in the original scene print too dark, and objects that were blue in the scene print too light. For example, red lips and ruddy complexions are too dark, blue eyes are too light, and blue skies with white clouds lack detail.

***Kodak Panalure* Paper.** When a color negative is printed on Kodak Panalure paper—sensitive to red, green, and blue light—all the colors in the picture are rendered in appropriate tones of gray. The effect is then similar to that obtained when a print is made from a panchromatic film negative.

You can produce excellent black-and-white prints from color negatives with Kodak Panalure paper. Color negatives from Kodacolor films and Kodak Vericolor professional films have an overall orange cast, and the colors recorded in the negative are the complementaries of those in the original scene. Panalure paper has a panchromatic emulsion; that is, it is sensitive to all colors. This enables the paper to reproduce subject colors as gray shades that appear in their correct tonal relationship in the print. The quality of a print made on Panalure paper will be as good as if you had taken the picture on panchromatic black-and-white film.

There are two kinds of Panalure paper: Kodak Panalure paper F—smooth, white, glossy, single-weight, and warm-black in tone—is for general purposes. Kodak Panalure portrait paper E—white, fine-grain lustre, and double-weight—is for portraits or other subjects that require a brown-black image tone.

Safelight. Handle Panalure paper by the light of a Kodak safelight filter No. 10 (dark amber) in a safelight lamp with a 7½-watt bulb kept at least four feet from the paper. For greater working illumination, use a No. 13 (amber) safelight filter with a 15-watt bulb at the same distance. Be sure to use one of these safelights, or process the paper in total darkness, because the safelights normally used for processing black-and-white papers will fog Panalure paper.

Enlargements. You can expose Panalure paper in an enlarger without using filters if the enlarger has a tungsten light source such as a photo enlarger lamp No. 302 or No. 212, or a similar lamp. With other enlarger light sources, you may need correction filters to produce a normal tonal relationship in the print.

Exposure. The exposure needed for an average Ektacolor negative is between five and ten seconds with normal enlarger illumination at a magnification of 2×. To find correct exposure, make a step test on a strip of Panalure paper and use seven seconds as the midpoint in the series of test exposures.

Before you make your prints, make sure your negatives are clean and dust-free. Remove all dust and lint from the surface of the negative with a camel's-hair brush.

Making Contact Prints

You can make contact prints with Panalure paper on a contact printer if you reduce the illumination in the printer. This adjustment is necessary because Panalure paper is more sensitive to light and requires less exposure than contact-printing papers. Reducing the illumination makes the exposure times longer and therefore more controllable. You can reduce printer illumination by using low-wattage lamps in your printer, or by placing white bond paper between the lamps and the negative. Do not put the bond paper in contact with the negative.

In making contact prints, you can control print exposure better by using your enlarger as the light source. You'll have more control over exposure because you can adjust the height of the enlarger and the size of the enlarger lens opening. When you expose the paper this way, place the negative and paper, emulsion-to-emulsion (with the negative next to the glass), in a printing frame on the enlarging easel.

You can make passable prints from color negatives on ordinary photographic paper. A No. 3 contrast grade paper is usually suitable. However, conventional black-and-white photographic papers will not reproduce print tones in their proper relationship because ordinary printing papers are not sensitive to red light. For example, red objects in the scene will appear too dark in the prints, and blue objects will appear too light. (Do not use some types of contact-printing papers that are sensitive to blue light only, such as Kodak Azo paper.) Furthermore, printing times will be extra long because the orange color of the negative acts as a filter affecting the printing light source.

Development Recommendations for *Panalure* Papers

Because the level of safelight illumination is too low, Kodak Panalure papers cannot be developed by inspection in the same way as ordinary black-and-white papers. Development must be by time and temperature correlation.

The emulsion of Panalure paper is designed to yield normal-contrast prints from average color negatives. Occasionally, however, the contrast may be too high to suit your needs. See the accompanying tables.

Toning Recommendations: Panalure F—Kodak brown and rapid selenium toners. Panalure E—Kodak Poly-Toner and rapid selenium toner.

Using Filters with *Panalure* Paper

When you print color negatives on Panalure paper, you have the advantage of being able to control tone rendition by using a filter with your enlarger when you expose the print. This creates the same effect that would have resulted had you used panchromatic black-and-white film and a filter over your camera lens when you shot the picture. For minor changes in tonal balance, use color compensating filters. For more abrupt changes or dramatic effects, use the same filters as for ordinary camera work.

The rules for using filters with Panalure paper are the same as those for using filters on your camera when you photograph the original scene on panchromatic black-and-white film. To lighten an original subject color, use a filter of a similar color; to darken an original subject color, use a filter of a complementary color. For example, you can expose your print through a No. 15 (G) deep-yellow filter to darken a blue sky.

Remember, however, that when you change the rendering of one color, you also change the rendering of other colors in the scene. For example, if the subject in a portrait has deep-red lips and blue eyes, the lips may be too dark in the black-and-white print. You can lighten the lips with a red filter, but at the same time, you darken the eyes. In a case such as this, a CC40 red filter yields about the maximum correction that can be applied without making the eyes too dark. If you require a strong orthochromatic rendering, use two CC50 cyan filters over the enlarger lens.

***PANALURE* F**
(at 20 C or 68 F)

Kodak Developer	Dilution	Development Time in Minutes		Purpose
		Recommended	Useful Range	
Dektol	1:2	1½	1 to 3	Normal tones
Ektaflo, Type 1	1:9	1½	1 to 3	Normal tones
Ektaflo, Type 2	1:9	2	1 to 3	Warmer tones
Selectol	1:1	2	1 to 3	Warmer tones
Selectol-Soft	1:1	2	1 to 3	Lower contrast

***PANALURE* PORTRAIT E**
(at 20 C or 68 F)

Kodak Developer	Dilution	Development Time in Minutes		Purpose
		Recommended	Useful Range	
Selectol	1:1	2	1½ to 4	Warm tones
Ektaflo, Type 2	1:9	2	1½ to 4	Warm tones
Selectol-Soft	1:1	2	1½ to 4	Lower contrast
Dektol	1:2	1½	1 to 3	Colder tones
Ektaflo, Type 1	1:9	1½	1 to 3	Colder tones

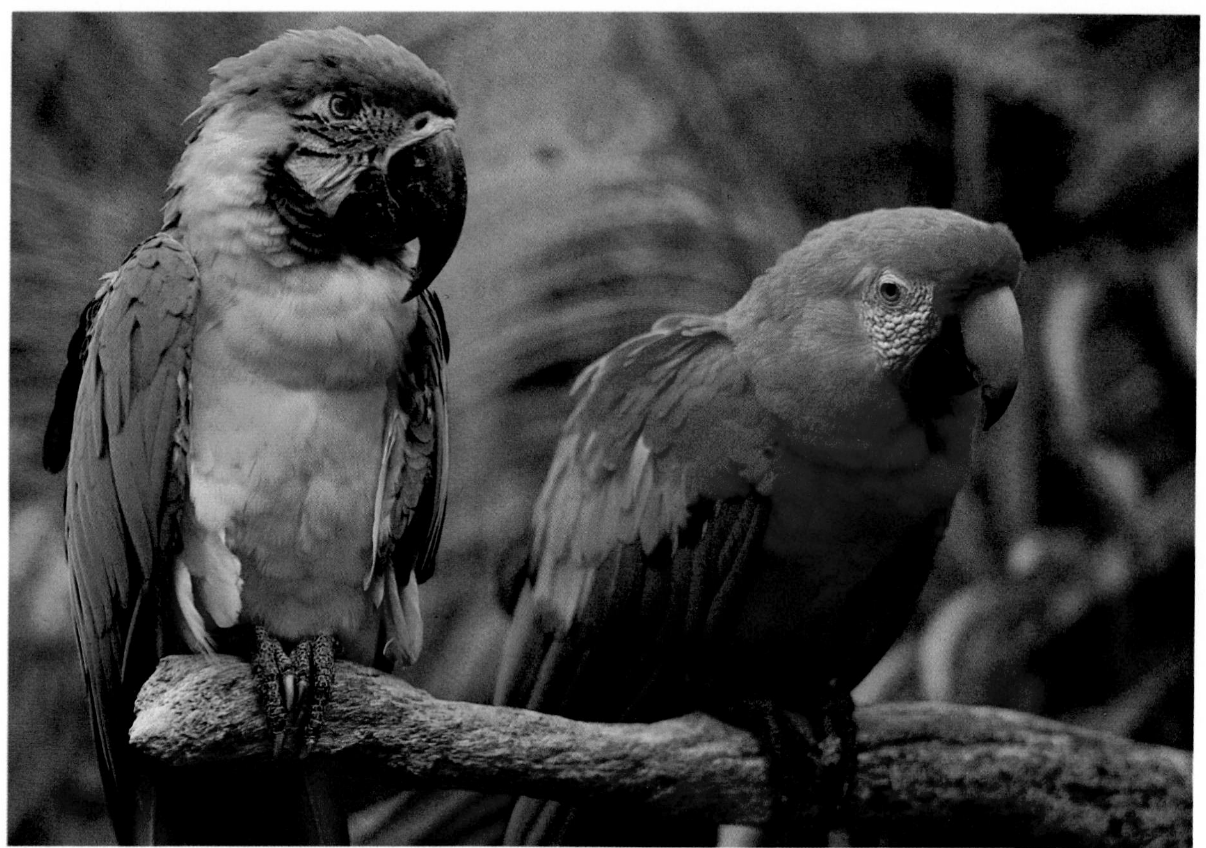

Black-and-White Prints from Color Transparencies

Since a color transparency (or slide) has a positive image, you'll have to make a black-and-white negative before you start making prints. There are several ways to do this.

First, and easiest, load your camera with an ordinary black-and-white panchromatic negative film. Set up your slide projector and project the slide you want to print on a screen or a white matte wall. Position your camera as close as possible to the projector lens-to-screen axis. Determine your exposure by taking a reflected-light reading of the projected image from the camera position. Hold your meter so that you don't shadow the screen or read any of the black border around the image. When you develop the film, you will have a black-and-white negative to use for printing.

Another easy method that may give you better quality is to use a slide-duplicating device that fits on the camera lens or camera body. These are available for many small-format cameras, usually at a reasonable cost. Again, load your camera with an appropriate black-and-white negative film. Fit the slide duplicator to the camera, determine exposure by following the directions packed with the duplicator, focus, and take a picture. Process the film, and you're ready to start printing.

Probably the most accurate, though not the easiest, way to make a black-and-white negative from a color transparency is to use an enlarger. You might have to remove the transparency from its cardboard or glass mount to fit it into the enlarger negative carrier. Focus and compose the projected image on the enlarging easel. It's helpful if you compose the image so that the resultant negative will fit a standard negative carrier.

Eliminate all stray light from the enlarger. If necessary, cover the enlarger lamphouse with a black hood or cloth. To prevent overheating the

Choice of the black-and-white film used to record the transformation from color is most important. The orthochromatic film used to make the black-and-white print (below) is insensitive to reddish colors, and records them in similar tones of gray. Panchromatic film (bottom), however, is sensitive to the full spectrum and records tonal values in a manner more closely related to the original colors.

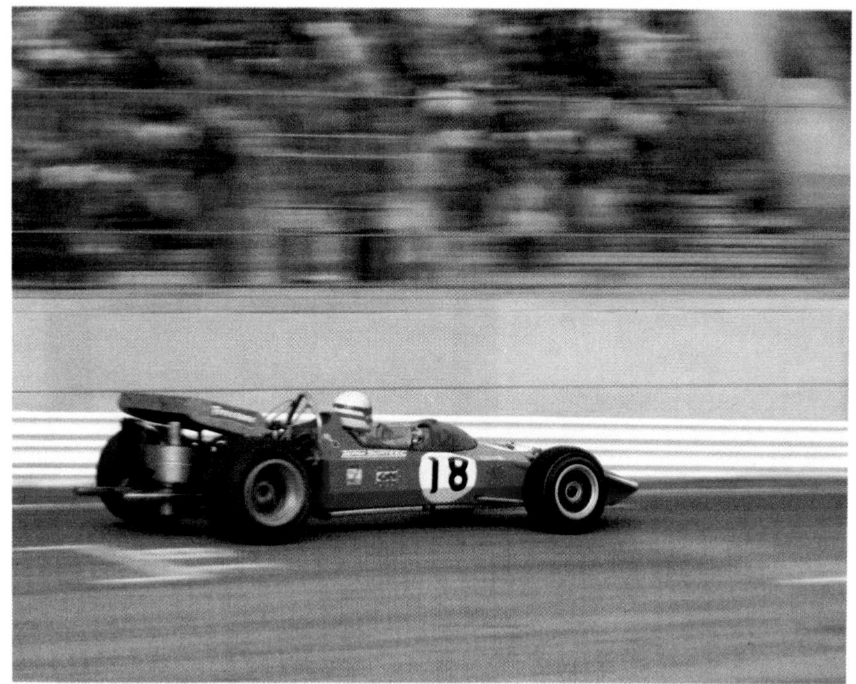

Black-and-white conversions can often be improved by using filters with the enlarger or slide duplicator. The color of the filter chosen would depend upon which colors in the original transparency were most in need of correction. (For more information, see the article on Filters.)

hooded lamphouse, keep the enlarger on for short periods only during focusing and composing. If your enlarging easel has a white surface, cover it with black paper; this prevents any stray light from striking the white surface and possibly fogging the film on the easel.

Turn off all the lights and place a sheet of black-and-white panchromatic negative film, such as Kodak Super-XX pan film in the enlarging easel, emulsion side up. Turn on the enlarger and make a test exposure. (A 3× enlargement from a normally exposed transparency on Super-XX pan film will usually require a one- to three-second exposure at *f*/16.) When you've determined the exposure, you're ready to make a negative.

After exposing, processing, and drying your new black-and-white negative, you're all ready to make a black-and-white print.

Sometimes you can improve your pictures by using filters with the enlarger or slide duplicator. You can also fit your camera with filters if you're copying a slide from a projection screen. Follow the same rules as for photographing the original scene on panchromatic black-and-white film.

Further Reading: Carroll, John S. *Photographic Lab Handbook,* 4th ed. Garden City, NY: Amphoto, 1977; Nibbelink, Don and Rex Anderson. *Bigger and Better Enlarging.* Garden City, NY: Amphoto, 1974.

Black-and-White Slides and Transparencies

Slides and large-format transparencies may be made in black-and-white by two basic methods: copying on color film, or reversal processing of black-and-white film.

If the original subject is black-and-white—a photographic print or an etching, for example—it is simple to copy it on color transparency film. It is only necessary to make sure that the illumination is matched to the color balance of the film emulsion. Details of setup, lighting, and exposure are given in a separate article. (*See:* COPYING.)

There are certain limitations to this approach. It obviously will not produce black-and-white slides of color subjects. Certain paper emulsions and printing inks that appear black to the eye reproduce with a bluish or brownish tinge on color film. And some papers that look white may photograph with a color tinge because of dyes or fluorescent "brighteners" used in their manufacture.

A far more flexible method, which may be used with all subjects, is to photograph on a black-and-white film and develop the image as a positive transparency by the procedure known as reversal or direct positive processing. There are also direct-reversal films for this which use standard processing. Not all films produce satisfactory results when reversal-processed, especially those with thick emulsions or high speed. There are two films in particular that do produce excellent black-and-white slides. Kodak Panatomic-X film is convenient for small quantities of slides because it is available in standard-length 35 mm magazines. Kodak direct positive panchromatic film is available in 100-foot rolls and is the preferred choice for large-quantity production of black-and-white slides.

Small amounts of film may be processed easily by using the chemicals supplied in the Kodak direct positive film developing outfit. Detailed procedures for using this kit are included in the article DIRECT POSITIVE PROCESSING. For larger-scale production, it is easier and more economical to mix your own solutions. Formulas and procedures are in the article REVERSAL PROCESSING.

• *See also:* COPYING; DIRECT POSITIVE PROCESSING; REVERSAL PROCESSING.

Black Body

A black body is a theoretical object that has the properties of being both a perfect absorber and a perfect radiator of radiant energy. That is, it will absorb any and all radiant energy falling upon it, reflecting none; at the same time, if it is heated to a given temperature, it will radiate all the energy generated. No such body exists, but it can be approximated using a box made of completely black material, with a small hole in one side, from which radiation is emitted. When a black body is heated to a certain range of temperatures, part of the radiated energy is in the form of light. This light varies in color from a dull red at approximately 500 to 550 C (932 to 1022 F) to bright red at 850 to 950 C (1562 to 1742 F), to yellow at 1050 to 1150 C (1922 to 2102 F), and so on. Thus the color of a light source can be specified in terms of a black body heated to some temperature at which its radiation will match, in color, that of the light source being measured. The temperature is measured in Kelvin degrees, which are the same temperature intervals as Celsius degrees, but zero degrees Kelvin is at − 273 C.

• *See also:* COLOR TEMPERATURE; COLOR THEORY; MIRED.

Black-Light Photography

This article covers the basic techniques for making illustrative pictures by ultraviolet energy or "black light." For more specialized uses and more detailed procedures, see the article ULTRAVIOLET AND FLUORESCENCE PHOTOGRAPHY.

The delicate and dramatic colors of this still-life composition are entirely the result of reflected light. Large pieces of colored fluorescent paper were hung around the room and illuminated with black light. The shiny surfaces of the objects reflected the colors. Photo by Albert L. Sieg.

The "Blacklight Blue" fluorescent tube. Be sure to get the dark blue "BLB" lamp—not the "BL," which is white.

To understand how to use black light for photography, first consider light—or radiant energy. Radiant energy that the human eye can see is called "white light" and is made up of the colors ranging from the violets to the reds. Radiation that is just beyond the blue wavelengths that the eye can see is called ultraviolet. It is composed of short, medium, and long wavelengths.

The long wavelength, or black light, is the most useful ultraviolet radiation for photography. It is also safe, causing no harm to the skin or eyes.

Every substance is composed of millions and millions of atoms. When invisible black-light rays hit certain of these atoms, the energy of the rays is absorbed and the atoms become excited; they move around trying to rid themselves of this extra energy. As they slow down, the extra energy is released as visible light in various colors that you can see and photograph. This is called fluorescence. As soon as the black light is shut off, the substance stops glowing.

Substances that exhibit this phenomenon are said to be fluorescent; there are more than 3000 of them. Many are readily available today as inks, paints, crayons, papers, cloth, and plastics.

Since the kind of fluorescence you will be photographing is generally weaker than most normal room lighting, you should work in a darkened room so that the colors aren't overpowered by bright room lights.

In addition to a fluorescent subject, you will need only a black-light source and a filter for your camera lens to start trying black-light photography.

Light Sources

There are many sources of long-wave ultraviolet illumination, but the easiest to obtain and use are black-light fluorescent tubes.

Fluorescent Tubes. Several sizes are available from electrical supply, hardware, and department stores. The 15-watt size fits easily into a desk lamp or a strip fixture, and two tubes will supply ample

Subjects for black-light photos may be found anywhere. These musical notes were cut from soapboxes and pasted on a glass sheet; the toy horn was found in a child's toy box. Photo by Albert L. Sieg.

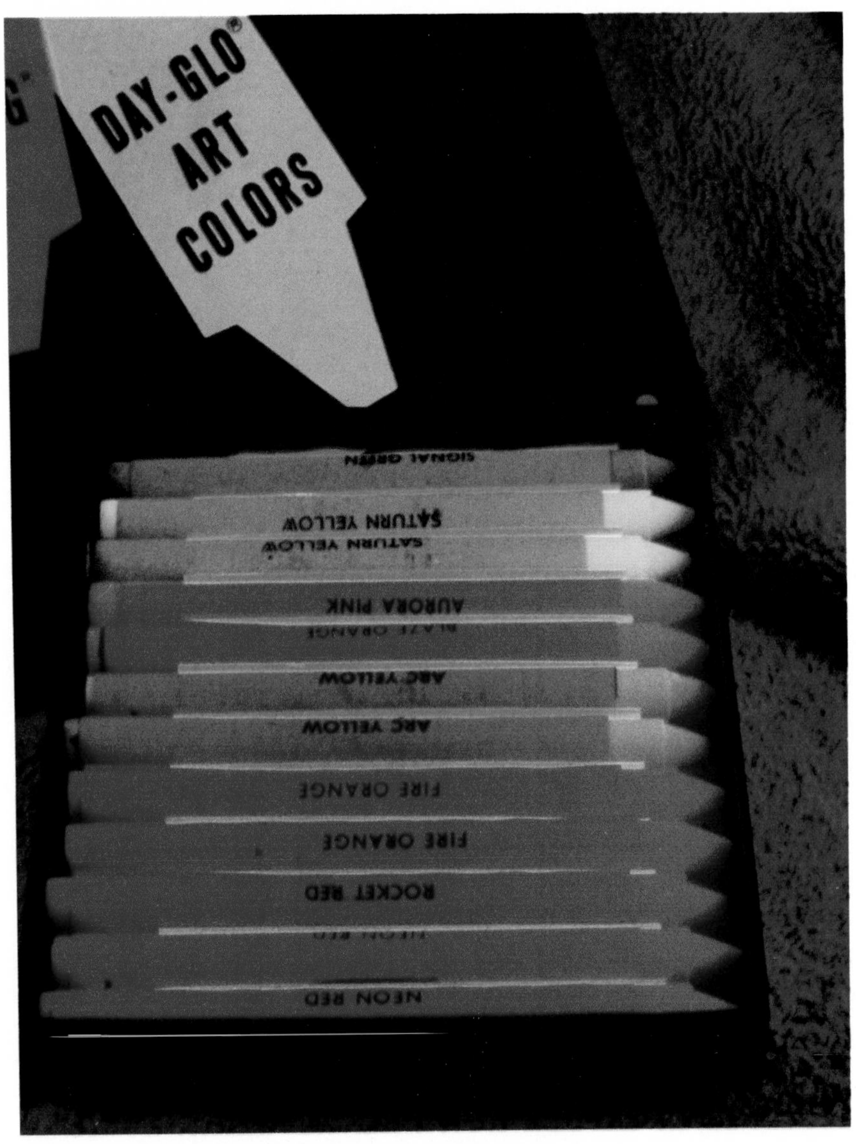

Fluorescent crayons shown under black light. Photo by Albert L. Sieg.

light for photography. These tubes are made by all the major lamp manufacturers and are identified by the code F15T8-BLB.

Whatever length tube you buy, be sure it is marked BLB (Black-Light Blue). This lamp is dark blue in color and has a built-in filter that virtually removes all visible light. Do not use a BL lamp—it gives off white light as well as black light and is not useful for the purposes described here.

To control the light, you can fit aluminum-foil reflectors right on the tubes. These will shield the light from the camera lens and will also be useful for shading and for introducing lighting control.

Flashtubes. A second potent source of black light is the flashtube used in electronic flash units. The manufacturer places a filter in front of the flashtube (usually by building it into the transparent plastic cover) to remove much of the normal ultraviolet light, otherwise normal color pictures would be too blue. To achieve maximum ultraviolet output, remove this filter if possible. Whether or not you remove the built-in filter from the unit, placing a

Kodak Wratten ultraviolet filter No. 18A in front of the flashtube will make your flash unit a convenient, portable, action-stopping source of sufficient ultraviolet illumination for black-light applications.

Exposure suggestions are given later in this article. Experiment with your exposures and record them so that you can determine your own guide numbers for your converted flash unit.

Eye protection is generally not necessary when you use long-wave ultraviolet, or black light, because this radiation is considered harmless. If you look directly at the lighted tubes, the eye fluids will fluoresce, causing some discomfort, so it's best not to look directly at the tubes for any length of time.

Materials

Fluorescent materials are just about everywhere. Many items around the house already fluoresce and are just waiting to be photographed.

A search through the kitchen, children's toy boxes, and closets with your black-light source turned on will light up countless fluorescent items.

Tempera or poster fluorescent paints. The blue background is a towel that had been laundered in a detergent containing a whitener. Photo by Albert L. Sieg.

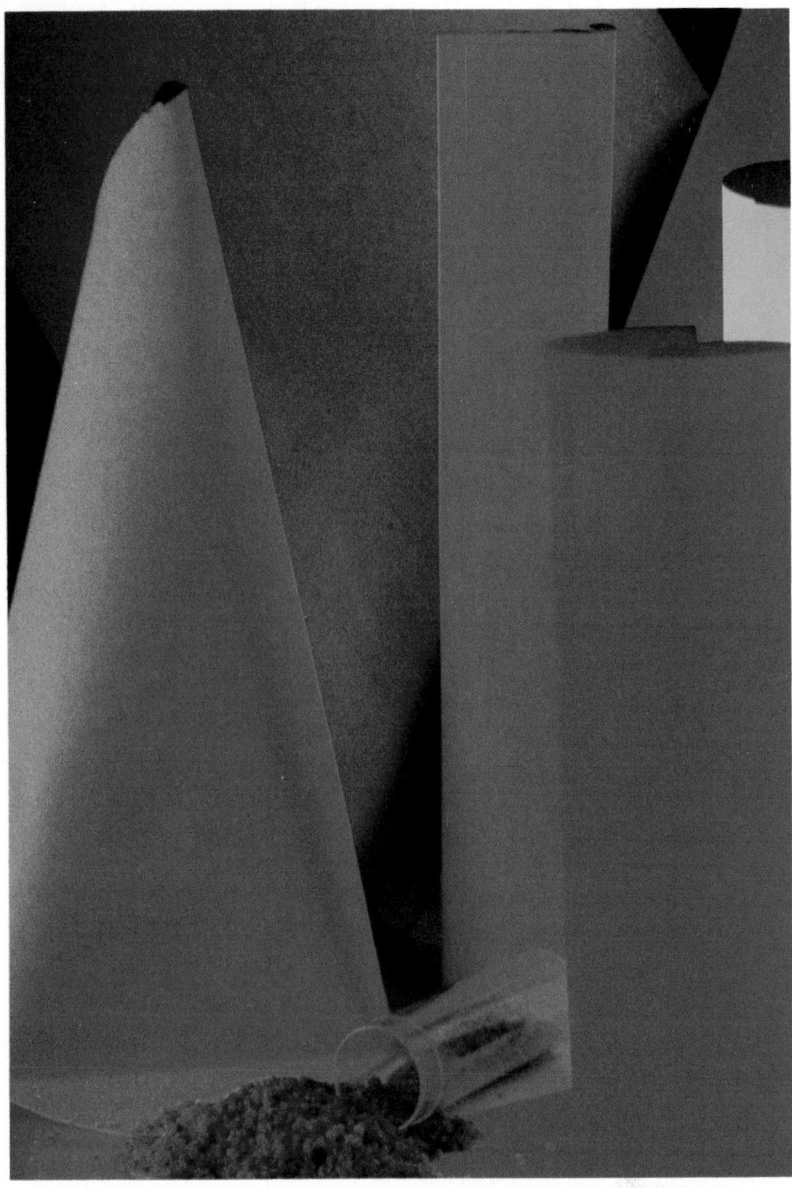

Fluorescent paper folded in geometric shapes. These were photographed on a daylight film that accented the warm colors. Photo by Albert L. Sieg.

Plastic building blocks, jump ropes, plastic items of many descriptions, items of clothing, boxes with bright-colored printing, detergents, and petroleum products are just a few typical examples.

If you want to photograph things that don't ordinarily fluoresce, you can apply fluorescent paints, chalks, and crayons. Art supply stores, arts and crafts shops, variety and discount stores, and hardware stores are all likely places to purchase items such as fluorescent spray paints, water and oil paints, crayons, chalks, coated papers, and brush pens. Most of these items are also available by mail order from Edmund Scientific Company.

Filters

The only other item you need for black-light photography is an ultraviolet filter, to be used over the camera lens.

In general, all films are sensitive to ultraviolet radiation. In almost all of your black-light photography, much reflected ultraviolet radiation will be entering the camera lens along with the visible light from the fluorescing subject. If this unwanted ultraviolet is not filtered out, your pictures will take on an overall blue cast and the colors will be washed out (on some occasions, however, this "mistake" can be used in a creative way to produce very pastel, bluish effects). The best filters for blocking unwanted ultraviolet light are the No. 2 series, such as 2A, 2B, 2C, and 2E. The 2A is the most readily available filter from camera stores.

In a pinch, you can use a No. 85 filter (the orange filter used to convert type A films for use in daylight) or a No. 8 (K2) filter, the widely used yellow filter employed to darken skies in black-and-white photography. These last two filters, while useful, will absorb the blues in your pictures and should be used only when you have nothing else available.

Films

Both daylight and artificial-light films can be used successfully for black-light pictures.

The same papers photographed on an artificial-light film that intensified blues and greens. Photo by Albert L. Sieg.

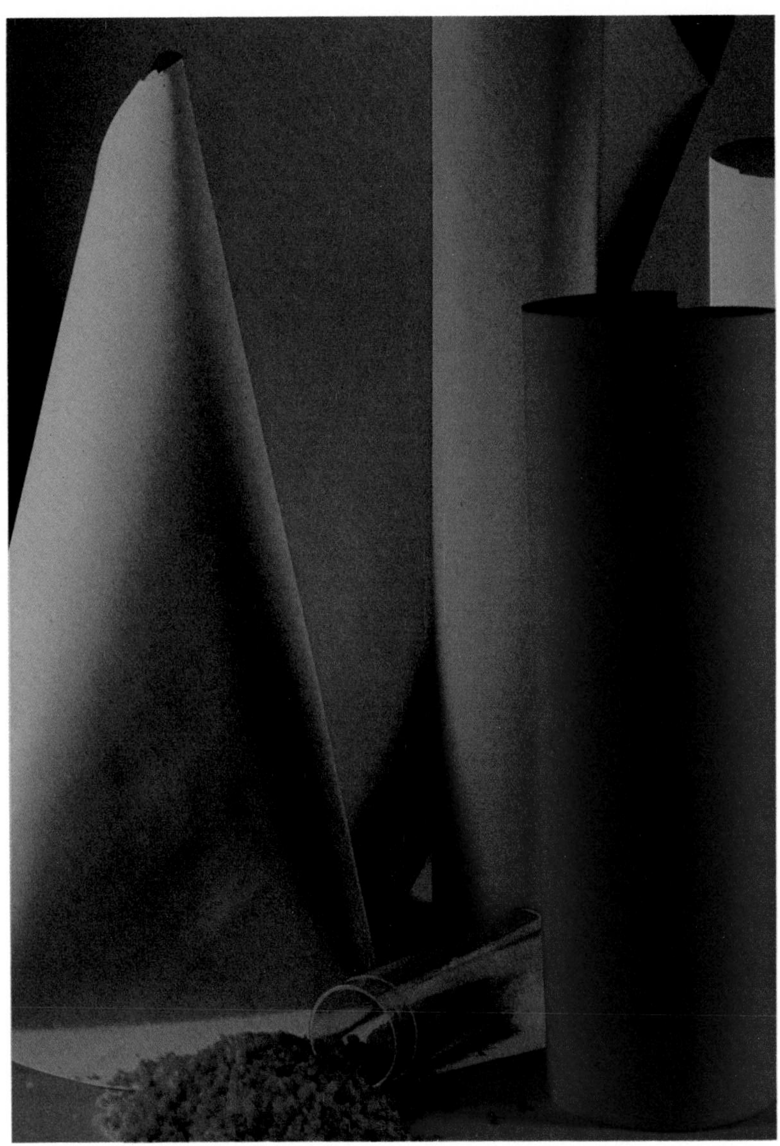

Daylight films all give strong, warm colors, accenting the reds and yellows.

Artificial-light films accent the cooler colors, giving very good renditions of the greens and blues.

Exposure

To determine exposure for photographing fluorescing subjects, make a few simple test exposures. Individual situations will vary in much the same way as some situations you encounter in other types of picture-taking.

As a starting point, place two 15-watt BLB fluorescent tubes 12 to 18 inches from your subject, and set the lens opening at *f*/16 with an ASA 64 film. With this setup, a five-second exposure will usually produce acceptable results. Bracket your basic exposure by making exposures at both *f*/11 and *f*/22.

A sensitive reflected-light exposure meter is helpful in determining correct exposure. Just set the meter for the normal ASA speed rating for your film.

But you must be careful. The reflected ultraviolet radiation that can affect your film so adversely without a filter over the camera lens will also cause your meter to give incorrect readings. Therefore, make your meter reading through the same filter that you intend to use over the camera lens.

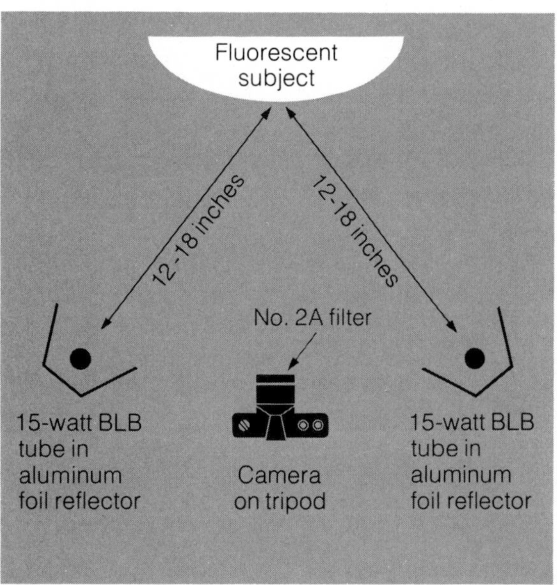

Frequently in black-light photography, the backgrounds are very dark, so you should take close-up meter readings of only the subject areas that are actually fluorescing. If your meter is built into the camera, move in close to the subject to make the reading.

Even when you use an exposure meter, it's a good idea to bracket one stop over and one stop under the meter's recommended exposure, at least until you become familiar with the technique.

Most color films exhibit a reciprocity effect, which decreases the effective film speed when the lens is open for one or two seconds or longer. Essentially, this means that you may have to give approximately twice the exposure indicated by the meter when this exposure exceeds a second. This is another good reason for bracketing your exposures. For specific information on the reciprocity characteristics of color films, see the data sheets available from your photo dealer or the film manufacturer.

Uses and Ideas

The uses of black light in photography are limited only by your imagination and willingness to try something new. Once you have mastered the basics, you can explore all kinds of ideas.

Geometric Patterns. Geometric patterns are easily built with a toy called the Space Spider, available in most creative toy departments or from Edmund Scientific Company. You can make many interesting designs with the fluorescent strings provided.

If geometric shapes intrigue you, photograph other toys such as D-Stix. Here you will have to add the fluorescent color by painting the sticks. Fluorescent spray paints come in a variety of colors and are easy to apply to these intricate forms. Once your setup is constructed, be sure to photograph it from many angles. Unusual angles frequently produce the best picture composition.

Glassware. You can make some strange and brilliantly colored pictures of glassware filled with

(Left) Test exposure setup for photographing a fluorescent subject. (Right) Glassware was filled with fluorescent chalk, then partially filled with water. When chalk settled, upper edges of glassware were rubbed with petroleum jelly to produce blue outline. Photo by Albert L. Sieg.

PYREX

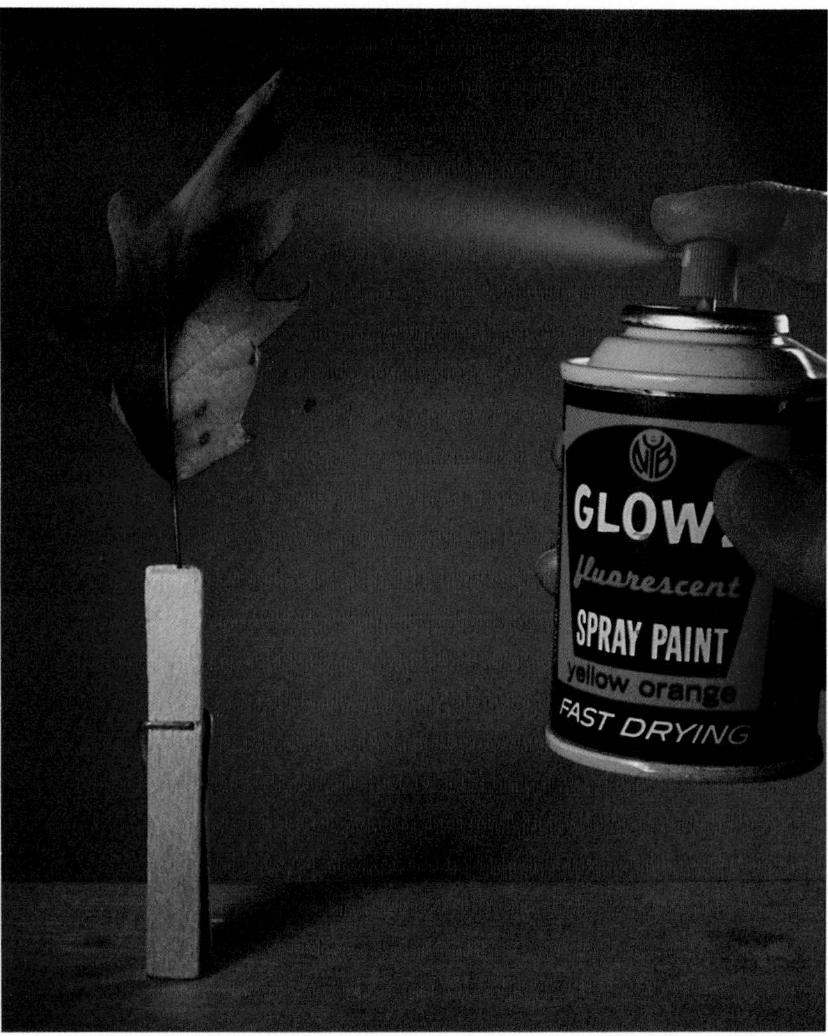

Depending upon the type of article to be painted, either spray or brush may be used. (Left) All the leaves in this photo were spray-painted. A brush was used to paint the branch. (Right) Spray paints are particularly useful for odd-shaped objects such as this leaf, and can be applied quickly and easily. Photos by Albert L. Sieg.

water to which some of the fluorescent watercolors have been added.

Another technique is to fill the bottom of the glass piece with grated fluorescent chalk and then partially fill it with water. After the chalk has had a chance to settle, a transparent color will form under the black light. This transparent quality differs from the more opaque quality of color produced by watercolors.

To add highlights to the glassware, touch up the sides and rims of the containers with fluorescent paint of the same color as the water inside, or rub them with petroleum jelly to outline them in blue. This adds new interest and sparkle.

Tabletops. Traditional tabletop setups are fun, but try adding the punch of brilliant color by painting your props with fluorescent paints. You can enliven almost any tabletop setup by using this painting technique and black light.

Applying Fluorescent Paint. When painting materials such as glass, plastics, metal, and wood, you can usually get better adhesion of the fluorescent paints and better color saturation if you first use a base coat of flat white latex paint.

When you mix colors, do it under black light. You will probably be disappointed with the results if you mix the paints in normal light and then see them under black light.

People and Action—with Flash. One of the newest and most exciting areas of black-light photography is photographing motion by using an electronic flash converted to a black-light source with a Kodak Wratten ultraviolet filter No. 18A. With this portable high-speed black-light source, you can open a new, vivid world of color and motion.

An exciting and colorful application of high-speed black-light photography is the photographing of go-go dancers in fluorescent costumes at discotheques.

Or closer to home, you can take pictures of your family suitably made up. Many cosmetics fluoresce, and rubbing petroleum jelly into the skin will cause it to fluoresce an eerie blue. Many bright-colored clothes also fluoresce.

Special Effects. It is possible to extend black-light photography even further by combining it with other techniques. You might try bubble pictures lighted by black light. Place your subject in an aquarium or other clear transparent container, cover the subject with water, and then add club soda (approximately 1 part of club soda to 40 parts of water). In about an hour, you will obtain an unusual effect from the bubbles that form on the surface of

(Above) Action black-light photography is possible if electronic flash is converted to a black light by using a Kodak Wratten UV filter over the unit. Black light at 1/1000 sec. stopped this dancer, whose clothes were made from fluorescent materials. (Left) These "demons" are halloween masks arranged in glass wool that was spray-painted with red fluorescent paint. Photos by Albert L. Sieg.

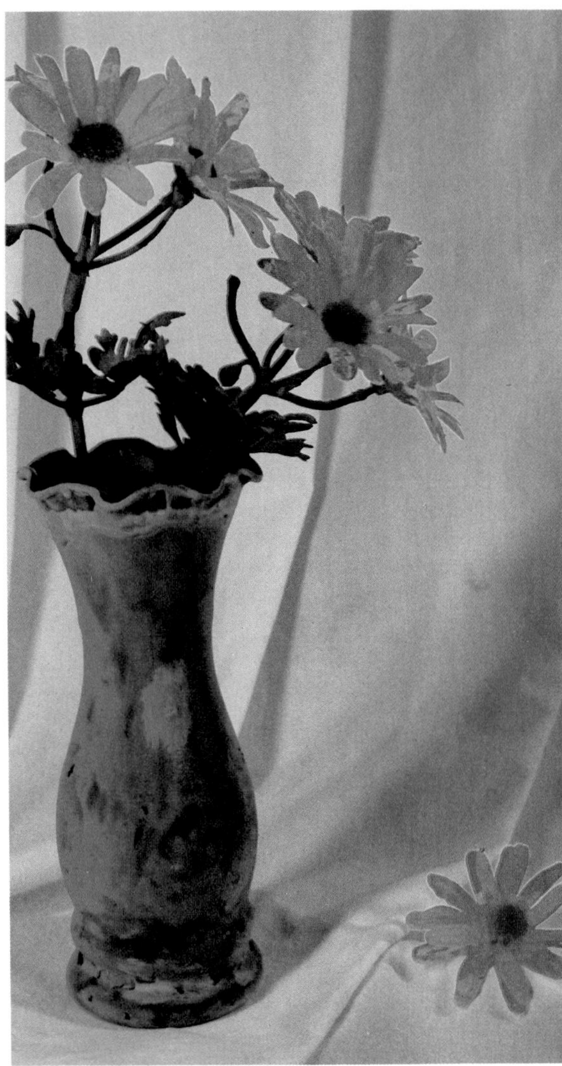

(Left) A still-life photographed under black light with Kodak Ektachrome-X film. (Right) A similar composition and light source, photographed with infrared film and a color filter over the lens. Photos by Albert L. Sieg.

the subject. Or you might go way out and use Kodak Ektachrome infrared film and a No. 15 filter.

Reflected black light either alone or combined with ordinary visible light can be useful to illuminate shiny objects, such as metal and glassware. You might even try the black-light flash method on such subjects as tropical fish for unusual nature pictures. For surrealistic effects, combine water and oil paints with powders and crayons. This mixture can be painted, poured, or smeared onto black construction paper and photographed both wet and dry.

• *See also:* ULTRAVIOLET AND FLUORESCENCE PHOTOGRAPHY.

Further Reading: Eastman Kodak Co., ed. *Infrared and Ultraviolet Photography.* Rochester, NY: Eastman Kodak Co., 1972;———*Ultraviolet and Fluorescence Photography.* Rochester, NY: Eastman Kodak Co., 1974.

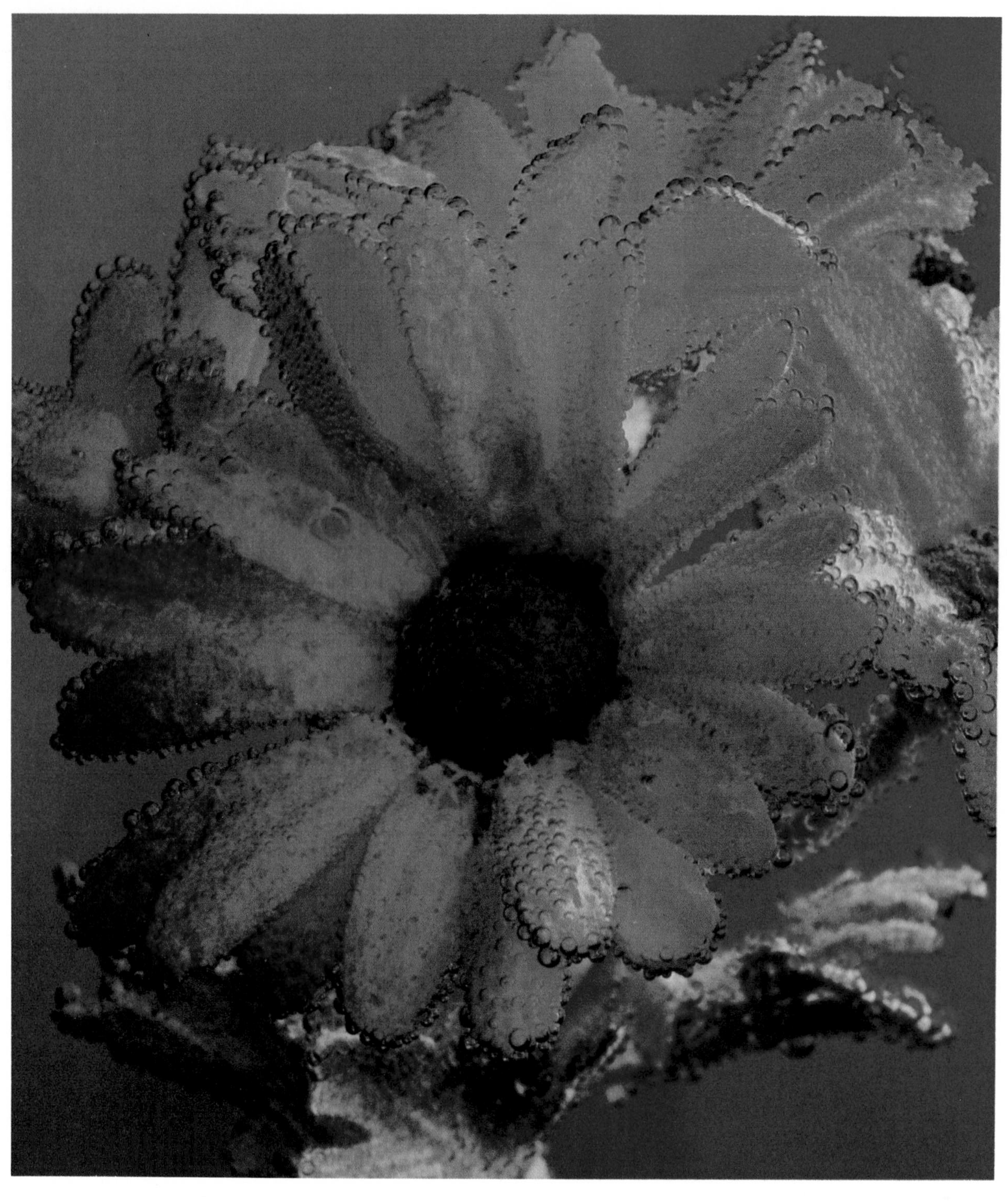

The subject was placed underwater in a fishbowl and club soda was added. The bubbles that formed gave a new texture to the black-light effect. Photo by Albert L. Sieg.

Bleach-Fix

Bleach-fix is a combination solution used in the final stages of some color film and print processes to remove the silver images after the corresponding color image has been formed; that is, to bleach and fix them. As the bleaching takes place, the fixing action of the solution simultaneously dissolves away all unused silver halides in the emulsion. Bleach-fix is not simply a combination of potassium ferricyanide and sodium thiosulfate (Farmer's Reducer), which would have a very short life, but a more complex solution not conveniently prepared in individual darkrooms. Bleach-fix is generally available as part of a complete set of color-processing chemicals and solutions.

• *See also:* COLOR FILM PROCESSING; COLOR PRINTING FROM NEGATIVES; COLOR PRINTING FROM TRANSPARENCIES.

Bleaching

A silver image may be chemically reduced to a colorless state as a preliminary step in a number of processes. In this state, the image may be reconstituted, or it may be removed completely from the emulsion.

For intensification or reduction, the bleached image can be conventionally redeveloped to a greater or lesser density range. For toning, it may be redeveloped in a solution that produces a color image. Localized bleaching is one means of retouching negatives or prints. In various dye, pigment, and transfer processes, bleaching makes the gelatin receptive to pigments or dyes in proportion to the strength of the original image.

In reversal processing, the negative image is first developed and bleached. The bleaching changes the silver image into a silver halide image. Then the remaining halides in the emulsion are re-exposed and developed to form a positive image. In color slides, dyes are formed along with the positive silver image and remain when both negative and positive silver images are bleached away.

Bleaches are also used to remove stains and fog from images, and to clean darkroom equipment.

Among the most common bleaching solutions are: potassium ferricyanide and sodium thiosulfate (Farmer's Reducer); potassium permanganate and potassium metabisulfite, or permanganate and sulfuric acid; and potassium bichromate and sulfuric or hydrochloric acid.

Frequently, a bleach leaves coloration in the emulsion, which can be removed by a clearing bath —a 5–10 percent solution of sodium sulfite, or sulfite and sodium bisulfite. Formulas and use of various bleaches are included in the articles about the processes to which they apply.

• *See also:* REDUCTION; RETOUCHING.

Bleed

To bleed is to print, mount, or trim an image so that it runs completely to one or more edges of the support material. A bleed print is a borderless print. "Bleed" also refers to printed reproductions that run to the edge of the page.

This photograph has been printed to bleed at the right and bottom of the page.

This overexposed and overdeveloped negative is much too heavy and contrasty. A proportional reducer will remove density from both highlights and shadows.

The proportional reducer has lowered both density and contrast to get a negative that will print on normal paper. Photos by John S. Carroll.

Blocked Highlights

Overdevelopment—especially in combination with overexposure—causes highlight details to build up excessive density in a negative. As a result, if the print is exposed for the shadows and midtones, the highlighted areas on the print do not receive enough exposure to print, so those areas are left blank, showing only the color of the print base material. Often, the use of a softer grade of paper will provide a better match for the density range of the negative and will allow the highlights to print with tone separation.

It is generally a good procedure to adjust development according to the subject brightness range and the exposure given the film. In some cases, treating the processed negative in a superproportional reducer will remove enough silver from the highlights so that the negative density range is made printable.

• *See also:* DEVELOPMENT; REDUCTION.

Block-Out

Block-out means to eliminate details or portions of an image. Photographically, opaque retouching fluids are used to block out parts of a negative; visually, opaque pigments are used on a print. A blocked-out print is usually rephotographed in order to make copies in which the treatment is not visible on the surface. Print details may also be removed by selective bleaching.

Common uses of block-out include eliminating unwanted shadows or backgrounds, isolating elements for silhouette presentation or combination printing, and concealing setup and support structures in exploded views.

Block-out can also be done photographically by the use of extremely high-contrast films, such as one of the Kodalith ortho films. They can be contact-printed to the original negative to create a blocked-out positive. Some opaquing and bleaching is usually required. If it is known at the time the picture is taken, and a view camera is being used, an original blocked-out negative can be made in the camera. The positive is made by contact-printing the camera blocked-out negative. This technique is especially useful in exploded-view photographs for instruction manuals.

• *See also:* BACKGROUNDS, ELIMINATING; EXPLODED VIEWS; RETOUCHING.

Blueprint Process

The ferroprussiate process, popularly known as "blueprint," is commonly used for duplicating mechanical drawings that have been made on tracing cloth or other transparent substances. The tracing cloth or transparent substance is placed right side up on the commercially obtained blueprint paper and printed through the back to obtain a print of white lines on a blue ground. For additional formulas and variations for printing from photographic negatives or positives, see the article CYANOTYPE. Printing is slow, and either sunlight or a strong artificial light is used. Print by inspection until the ground color appears bronzed. The process is completed by simply washing in three or four changes of water until the print is cleared, showing white lines on a blue ground. The print is stable unless exposed to bright light for a long time. If it fades, it can be restored by keeping it in a dark, damp place. As perspiration is always alkaline, fingerprints will show up on blueprints if they are handled with moist hands. Correc-

To block out extraneous details in the picture at left, opaque pigments were used on another print. That print was then rephotographed, resulting in the picture at right.

tions can be made on blueprints by using Prussian blue watercolor for the ground and a pen dipped in a 20 percent solution of neutral potassium oxalate thickened with a little gum arabic for the whites. For an emergency job, a five per cent solution of oxalic acid can be used for the whites, but this rapidly corrodes the pen.

Blueprint Paper

Blueprints are made commercially in continuous operation from rolls of sensitized paper, which is carried, together with the drawings in contact, on an endless belt around a glass cylinder lighted from within.

As the drawings are likely to be larger than available printing frames, occasional work is done by placing the drawing and the sensitized paper under a sheet of plate glass on a drawing board and exposing to the sun.

When printing from negatives, the paper should be placed in contact with the emulsion side of the negative. The range of tones of a blueprint is so short that except for special effects, it is not suitable for anything but line negatives, but very handsome effects are sometimes obtained by using it for pictures of suitable subject matter. There is a marked falling off in the depth of the image when washing the print, and this should be taken into account when printing.

Commercial blueprint paper is just about unobtainable today; engineering and architectural plans are now commonly printed by the Ozalid process, which has certain advantages. Blueprint paper is easy to make, however, and the sensitizer can also be used for fabrics. The sensitizer is painted on the paper with a wide brush; fabrics are sensitized by immersion. The sensitizing may be done in room light, but the coated paper should be dried in the dark. The sensitizing solution should be prepared in small quantities as it deteriorates rapidly; left-overs should be discarded.

Ferroprussiate Sensitizing Solution

Solution A
Ferric ammonium
citrate (red) .... 250 g
Water .... 1000 cc
Filter after solution is complete.

Solution B
Potassium ferricyanide........ 200 g
Water .... 1000 cc
Filter before use.

The ferricyanide must be perfectly clear ruby-red crystals and should be freed from any adherent yellow powder. To do this, allow a little more in weighing out and place the crystals in a flask; pour in some distilled water, shake, pour off the water, and repeat this operation; then add the water for the solution and heat until dissolved. Mix the two solutions in equal volumes and filter. Either float the paper on the solution for three minutes, or paint on the solution freely with a broad flat brush. After applying the solution, dry the paper as quickly as possible, preferably by heat.

A much more sensitive paper is obtained by using the green ammoniocitrate of iron; then the solutions should be:

Solution A
Ferric ammonium
citrate (green).............. 125 g
Water .... 500 cc
Filter and add:
Solution B
Potassium ferricyanide.......... 45 g
Water .... 500 cc
Filter before use.

The separate solutions keep fairly well in brown bottles; once mixed, they deteriorate rapidly. Mix only as much as is needed to coat the amount of paper you intend to use within a day or so; the coated paper also deteriorates.

For use, mix equal parts of the two solutions and coat paper with a wide brush having no metal in the mounting. You can obtain brighter prints by adding a small amount of oxalic acid solution to the above, and the paper can be given better keeping qualities by adding a trace of potassium bichromate to the solutions. Printing is done by daylight or by the light of a Type RS sunlamp bulb.

You will note that with long exposures, the background, which first turns blue, starts to lighten again and becomes a grayish color. The blue color returns when the paper is washed after exposure, and the deepest blues are obtained by exposing until the darkest parts of the image are gray rather than blue. In all cases, the image loses considerable density in washing, so exposure should be longer than needed to produce a good visible image.

No treatment other than washing is required; after washing, dry normally. Fabrics should be ironed lightly with a warm iron while damp.

• *See also:* CYANOTYPE.

Borax

Sodium tetraborate, sodium pyroborate, sodium biborate

A mild alkali used mainly as accelerator in developers of low pH, such as Kodak D-76. It is also used as a buffer in fixing baths and hardeners. It increases the rate of deposition of gold in gold toning baths.
Formula: $Na_2B_4O_7 \cdot 10H_2O$
Molecular Weight: 381.37

White crystalline powder, soluble in water and glycerin, insoluble in alcohol. Solutions are weakly alkaline.

• *See also:* ALKALI.

(Below) A weak flash is bounced off a white umbrella for a combination of available light and flash illumination. Photo by Don Nibbelink. (Right) The resulting portrait is softly shadowed, as with natural light; however, shadowing has been controlled by the photographer's ability to aim flash so as to provide some modeling. Photo by Steve Schlosser.

Boric Acid

Boracic acid, hydrogen borate, orthoboric acid

Weak acid, used as a buffer in fixing baths and some developers.
Formula: H_3BO_3
Molecular Weight: 61.84

Fine white crystals or fluffy white powder, soluble in water and alcohol. The powdered variety floats on water and is difficult to dissolve, so for photographic uses, the crystalline form is generally preferred.

Bounce Light

In photography, direct light is produced when a light source is aimed directly at the subject. Bounce light is the illumination produced by instead aiming

lamps or a flash unit at a reflective surface such as a wall, a ceiling, or a folding umbrella-type or other reflector.

There are several good reasons for taking pictures by bounce light. First of all, it's easy. Second, it produces a very "soft" and natural type of lighting —there are no dark shadows. Third, by aiming the light toward the ceiling, you'll obtain even lighting in the general vicinity of the light. This means that in many rooms, you won't have to change exposure settings on your camera when your subject moves around the room.

While shadows are soft with bounce light, you can control them somewhat based on where you aim the light source. A side wall will reflect light only on one side of the subject, providing some "modeling," which gives a feeling of roundness and solidity. If the color balance can be adjusted, bounce light is a good way to fill in the shadows when the main illumination in a room is sunlight coming through windows. Light bounced from the ceiling will wash gently down over all the frontal surfaces of the subject. For greatest efficiency and spread of light, aim the source into a corner so that you have three reflectors working for you: the two walls and the ceiling.

Bounce light can be achieved with flash units as well as with continuous-burning sources such as photolamps. (*See:* FLASH PHOTOGRAPHY.) You can take pictures with bounce light if you have an adjustable camera with a fast lens (*f*/1.9 or *f*/2.8). You can use any reflector-type photolamp; a movie light works fine. If you're taking color pictures, the ceiling must be white or a light gray. A colored ceiling will reflect its color onto your subject.

For a start, point your photolamps at the ceiling, aimed slightly forward of the camera position. Just don't let light fall directly from the lamps onto the subject. Of course, because the light is reflected, your subject won't be as brightly lighted as when the lights are pointed directly toward it. For this reason, it's a good idea to use a fast film, such as Kodak Tri-X pan film for black-and-white prints, or a Kodak high speed Ektachrome film (tungsten) for color slides. If your camera isn't automatic, use an exposure meter to determine the correct shutter speed and lens opening. If you don't have a meter, try the settings in the accompanying table.

This table is based on the use of a 625- or 650-watt tungsten-halogen movie light (3400 K) aimed at a white ceiling. These same exposures apply to a three-lamp movie light using 300- or 375-watt reflector photolamps. If you use two 300- or 375-watt reflector photolamps, try a lens opening one-half stop larger than that shown in the table.

SUGGESTED EXPOSURES

Film Speed (ASA)	Shutter Speed	Lens Opening
25	1/30 sec.	*f*/2
40	1/30 sec.	*f*/2
100	1/30 sec.	*f*/2.8
125	1/30 sec.	*f*/2.8
250	1/30 sec.	*f*/4
400	1/60 sec.	*f*/4

• *See also:* LIGHTING.

Bracketing Exposures

Bracketing is carrying out a procedure to the normal degree and to greater and lesser degrees for purposes of testing or to ensure satisfactory results under unfamiliar conditions. The most common example of bracketing is in the exposing of film. In addition to the normal, or meter-indicated exposure, greater and lesser exposures are made at consistent intervals. It is common to bracket negative films in one-stop intervals, and transparency films in half-stop intervals because of their smaller exposure latitude. The changes can be made by adjusting the lens aperture setting or the shutter speed, or by changing the speed rating of the film and calculating exposure anew. Doubling the speed rating produces an exposure one stop less than normal; halving the rating produces one stop more exposure.

Bracketing is used in printing to see the effects of various exposure times, as in a series of test strips, or to see the results of varied filtration, as in a color print ring-around.

Development is bracketed by processing identically exposed materials at normal, greater, and lesser times or temperatures. The combining of exposure and development bracketing produces a valuable ring-around for evaluating negative-making procedures.

• *See also:* RING-AROUND; TESTING.

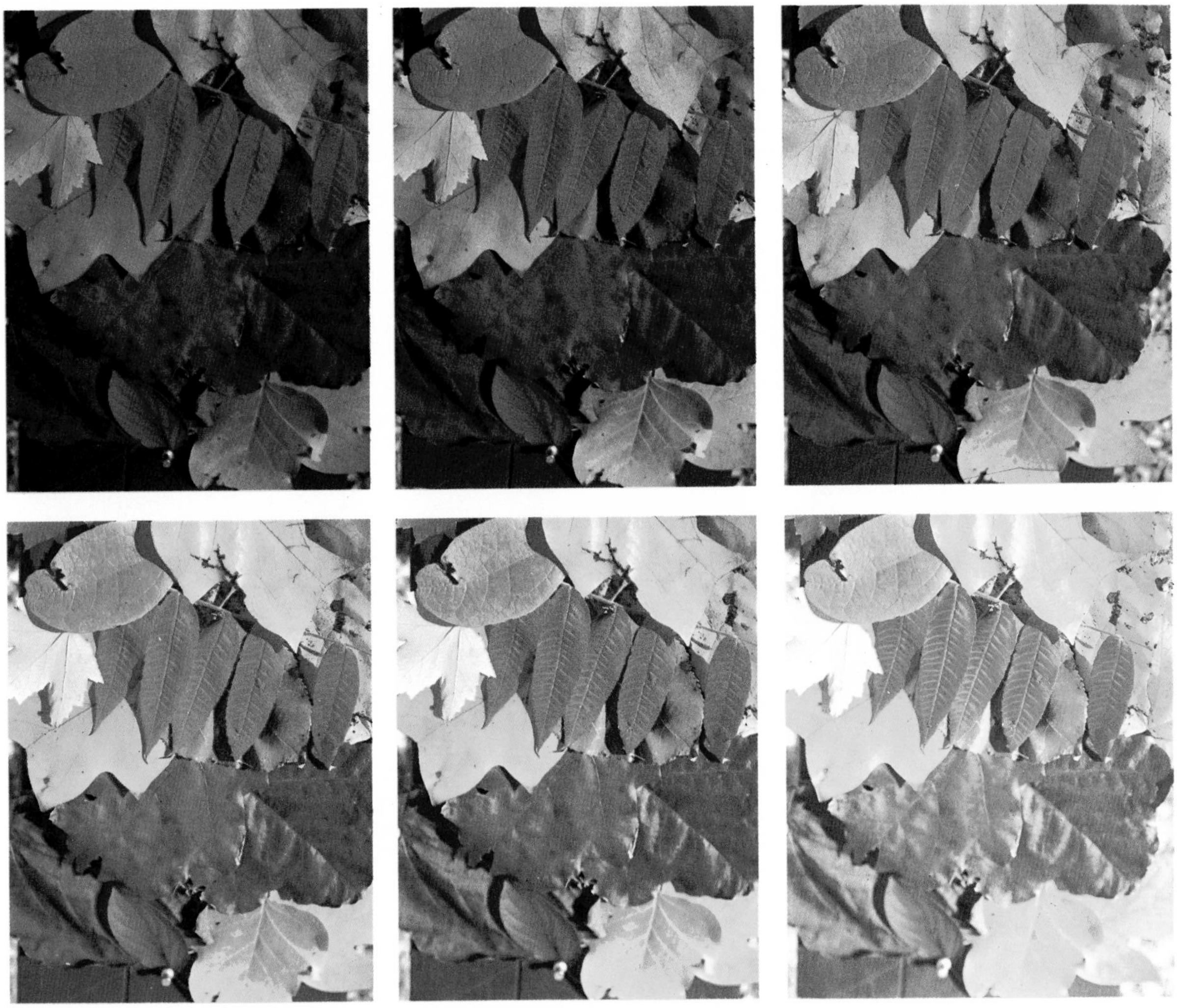

Under controlled circumstances, difficulty in visualizing the final effect of a photograph can be solved by bracketing. Although the darkest and lightest exposures here would probably be rejected, each of the remaining four is a valid representation of the subject. Photos by Andreas Feininger.

Brewster, Sir David

(1781–1868)
Scottish scientist and optician

Brewster was the author of an early book on optics and photographic lenses. He invented the refracting stereoscope in 1844 and the twin-lens stereo camera in 1849. He also built reflecting stereoscopes, used for studying large-size stereo images.

Bright-Field Illumination

Generally, a lighting arrangement that provides a single-tone, shadowless background (surrounding field) that is brighter than the subject is termed bright-field illumination. It is a specific technique in close-up photography, photomacrography, and photomicrography for obtaining a full or partial silhouette image. The field may be opaque material lighted from a frontal angle, diffusing material lighted from behind, or the direct rays of the light source focused into the lens field of view by a condenser system. The degree of silhouette effect varies according to the transparency of the specimen, which may transmit some of the field brightness, or according to the amount of frontal light directed onto the subject.

• *See also:* DARK-FIELD ILLUMINATION; PHOTOMACROGRAPHY; PHOTOMICROGRAPHY.

Brightness

Brightness is the term used for the luminous intensity of a surface in any given direction from that surface, as seen by the eye. It applies only to extended sources or reflective media, whereas *intensity* refers to the light emitted by a source of zero dimensions (a point source). Measured brightness is called luminance. Luminance units are the candle per square foot, or candle per square centimetre (known as the *stilb*). Other units of luminance are the lambert, which is equal to $1/\pi$ stilbs, and the footlambert, which is $1/\pi$ candles per square foot (which is also equal to one lumen per square foot).

• *See also:* EXPOSURE; LIGHT.

Brightness Range

Brightness range is the difference in intensity of light reflected from the darkest and the brightest parts of the subject. It is commonly expressed as a range of so many stops, or as an equivalent ratio. While technically this is the luminance range, photographers usually use the term brightness range. To measure the brightness range, take a reflected-light reading of the darkest part of the subject to be reproduced, and note the *f*-stop called for at any convenient shutter speed. Then take a reading of the brightest part of the subject to be reproduced and note the *f*-stop called for at the same speed. The difference between the two readings is the brightness range in stops.

For example: darkest area reads *f*/2.8 at 1/125 sec.; brightest area reads *f*/16 at 1/125 sec. The brightness range is five stops; the equivalent brightness ratio is 32:1.

BRIGHTNESS RANGE

Brightness (Luminance) Ratio	Log Luminance Range	Brightness (Luminance) Range (stops)
2:1	.3	1
4:1	.6	2
8:1	.9	3
16:1	1.2	4
32:1	1.5	5
64:1	1.8	6
125:1	2.1	7
250:1	2.4	8
500:1	2.7	9
1000:1	3.0	10

If fill-in light is used, it is important to choose a subject area that is illuminated by both the main light and the fill for the bright-area reading. Reflected-light readings from a gray card held at various subject positions, or incident-light readings, do not measure the brightness range because they do not take into account subject reflectivity; instead, they measure the lighting ratio, or illumination range. This is why the lighting ratio could be 3:1 while the subject brightness range is 125:1.

The brightness range must be within the exposure range of the film to secure suitable image densities without special processing. Generally, a black-and-white panchromatic film will accommodate a brightness range of over ten stops, a color transparency film will accommodate a range of up to seven stops. If the subject brightness range does not coincide with the exposure range of a black-and-white film, development can be changed within limits to obtain better results. When the subject range is shorter, increased development will render individual tones with greater negative densities, thus increasing their visual separation and overall contrast in a print. When the subject range is longer than the film exposure range, reduced development will hold upper values within the range of printable densities in the negative.

• *See also:* EXPOSURE; LATITUDE; LIGHTING; SENSITOMETRY.

Broad Lighting

An arrangement in which the main light fully illuminates the plane of the subject turned toward or nearest the camera is called broad lighting. It is commonly used in portraiture to deemphasize facial textures, and especially to make thin or narrow faces appear wider.

• *See also:* LIGHTING; PORTRAITURE; SHORT LIGHTING.

Broad lighting, as illustrated here, was at one time frequently used for portraiture.

Bromcresol Purple

Dibromo-o-cresol sulfonphthalein

A dyestuff that has the property of changing color according to the acidity of the solution in which it is contained (chemically, an "indicator"). It is used in stop baths for printing papers, to indicate the exhaustion of the bath.

Formula:

$$SO_2 \overset{C_6H_4}{\underset{O}{\diamond}} C = [C_6H_2Br(CH_3)OH]_2$$

Molecular Weight: 540.02

Light-pink crystalline powder. It is insoluble in water but dissolves in solutions of alkalies, also soluble in water. The solution is purple at solution acidities (pH) of 6.8 or higher, yellow at 5.2 or less. Since on the pH scale the neutral point is 7.0, the solution will turn purple just before it changes from acid to neutral. In stop baths, then, the normal color is yellow, which is not visible under the usual safelight; the bath turns purple as the acid is exhausted, and appears black under the safelight illumination. To prepare a solution of bromcresol purple, dissolve 0.1 gram of the dye in 9.25 ml of N/50 sodium hydroxide solution, then dilute the mixture to 250 ml with distilled water. Add a few drops of this solution (which will be purple) to the stop bath, which will turn yellow, reverting to the purple color when the bath is exhausted.

Bromide

A salt of bromine in which the other ion is usually a metal. In photography, silver bromide is the primary light-sensitive compound in film emulsions, and it is used in combination with silver chloride in print material emulsions. Potassium bromide and ammonium bromide are used as restrainers in developers and bleaches.

• *See also:* DEVELOPERS AND DEVELOPING; EMULSIONS; HALIDE; and individual chemical listings.

Bromoil Process

In this obsolete printing method the positive image on special bromide-emulsion paper was bleached, leaving the emulsion absorptive to oil paints or special greasy inks. The colors were applied by a stippling brush and absorbed in proportion to the densities of the original image. The tones could be darkened or lightened by control of the pigments, giving a large degree of manual control. In the transfer process, the image was transferred to a second support by contact under pressure before the pigments had dried.

BSI Speeds

The BSI Film Speeds are a system of speed ratings for sensitized materials, issued by the British Standards Institute in British Standard No. 1380–1947.

Like the original ASA system, there was a BSI Speed, distinguished by having a 0 in front of the first significant digit, thus 0500, and a BSI Exposure Index, intended for use on various exposure meters calibrated for it. The BSI system differs from the current ASA system in that two Exposure Index systems are used: one has an arithmetic series of numbers, which are identical with the ASA Exposure Indexes; the other uses a logarithmic scale, which is related to the arithmetic system in the following way:

$$\text{BS Log} = 10 \text{ Log BS Arith} + 11$$

Thus a film speed of ASA 200 would convert as follows (log 200 = 2.3):

$$\text{BS Log} = (10 \times 2.3) + 11 = 23 + 11 = 34$$

Because the log of 2 = 0.3, BS log values increase by a factor of three for every doubling of film speed; that is, a BSI speed of 34 is twice as fast as one of 31 and half as fast as one of 37.

• *See also:* ASA, ASAP SPEEDS; DIN SPEEDS; GOST SPEEDS; SENSITOMETRY; SPEED SYSTEMS.

Buffer

A chemical that acts to maintain the pH (acidity or alkalinity) of a solution within a narrow range. A buffer counteracts increasing acidity by combining with some of the hydrogen ions; it counteracts increasing alkalinity by releasing hydrogen ions. Buffers prolong the useful life of some developers and fixing baths and are essential for maintaining the performance of several color-processing solutions.

• *See also:* ALKALI; FIXERS AND FIXING; pH.

Bulb, "B"

Bulb, "B", is a shutter-speed setting at which the shutter remains open as long as the shutter release is depressed, and closes as soon as the release returns to its normal position. The name originated with old squeeze-bulb, air-actuated shutter releases. It is used for brief time exposures. With cameras that do not have a "T" (Time) setting, longer exposures can be achieved by using the "B" setting and a locking cable release; the plunger is locked in the depressed position until the desired exposure has been achieved. The term *brief* is currently a more common term used to identify the "B" on shutters.

• *See also:* SHUTTERS.

Burning-In

Burning-in is the procedure of giving additional exposure to selected areas of a print after the basic exposure has been made in order to darken them. It is most often used to produce tone or to print details

When burning-in a highlight or a dense area of the negative, avoid letting the exposure spill over into adjacent areas. Otherwise, an unsightly dark ring will result.

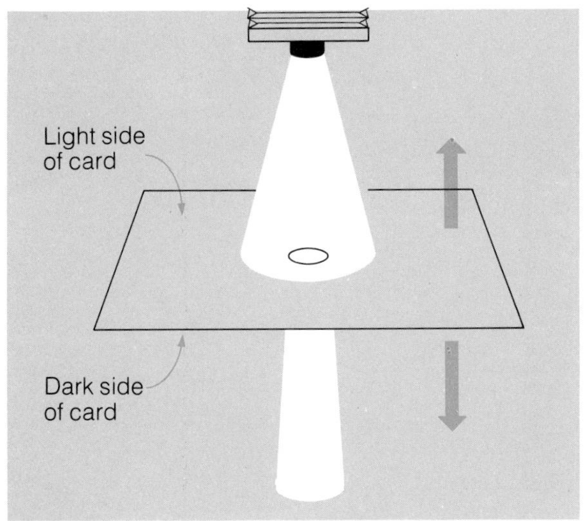

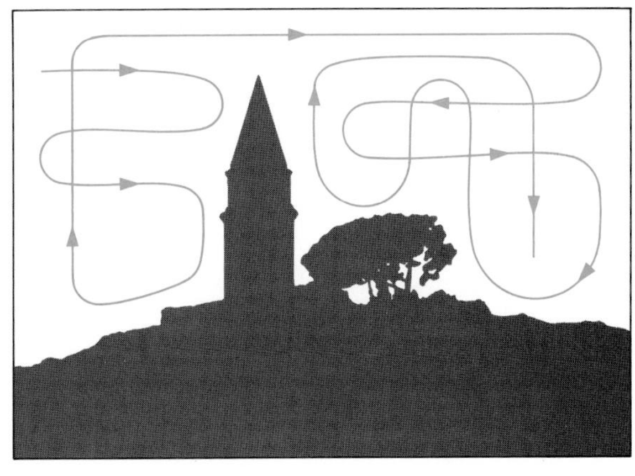

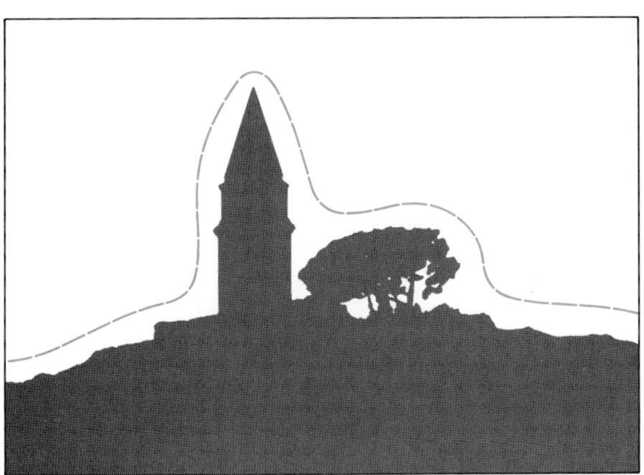

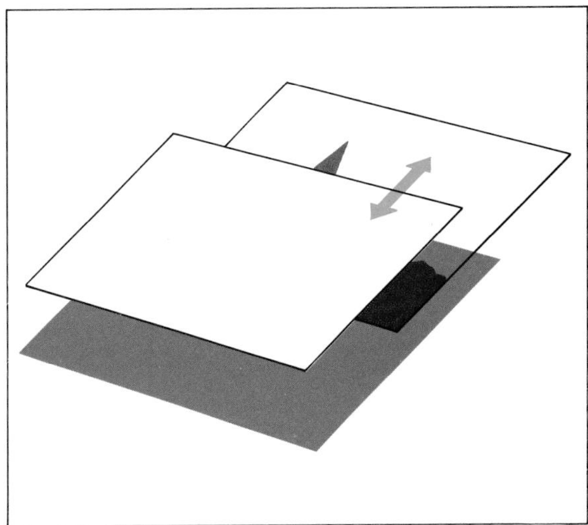

Burning-in techniques. (Top left) Raise or lower an opaque board to vary the size of the area covered by light passing through the hole. (Top right) Keep the light moving in overlapping paths to cover large areas. (Bottom left) Finish by using a small spot of light close to objects to eliminate the brighter "halo" where overlapping seldom occurs equally. (Bottom right) Use the edge of the board for burning-in large areas, and darkening edges or corners of the image. Keep the board moving to avoid a shadow image; work progressively outward for graduated darkening toward the edges.

more strongly in highlight areas, but can also be employed to darken middle range and shadow areas. (With reversal print materials, such as Kodak Ektachrome RC paper, burning-in has the opposite effect: additional exposure lightens the image.)

To burn-in, use your hands or a piece of opaque board with a hole in the center to shadow most of the print and permit light to fall only on the area you want to expose. A light-toned board makes the projected image from the enlarger visible on its upper surface so you can easily see where to move the hole; the lower surface should be dark to prevent reflections from the paper fogging other areas. Use a board somewhat larger than the size of the print so that when you burn-in a corner or edge, the opposite side of the print remains covered.

The paving blocks in this photograph of Red Square are too light, yet the Kremlin Wall and the people waiting on line are correctly exposed.

By holding back the upper section of the print and burning-in the street, an acceptable print was made. Photos by Karl Rehm.

To increase the spread of the light, raise the board toward the enlarger lens; to cover a smaller area, lower the board toward the print. A hole about one inch in diameter is a convenient size; if you need a smaller opening, partly cover the hole with a smaller card. Note that small holes act like small apertures—they reduce the amount of light passing through and thus lengthen the required exposure. Different shaped holes can be used to burn-in odd-shaped areas; cards without holes are used to burn-in the edges of a print.

During burning-in, keep the beam of light moving over the area being exposed, otherwise a shadow image of the hole will be produced. With variable-contrast materials, you can gain an extra degree of control by making the basic exposure through one filter, and burning-in through a different filter, usually of lower contrast. You can burn-in through filters to control results in color printing.

• *See also:* BLACK-AND-WHITE PRINTING; COLOR PRINTING FROM NEGATIVES; COLOR PRINTING FROM TRANSPARENCIES; FLASHING.

Business Methods in Photography

Making a business of photography—earning a living from your work—requires a much greater variety of skills and many more kinds of effort than taking pictures solely for personal purposes. A knowledge of photography is basic, of course, but skill as an amateur is not the same as the technical competence required of a professional. In business, you are working to satisfy others—your customers or clients. You must be able to deliver (a) the pictures that are wanted or expected, (b) on time, and (c) with consistent quality. You must be able to do this on a day-in, day-out basis in order to succeed.

In addition, you must be able to handle business details. These include making contracts or sales agreements with publishers, clients, or customers; hiring assistants and models; purchasing equipment, supplies, and props; protecting your rights in the pictures you produce; planning and promoting your activities; and, above all, keeping the records that are required for legal, tax, and business-management purposes. Accurate records are essential, for they are the only way you will know whether you are truly making a living and earning a profit, or whether you are heading for bankruptcy. You can hire some business assistance—bookkeeping and accounting, legal counsel, and tax advice, for example—but the planning and running of the business, and knowing what advice and assistance to obtain, all are your responsibility.

There are two major aspects of being in the business of photography: establishing the business in the first place, and operating successfully once you

The successful commercial photographer must know how to present a client's product to make it irresistible to the consumer. Here, a simple photograph of the vitamin bottle would not suffice. Instead, an arrangement of highly nutritious foods tells the consumer of the product's virtues. Photo by Stephen Stuart.

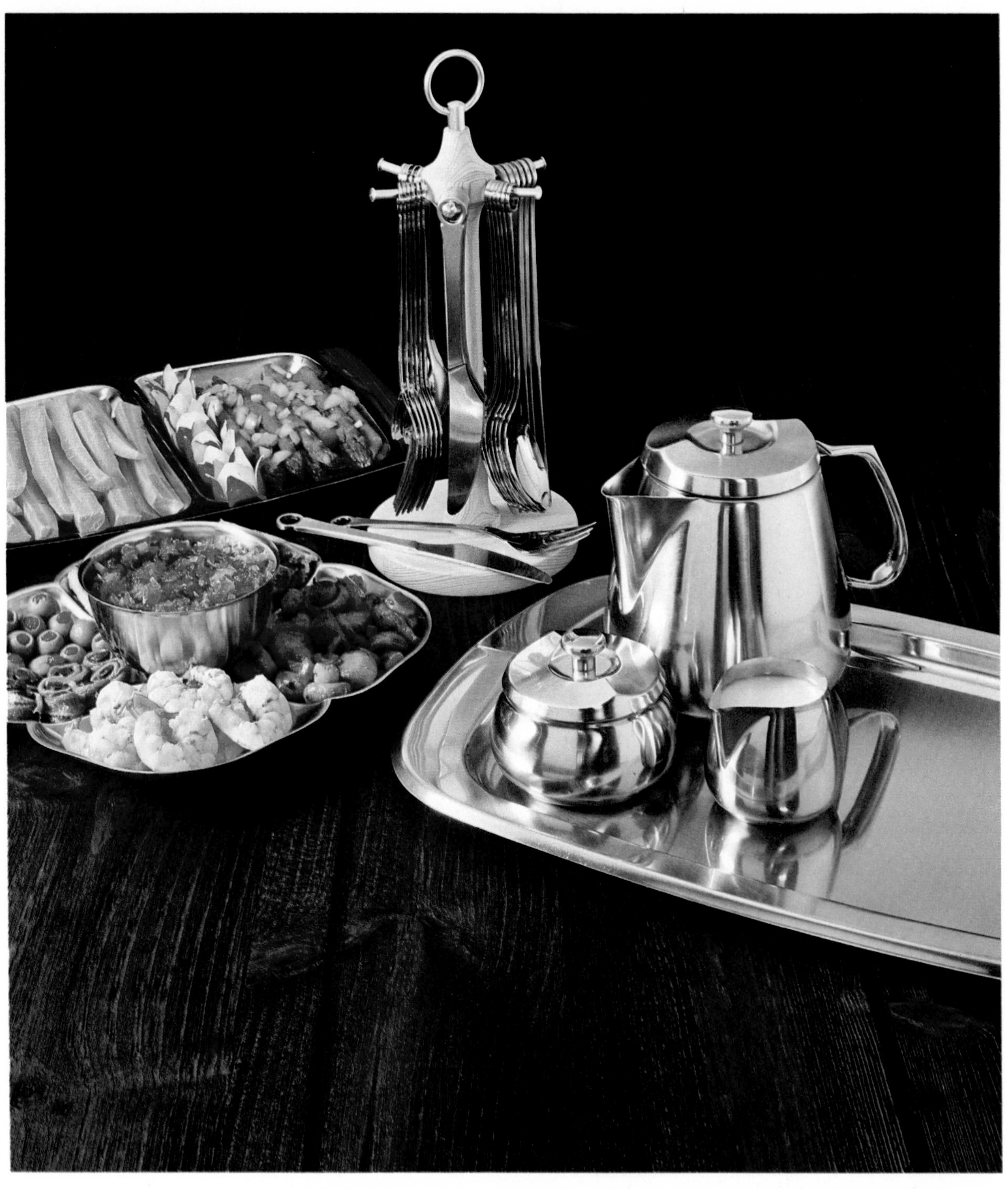

The photographer's ability to display a product attractively must be apparent to prospective clients. This is an excellent portfolio photograph, because it shows that the photographer can work with tableware and food. Art directors and editors of home and entertainment magazines would be interested in a photograph such as this. Photo by Stephen Stuart.

have started. Many of the major factors in both these aspects are discussed here. A number of related topics are discussed in more detail separately; see the list at the end of the article.

Establishing a Business

It is possible to slide into business: You sell a few pictures, then a few more, volume slowly increases, and finally you are spending most of your time in, and receiving most of your income from, photography. That seems the easy way, but it is likely to take far longer than necessary, which is expensive in terms of lost income and opportunities. And it is almost certain to let some bad practices become part of your habitual working methods.

Success is far more likely to come from analysis and planning of what you want to do, followed by positive action. Analysis consists of finding the answers to questions that probe the true nature of the matter. Finding the answers helps you define specifically where you want to go professionally, and how to start getting there. Basic questions about a photographic business should include:

What kind of photographer do you want to be? A freelance, requiring little more than a telephone and a darkroom or a reliable lab? Or a studio photographer, working under controlled conditions, perhaps with a staff of assistants? What kinds of pictures do you want to take—fashion, news, portraits, advertising, industrial? Which type will greatly affect how you go about getting started?

Do you have the necessary skills? Do you really know what is involved in the kind of work you want to do? And do you know enough about the business aspects? This is a critical question. You cannot afford to pay for your own on-the-job training in everything. Working for a year or so as an assistant to an established professional is one of the best ways to learn what needs to be done and how to deal with all aspects of doing it. The pay may not be much, but you will more than make that up in the mistakes you learn not to make when you are on your own.

Is starting your own business the best solution? Often it is not. If you want to be a technical or scientific photographer, for example, the initial investment in special equipment and facilities could be out of the question, or your capabilities might be severely limited by whatever you could afford. In such a case, looking for a position in industry or with a research organization or university would provide far greater opportunities and facilities. Even where technical considerations are not a limitation, there still may be an advantage to entering an existing business, perhaps investing as a partner or buying the business outright. This course provides immediate facilities and an established list of clients—two essential assets that take a long time to acquire when starting a business from scratch.

What kind of business should it be? There are three major choices: As an *individual or sole proprietor,* you have the greatest freedom of action, and all income is yours alone. But so is all responsibility and all liability. If you fail, your personal assets, such as a car and a house, may be claimed to pay off your business debts. A *partnership* shares responsibility and liability; it provides additional capital to start and operate with; and it increases the pool of skills and talents the business has at its disposal. If you are an experienced photographer but weak in other areas, acquiring a business-wise partner could be an extremely valuable move. A *corporation* is not necessarily a giant organization; it can be composed of only one or just a few individuals. Legally, it is an individual in itself. Incorporating may provide you with a number of tax and legal advantages. Almost certainly you should seek professional advice from an accountant or a lawyer in answering this question. A small investment in counseling at the early stages of your business planning is worth many times its cost.

Can you carry out your kind of business in your present location? Is there a market in your location for your specialty—say, fashion pictures, photojournalism, or portraiture? Or will you need to operate where there is more business activity in buying or publishing pictures, more population to provide clients for a studio? Could you commute to another location if necessary, or would you have to move? What is the competition—how many photographers are already trying to split up the available market for the kind of photography you want to do? This kind of market survey is essential. You can begin it by looking at the "Photographer" listings in local business and classified telephone directories and by discussion with the Chamber of Commerce or Better Business Bureau in your target area.

Can you afford it? Do you have the money not only to get started, but to keep operating for up to

Taking family portraits provides steady employment for some photographers. Word-of-mouth recommendations, as well as print advertising, are important methods of attracting clients in this field.

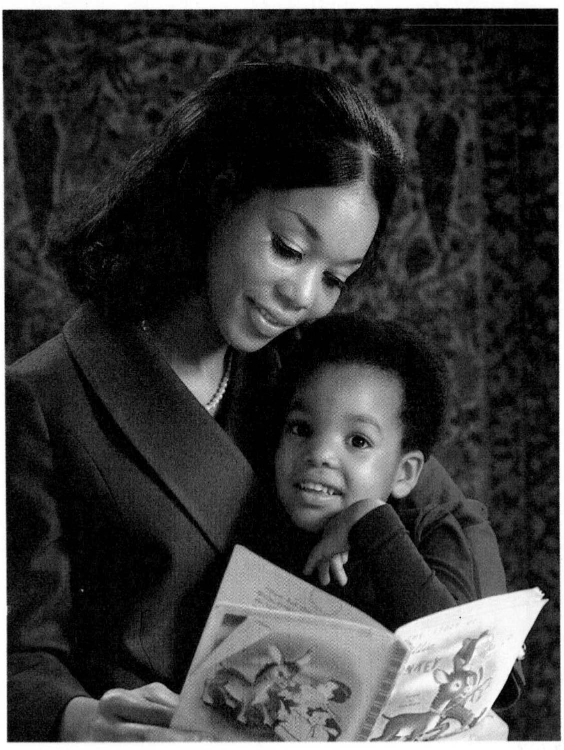

a year? If you begin operation part-time, with another source of primary income, you may be able to build up enough business to make the transition more easily. But your chances of success may well be improved by devoting all of your time to the new business. That means you need start-up and operating money for a year—the earliest you can reasonably expect to show a true profit—plus enough money for your personal living expenses. In figuring how much money you need, there are two major categories: initial capital, most of which goes for nonrecurring equipment and facilities investment; and operating capital. A six-month period is the shortest you should estimate for in detail; you can double your totals to get a yearly figure.

Initial Capital

Photo Equipment (Cameras, Tripods, Lenses, Lights, Backgrounds). The cost of anything directly involved in taking pictures that must be purchased in addition to what you already have must be considered. If you will pay cash, list the total price; if you will buy on time, list the down payment plus the first six installments.

Darkroom Equipment. Everything you will purchase for the processing and printing of pictures is another cost factor. Again, list the total cash cost, or the down payment plus six installments.

Photo Supplies (Film, Paper, Chemicals, Frames, Mounts, and so forth). This is initial inventory which you must have on hand to get started; it will be replaced and used as part of your operating expenses. Figure the cost of what you will need for a six-month supply.

Office Equipment and Supplies (Furniture, Typewriter, Stationery, and the like). List the price, or down payment plus six installments, for equip-

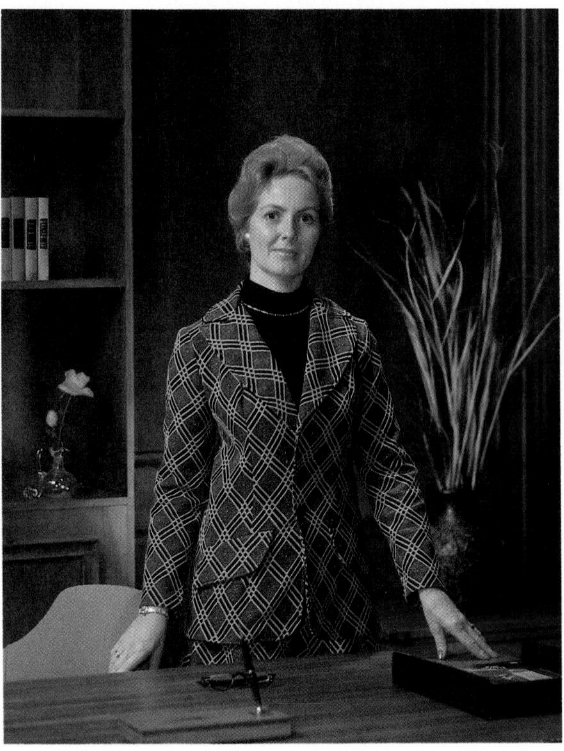

Some photographers specialize in portraits. Large corporations are excellent clients because many of them regularly want photographs of their executives for public-relations purposes.

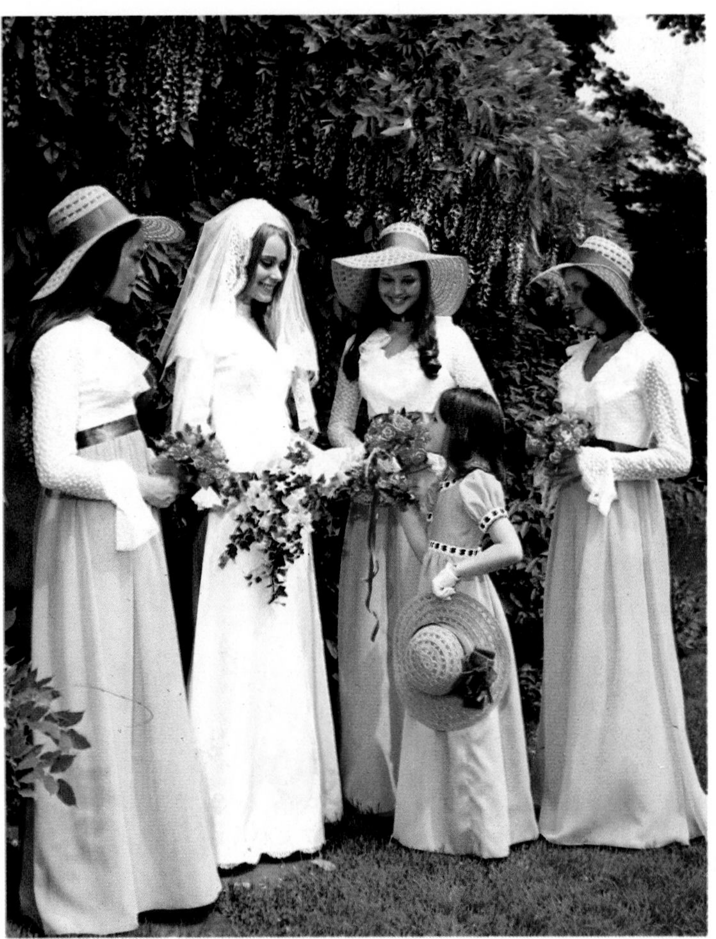

Weddings, as well as communions, bar mitzvahs, anniversary parties, and other social occasions, always need a photographer. Tie-ins with hotels, restaurants, and caterers may be particularly useful in this field.

ment; estimate the cost of a six-month stock of supplies. The expendable items will be replaced out of operating expenses.

Total the preceding four categories and add ten percent as an estimating cushion. This is your initial, nonrecurring capital requirement.

Operating Capital

Your operating costs will include all of the following items:

1. *Rent* for six months.
2. *Utilities*—heat, electricity, water, telephone—for six months.
3. *Salaries* of those who will be working regularly for you—six months.
4. *Taxes, permits, and other required fees.*
5. *Personal expenses*—how much you need to live on and meet all your personal and family expenses (food, housing, insurance, car payments, and such) for nine months.
6. *Other*—advertising, business insurance (property, theft, liability).

Total 1 through 6 and add ten percent as an estimating cushion. This is your estimated initial operating capital requirement.

Add the totals together to find the *minimum* six-month cost of starting your business. Double the amount to arrive at your first year's needs. You should have at least two-thirds of that amount in your own funds before seeking any outside loan or investment. If you turn to other sources, you must

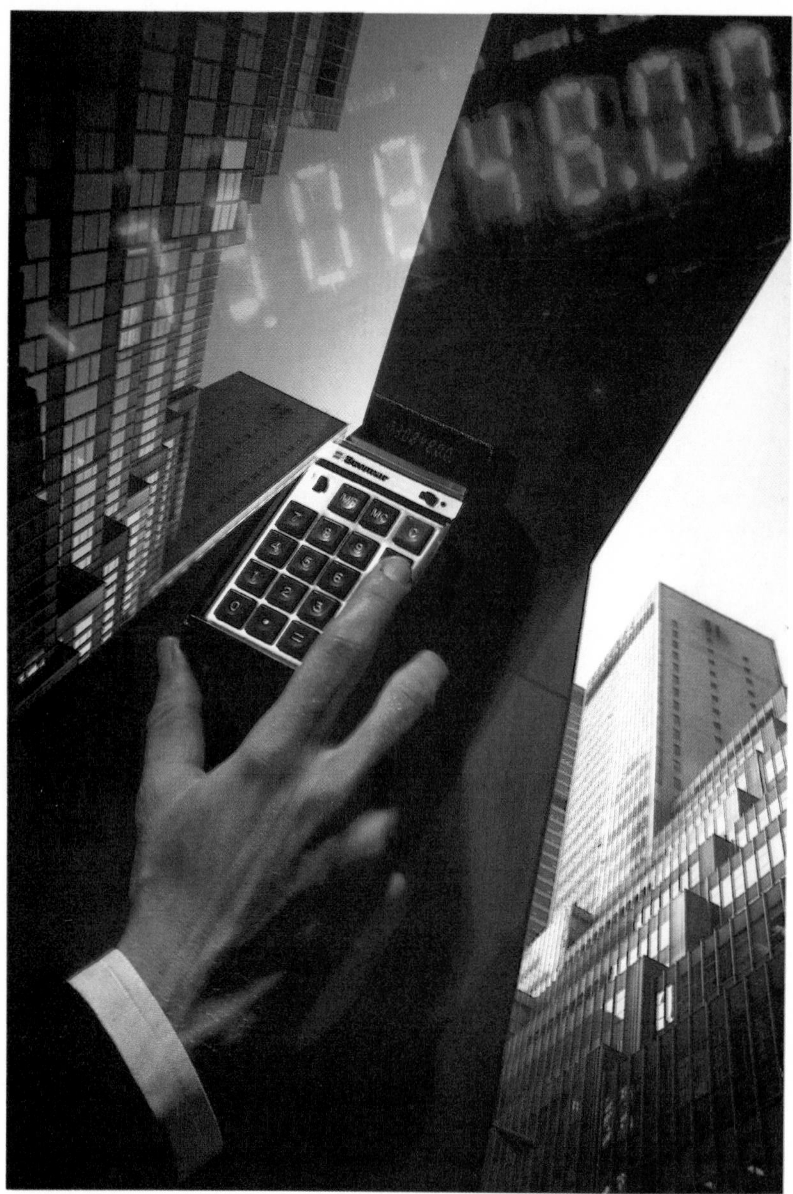

Selling industrial products is big business, and the commercial photographer must be able to present the product in a manner that is both eye-catching and informative. This triple-exposure implies the relationship between the product (the calculator) and big business (the skyscrapers). Photo by William Rivelli.

show this kind of analysis in detail as well as a market analysis—how many sales are possible, at what price and what profit—for any lender to give you serious consideration.

Note that the salary estimate (3) does not include payment to yourself; the inclusion of your personal needs in (5) ensures that you will be working at a personal break-even point, but the capital estimate assumes that you will be willing to work at a no-profit level in order to get the business underway. In further projecting your estimate of operating expenses, you will have to include a reasonable salary for yourself as you will in pricing your pictures and services (see the section on pricing). However, the personal-expense estimate is for nine months rather than six, to ensure that you will have some money to live on while finding work if the business should not succeed.

This kind of planning and analysis may seem tedious, and perhaps discouraging, but it is the only way to make a realistic estimate of your business potential.

Operating a Business

Once a business is started, operating it successfully so that it shows a profit depends on at least three major factors: personal effort, record keeping, and accurate pricing.

Personal Qualities. What you must bring to the business is more than technical skill and the willingness to work hard. You should be able to deal effectively with people (customers and clients, suppliers, and your employees); to be self-disciplined enough to organize your own work; to schedule the work and manage the activities of others so that each job is completed and delivered on time; and to plan ahead for effective advertising, promotion, and expansion.

Unless you have someone managing your sales counter, or calling on clients as your personal representative, it is your own contacts that will make or lose business. One of the best ways to get business is to make the customer feel that you are placing yourself at his or her service. This means, first, making every effort to understand the customer's needs clearly; second, determining the price range the customer has budgeted for; and, third, showing the customer how you can best meet the needs at or close to the customer's price. If the customer's budget is so low that you cannot do the job, or if it is out of your chosen range of work, explain this courteously and try to suggest where he or she can find help. You are not losing anything, and you may gain a great deal in public relations. Of course, that means you must know what your realistic price for a job should be; see the discussion on pricing later in this article.

Suppliers. Dealing with suppliers requires that you plan your needs and order sufficiently in advance so you can demand delivery on time. Rush orders get rushed handling, which often means careless handling and higher-than-normal rates. Your beginning business does not need any extra expenses. The surest way to get prompt service is to make your orders clear and accurate in all details, and to pay your bills promptly. Unpaid accounts make suppliers stop to evaluate how much more credit they are willing to extend, especially to a newly established business.

Prompt Payment. This is often a way to save money. Many firms offer a discount, indicated on their invoices in terms such as *2/10 EOM* (end-of-month), *net 30 EOM;* this means you can deduct two percent from the bill if you pay within 10 days of the end of the month of purchase, or you can take 30 days to pay without a discount. By taking the extra 20 days on a $100 purchase under such terms, you get the use of $98 at a cost of $2, the lost discount. That may seem a cheap way to get the use of some money, but actually it is very expensive. In fact, you are paying 2.04 percent (2/98) for the use

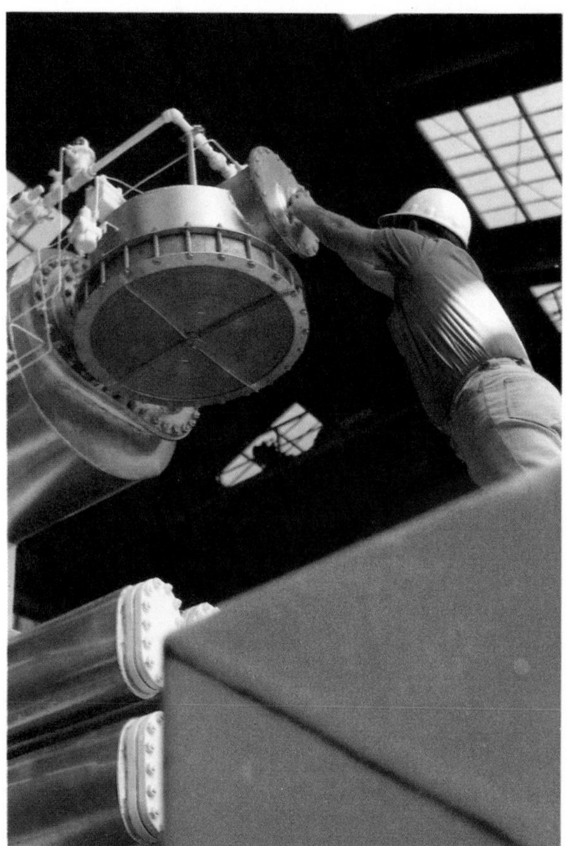

The assignment was to illustrate the annual report of a large textile manufacturer. Because industrial machinery is not especially colorful, the photographer added a large bolt of bright scarlet fabric to the foreground. Photo by William Rivelli.

of $98 for 20 days, or one-eighteenth of a year. In terms of annual interest, that is almost 37 percent (2.04 percent × 18), which is an impossible price to pay for operating funds. You should take advantage of all discounts offered, even if you have to borrow from a bank to do so. The interest paid to a bank is much lower than the cost of not taking the discount.

Managing Employees. Managing your employees, whether they are full-time or hired only for a specific assignment, is a matter of choosing those who have the abilities you need, and of making sure they are efficiently scheduled. A secretary-receptionist will often be the first contact outsiders have with your studio or business; the ability to deal pleasantly with people is probably as important in the person you hire as typing, filing prints and negatives, and basic record-keeping skills. Often such a person is required to spot prints, send out invoices, and pay bills as well.

Studio and darkroom assistants must know how to handle the equipment you have, and how to process film and make prints to your standards; you cannot afford to operate a training course in the basic aspects of photography. When something new comes along, your assistants should be able to grasp it quickly. Models, stylists, makeup technicians, and

Brochures and catalogs for department stores make up a considerable amount of the commercial photographer's business. For a fabric advertisement, it is not enough to show the fabric. The photographer may want to work with a model and a fashion coordinator to create a more appealing photograph. Photo by Norman Mosallem for Editorial Photocolor Archives.

Cosmetics manufacturers do a great deal of advertising. For such advertisements the client may provide its own models, make-up people, and stylist. Photographer and the art director then work out the best ways of displaying the model and the product.

other part-time help are usually hired on the basis of previous performance. After a while, you will have a stock of experience to draw on in selecting those who will work well for you; at the beginning, recommendations from other photographers, and a look at the individual's portfolio or resumé, will give helpful guidance.

Hired help are useful only when they know exactly what is required of them and when. Your job is to plan how you expect to handle each assignment, to divide the work among those available, and then to explain the operation to each individual. That may take only five minutes at the beginning of the day, or it may take some long sessions well ahead of time. Whatever the case, planning and briefing time is an investment that saves money. Once props are rented and models are in the studio, or you are on location with your equipment and assistants, any delays can cost three to five times as much as your planning time, and often much more. Large or small, you are carrying out an operation; anything you have not planned for can create on-the-job delays, which translate into expenses that you, not the client, may have to absorb.

Business Planning. Planning for your business as a whole is also important. You must target the kinds of events, seasonal activities, or anticipated developments with which your work can tie-in. Then you must make the contacts far enough ahead of time to allow others to consider your proposal,

"How-to" magazines always need photographs to display their finished products. This picture might appear on the cover of a needlework publication.

decide to use you, and make an actual agreement. You cannot initiate a campaign for Graduation Day pictures, or coverage of a new business opening, or cooperative holiday advertising just a week or two before the event. By that time, everyone else will have made arrangements, advertising and announcements will have long since been placed, and your answer will be, "Why didn't you ask me about that sooner?"

The same thing holds true for your own advertising and promotions. Be ahead in your thinking and arrangements so that your ads appear and your mailings go out on time. A moderate but steady flow in these areas is far more effective than one or two sudden spurts a year. It is the cumulative effect that counts in building steady business.

Record Keeping. The only way you can tell exactly what is going on in your business, and the only way to get the data you need to plan ahead, is to keep track of everything you do. Service records help you to keep your customers satisfied. Financial and work records are legal requirements as well as business essentials. If you do not have bookkeeping experience, a professional accountant can help you set up a workable system and show you how to use it, for a reasonable fee. Many small businesses find it profitable to hire a bookkeeper's or accountant's services on a quarterly, or even a once-a-month, basis. The business and tax savings that result from properly maintained financial records are greater than the cost of the service.

An important aspect of keeping useful records is identifying every job. In a portrait studio, the customer's name may be sufficient identification, but in other cases (and in portraiture too), assigning a *job number* is a good solution. If you start a new set of numbers each year, it will be easy to locate previous work quickly; you can even use the year as part of the job number. For example, in 1977, the sequence would begin 77–1, 77–2, and so on, and 78–1, 78–2, and so on the next year.

However you choose to identify each job, the following are some of the most important records you should maintain.

Expenses. Expenses are everything that is paid out, with a receipt or canceled check to verify each expense. If the expense is for a particular job, note the job number on the receipt. Keep a daily record and summarize your expenses each month, distributing them in various direct-cost and overhead categories (see the section on pricing later in this article).

Income. Record every payment received: amount, source and job number, date.

Payables. A reminder list of what you must pay in the next 30 to 60 days should be kept so that you can anticipate your expenses, listed by date; recurrent items, such as rent and taxes, can be listed far ahead of time, other items entered as the bills come in. As they are paid, mark them off and enter the payment in your expenses record.

Receivables. These are the payments that are owed to your business. Your list of them should include job number, total amount, balance due, date billed, date rebilled if payment is overdue. They must be marked off and entered as income when payment is received, or transferred to the next month's list of receivables if unpaid. A list of *items to be billed* can be incorporated in this record or kept separately.

Taxes. If you have regular employees, you will be responsible for withholding various amounts for income tax, Social Security (FICA), workmen's compensation, and other purposes. You must pay those amounts and certain employer's contributions to various government agencies. In addition, in most locations, you must charge sales tax and remit it to state and local governments. You need complete and accurate records for these purposes. Often, the kinds of records and the manner in which they are to be kept is prescribed by law. Get professional advice on these requirements at the very beginning.

Clearances and Protections. You must have written permission from each person in every picture you intend to sell or publish for commercial purposes. It is not only professional models who must sign such a release, but every recognizable individual in the picture (the only exceptions are in some public places and public events). (*See:* LEGAL ASPECTS OF PHOTOGRAPHY; MODEL RELEASES.) Be sure the job number or other identification is on each release. You must be able to assure clients that a release is available—and to supply a copy on demand—before they will purchase a picture. Selling and using pictures without permission can expose you and your client to expensive legal action and make you liable for damages.

You should also have written permission to use any privately owned premises, such as homes, offices, or commercial establishments, or privately owned objects for picture purposes. Having written clearance will prevent delay in gaining access and avoid interruption during shooting. It will also be essential for legal and insurance purposes if you or anyone with you should accidentally cause damage or if anyone should be injured.

Such releases and clearances protect you as well as others. In addition, you should protect your rights in the pictures you produce so they cannot be used without your permission. A stamp on the back of each picture reading:

J. Jones, Photographer
(address or phone no.)
Not to be used without permission.

offers some protection. You may wish to copyright your most important pictures, in which case you will want to keep a record of each picture protected. (*See:* COPYRIGHT.)

The primary service record a business needs is an efficient file of negatives and prints, indexed by job number and cross-indexed with the customer's name on a master list. This allows you to make additional prints and fill repeat orders with a minimum of effort.

Other useful service records include a list of what pictures have been submitted for approval to a client, when, and when returned; indexes of available locations and props (with a small photograph where useful); an illustrated file of models with notes on their specialties; and a list of special services—retouchers, model builders, animal rentals, freelance photo assistants, and the like.

Pricing. This is the crux of business operation. Prices must be low enough to be within reach of your market, but they must be high enough to cover all your costs plus a reasonable profit. There are two kinds of costs: direct, and overhead.

Direct costs. Direct costs are those specifically related to a job and chargeable only to that project. They include:

Wages of photo personnel, generally figured on an hourly basis and often with a percentage added to cover unproductive time.
Materials—films, chemicals, and the like—figured at actual cost plus a percentage to cover waste.
Your salary as a photographer or proprietor, at the hourly rate you charge for this service (you may charge differently for your administrative time, which is part of overhead).
Travel and related expenses.
Travel and waiting time, at the hourly rate for each person involved.
Model fees, prop and location rental, outside processing and services, such as retouching—each at cost plus your business markup, commonly 20 to 30 percent.

Overhead Costs. Overhead costs are all those which relate to keeping the business in operation. They include:

Wages of office and nonphoto personnel.
Office supplies.
Postage, packing, and delivery.
Petty-cash expenditures.
Advertising and promotion.
Rent.
Business fees, permits, and licenses.
Taxes.
Heat, light, water, and telephone.
Insurance.
Equipment investment, replacement, maintenance, and depreciation.
Accounting, bookkeeping, legal and similar services.
Bad debts, uncollectible accounts.
Your salary as administrator, based on the proportion of time you spend in nonphotographic activities.

At the beginning, you will have to estimate your overhead. After several months or a year of operation, you will have enough data to compute overhead accurately. The major problem is charging each job with the proper proportion of the overhead. There are two ways to do this.

For the first way, determine how many hours in a year (or a six-month period) were actually charged as job time. Divide the overhead for that period by the number of job hours, to get an overhead-per-hour rate. Add that to each job according to the number of hours it takes. For example, if last year you had 1,000 job-hours and $15,000 overhead, you would add $15 per hour to each job, along with the direct costs.

For the second way, determine the dollar amount of direct costs for a year; find what proportion that is of your yearly overhead. Add an overhead charge to the direct costs of each job in the same proportion. For example, if your job costs were $7,500, and your overhead $15,000, the proportion is 1:2. So for every dollar of direct costs on a job, you would add two dollars to cover overhead.

The total cost of a job (exclusive of sales tax) to the customer is: *Direct job costs + Overhead + Profit.* Profit is figured as a percentage of the combined direct costs and overhead on each job. It may range anywhere from 6 to 15 percent, or higher, depending on your volume and the prices your market will bear. Remember that your salary is already included in the job cost. The profit is the return on your total investment in time and money in the business; it adds to your equity, or the money value of the business you own. Some of the profit ought to be budgeted for investment in the business to provide growth, such as expanded facilities and additional equipment; the remainder is yours to use as you would the return from any other investment you might make.

Food photography presents its own special problems, including knowledge of truth-in-advertising laws which prohibit addition of colorings or other substances to the foods to make them look better or last longer. In addition to understanding the artistic problems of arranging colors and shapes, the food photographer must also know all the techniques to make the product look especially appealing. Photo by Stephen Stuart.

Job Estimates

If you do not have a business establishment, or if you operate as an individual, there is a simple way to estimate what you should charge for a job.

First, determine how many productive hours a year you might have. Say, 48 weeks (figuring two weeks for vacation and two more for holidays and other lost time) multiplied by 30 hours per week (which allows for lunches and other unproductive time). That equals 1,440 hours a year.

Next, determine what base income you want in a year, say, $15,000. Divide that by the hours-per-year to get a *personal hourly rate:* $15,000 ÷ 1,440 = $10.42, or $11 per hour. (Rounding off to the next higher dollar provides a little margin for error, especially in your first year's estimate.)

Estimate your yearly overhead and divide by the hours-per-year to get an *overhead hourly rate.* Say, $12,000 ÷ 1,440 = $8.33, or $9 per hour.

To figure the cost to the customer, add the personal and overhead hourly rates, multiply by the number of hours the job took (or you estimate it will take), then add any special expenses, such as travel, models, rental equipment, assistants, outside processing, and retouching. For example, a job that takes 5 hours and has $350 in special expenses would cost: (11 + 9) × 5 = 100 + 350 = $450.

Many photographers prefer to establish a day rate rather than an hourly rate by adding the desired yearly base income to the estimated yearly overhead and dividing by the number of probable work days, say, 48 weeks × 4 = 192 days. Jobs are charged at this rate, with a minimum charge of one-half day and a full day for anything over four hours.

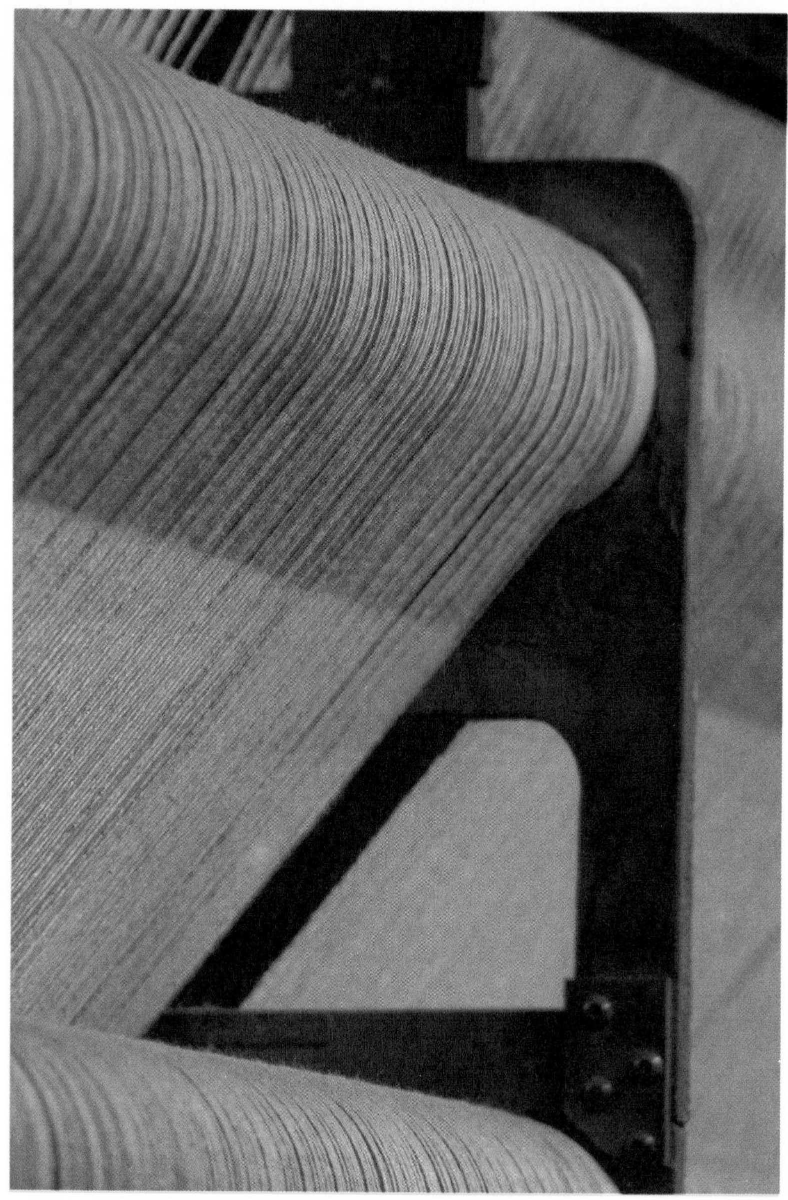

Industrial photographers often find themselves in the difficult position of having to make a purely utilitarian object look interesting and eye-catching. Here, a commercial loom is represented as a splash of brilliant yellow. Photo by William Rivelli.

The advantage of computing your personal rate separately from the overhead rate, especially in the first year, is that it makes it easy to adjust either one (usually the overhead rate) as soon as significant or corrected figures are available.

Evaluating Progress

If you keep complete and accurate records, you have all the information you need to compile the two basic financial reports used in successful business management: the balance sheet, and the profit-and-loss statement. Do not fail to prepare these two reports even if you are the only one who ever sees them. Without them, you are flying blind; with them, you can see whether your business is headed up or down. Prepare them monthly, or at least quarterly, in order to see where you are going in time to do something about it.

Balance Sheet. The balance sheet shows the condition of the business on a selected closing date of the records, usually the end of a month. You can see how much cash you have; how much inventory is on hand; how much customers owe you; how much you owe to others; and your equity, which is the money value of your interest in the business in excess of all claims against it. The balance sheet is so named because the total assets balance with the total liabilities and the owner's equity. (If they don't, you have lost track of something.) It shows that everything owned by a business is financed either through ownership or borrowed funds.

Profit-and-Loss Statement. The profit-and-loss statement is the summary of operations for a given period of time, usually from one balance sheet date to the next. It reflects operations by relating the income received during that period to the expenses necessary to bring in the income. The net result is a profit (or loss), which is available to the owner to retain in the business (net worth increase) or to withdraw for personal use.

(Net profit for each period becomes part of owner's net worth. A loss in a period reduces the net worth by that amount.)

• *See also:* COPYRIGHT; FILING AND STORING NEGATIVES AND PRINTS; LEGAL ASPECTS OF PHOTOGRAPHY; MODEL RELEASE; MODELS AND MODELING; RIGHTS.

Further Reading: Ahlers, Arvel W. *Where and How to Sell Your Photographs,* 8th ed. Garden City, NY: Amphoto, 1977; Gutenberg, Arthur W. and Val K. Albrecht. *Profitable Studio Management.* Garden City, NY: Amphoto, 1965; McDarrah, Fred, ed. *Photography Market Place.* Ann Arbor, MI: R.R. Bowker Co., 1975; Perry, Robin. *Photography for the Professionals.* Garden City, NY: Amphoto, 1976; Schwarz, Theodore R. *The Business Side of Photography.* Garden City, NY: Amphoto, 1969.

Relationship Between a Balance Sheet and a Profit-and-Loss Statement

BALANCE SHEET, as of (date)

Assets		*Liabilities*	
Cash	$5,000	Taxes Payable	$ 2,000
Accounts Receivable	6,000	Accounts Payable	2,900
Photographic Equipment	9,000	Notes Payable	6,000
Other Assets	6,000		
		Net Worth	
		J. Jones, Capital	15,100
Total Assets	$26,000	Total: Liabilities and Net Worth	$26,000

PROFIT-AND-LOSS STATEMENT, for the period ______ to ______

Sales		$60,000
Cost of Sales:		
Photographic Labor	$15,000	
Outside Services	3,600	
Photographic Supplies	10,800	
Total		29,400
Gross Profit (Sales less Cost of Sales)		$30,600
Operating Expenses *(in detail)*		26,400
Net Profit (Gross Profit less Operating Expenses)		$ 4,200

C

C

Callier Effect

The silver densities in a negative absorb some of the incident light falling on the negative and transmit the remainder. Each density scatters the transmitted portion of the light to some degree.

When the incident light on the negative is moving in parallel paths (specular light), more light is lost by scattering in areas of heavy density than in areas of less density. The light transmitted by each area is reduced by (1) the absorptive capacity of the density there plus (2) its light-scattering power. The density to specular light (specular density) is measured in terms of only the transmitted light that is traveling in the same path as the incident light; scattered light is not taken into account.

When diffused light, traveling in many different paths, strikes the negative, the degree of scattering in each area is equal—as much light is scattered into a given path or direction as is scattered out of

The density of a negative determines how much light will pass through it. Under specular light, increasing negative densities increases light scattering. Under diffuse light, the same increasing densities produce equal degrees of light scattering. Diffuse density measurements include all light transmitted, so will show less difference between two areas than specular density measurements which exclude scattered light. Greater printing contrast occurs with specular light, as in a condenser enlarger.

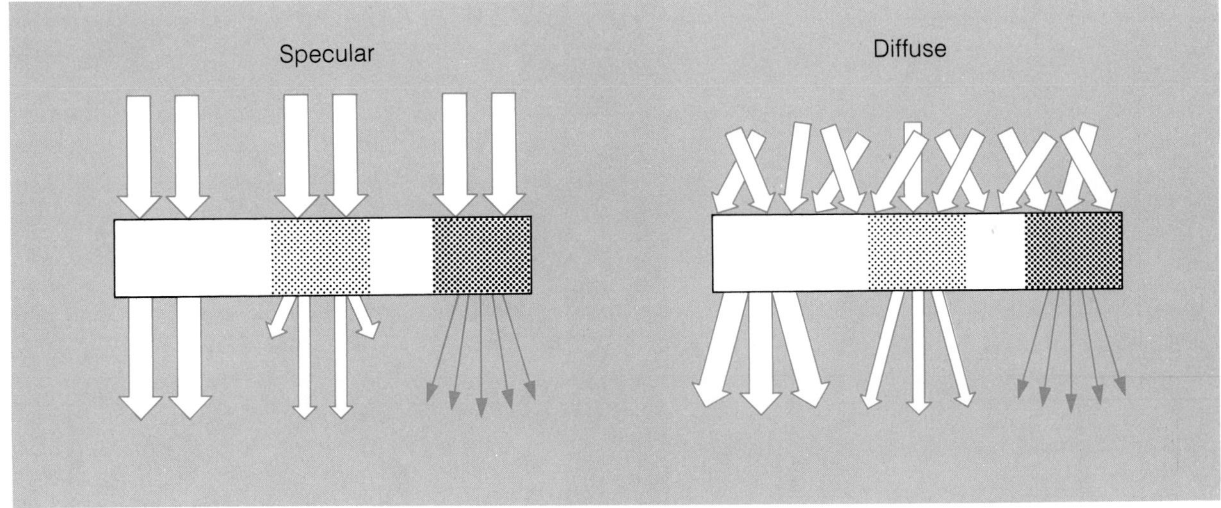

it. As a result, the differences in intensity of the transmitted light from area to area are in proportion only to the density variations; the light-scattering power is constant for all areas. The density to diffuse light (diffuse density) is measured in terms of all light transmitted by an area, regardless of its path.

When the diffuse density and the specular density of a single area are compared, the specular density will always be higher because scattered light is not measured, and therefore the effective light-stopping or light-dissipating power of the area is greater.

The relation between the two kinds of density was first investigated by André Callier in 1909. The phenomenon of greater scattering of specular light is called the *Callier effect.* The ratio of the specular density to the diffuse density is known as the *Callier coefficient,* or the *Q factor* of the area measured.

The Callier effect has practical consequence in photographic printing with diffusion or condenser enlargers. A condenser system with a point-light source provides illumination in relatively parallel paths, which is affected somewhat like specular light by the negative densities. When printing exposure is adjusted so that the clear portion of a negative produces the same black in either enlarger, the tones represented by increasing densities in the negative will print lighter in the condenser system than in the diffusion system because of the increasing amounts of light lost to scattering. The print from the condenser enlarger will show greater overall contrast (fewer separate tones or steps between black and white) and greater local contrast (a greater degree of difference between adjacent tones). Similarly, a contact print from the same negative will have less contrast than the print from the condenser enlarger because no additional light is lost by increased scattering in the denser areas.

Most enlargers are semi-specular in nature, and most use diffuse enlarging bulbs rather than a point-source type of bulb. Hence the contrast effect caused by the Callier effect falls somewhere between that of a diffuse enlarger and a true specular enlarger. The negative density range of a negative made for a typical condenser enlarger is usually about 75 to 80 percent of that required by a diffusion enlarger.

This means that in order to achieve comparable results on the same contrast grade of paper, negatives for condenser enlarging should be developed to a lower contrast index than those for diffusion enlarging or contact printing.

The Callier effect is of less importance in color printing than in black-and-white because the silver grains that scatter the light are replaced by transparent dyes which produce little scattering. In addition, most color enlargers use diffused light illumination.

• *See also:* CONTRAST INDEX; DENSITOMETRY; ENLARGERS AND ENLARGING; LENSES.

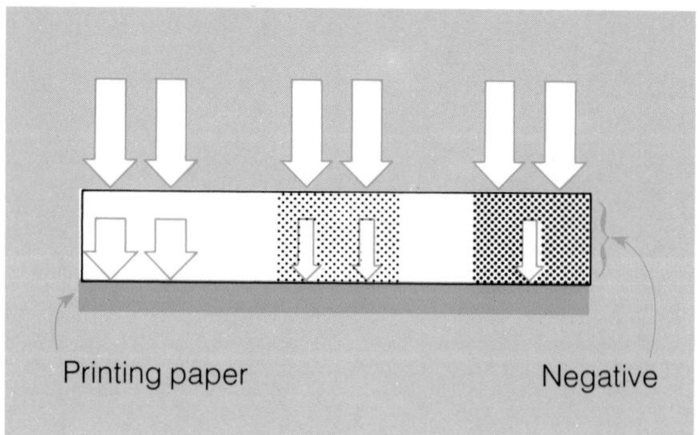

Contact printing is similar to diffusion enlarging. No scattering occurs, so printing contrast is in direct proportion to actual densities. All transmitted light reaches the printing paper emulsion.

Calotype

Calotype is the name coined (from the Greek *kalos*: beautiful, and *typos*: form) for the first negative-positive process in photography, patented in 1841 by the English inventor William Henry Fox Talbot, and later called the "Talbotype." (Not to be confused with the *collotype*, a photomechanical reproduction process; or the *kallitype*, a photographic printing process invented in 1899.)

In the calotype process, paper is sensitized for camera use to produce a negative by development; contact prints are made on a simple printing-out paper. The process may be duplicated today, but the method of producing negatives primarily has curiosity value nowadays because of the work involved in preparing the material. It is far simpler to use modern single-weight enlarging paper in place of film to obtain a paper negative. However, the printing material—generically called *salted paper*—produces interesting colors and tones that may have expressive value in some kinds of artistic photography. A great variety of paper stocks may be treated for printing this way.

Uncoated paper with high rag content is best. Thin sheets of good-quality watercolor paper work well for negatives; thick papers interfere excessively with the transmission of printing light. Heavier papers are suitable for prints. Unsized papers produce a maximum matte effect in a print because the surface treatment is absorbed deeply into the paper fibers. Sized papers reduce absorption, which helps to keep the image on the surface. Some art papers may be purchased sized; others may be sized with a thin solution of laundry starch or a light coating of a modern spray starch. Sizing must be carried out, and the paper completely dried, before any other treatment.

The side that will not be treated should be pencil-marked for identification before beginning. The paper may be floated on trays of solutions or fastened on an inclined surface (pinned to a board or taped at one end to a sheet of glass) and the solutions flowed over the surface by means of a thick, soft brush. The side being treated must be evenly saturated with the various solutions. Papers should be air-dried slowly to prevent ripples. Using a sheet larger than the intended image size provides a border for handling and reduces the chances that edge fluting will reach the image area. Treatment may be carried out under any safelight suitable for modern printing papers. Calotype materials should be dried and stored in darkness.

Negative Preparation

Prepare a stock of *iodized paper* ahead of time. It will later be sensitized for use. Treat paper one to two minutes with solution A, blot it, and dry it in the dark.

A. Silver nitrate (crystals)	4 g
Distilled water	60 ml

Float the nitrate surface of the dried paper on solution B for about ten minutes, or saturate it well by brushing. Rinse it thoroughly in plain water to remove excess iodide; then blot and dry. Store in darkness.

B. Potassium iodide	16.0 g
Sodium chloride (table salt)	1.6 g
Distilled water	237.0 ml

Sensitize the iodized paper surface with a combination of solutions C and D, one part of each:

C. Silver nitrate (crystals)	13 g
Distilled water	60 ml
Acetic acid, 28%	36 ml

Keep C in a dark brown bottle or otherwise protected from light.

D. A saturated solution of gallic acid crystals in a few ounces of water.

Only a small quantity of crystals will dissolve; either filter out undissolved crystals or carefully pour off liquid. This solution keeps only two or three days.

Just before use, mix equal quantities of C and D. Flow the solution onto the iodized surface of the paper. Treat for one to two minutes then rinse the paper in plain water and damp-dry it between blotters. It may be exposed while damp or soon after it is completely dry. Sensitivity decreases progressively after about 24 hours. Sensitivity may be increased somewhat by treating dried paper a second time with fresh C + D solution. Like conventional film, the sensitized paper must be protected from light and loaded into a holder for camera use.

The exposed image is developed by a combination of four parts solution D and one part E.

E. Silver nitrate (crystals)	4 g
Distilled water	30 ml

Flow the developer on, or bathe the negative in a tray of solution. Develop by inspection under safelight. Rinse the developed negative thoroughly in plain water, then fix it in a 30 percent solution of plain hypo—300 grams sodium thiosulfate dissolved in water to make one litre. Wash and dry it in the usual way.

To make the paper negative more nearly transparent for printing, use a cotton wad to coat the back evenly with a clear, lightweight oil. The paper must be dried thoroughly between blotters before printing to remove all excess oil that might otherwise affect the print. An alternate method is to rub the back of the negative with paraffin or clear wax, then cover it with clean paper and use a hand iron at moderate heat to melt the wax evenly into the paper fibers. The negative may be retouched with pencil, or drawing added on the back before being waxed or oiled.

Printing

Paper negatives may be printed onto modern papers. However, the salted paper of the calotype process is easily prepared and produces distinctive results.

Treat one side of the paper with a weak solution of common table salt in water. When dry, flow a solution of 4 grams silver nitrate in 30 ml water over the salted surface. Dry the paper in darkness. Sunlight or a strong ultraviolet source is required for contact-printing with this paper. Place the negative in a printing frame with the image side against the treated surface of the print paper. The image is printed-out by the action of the light alone; no development is required. The negative may be peeled back from time to time to inspect the progress of the print. When sufficiently exposed, fix the print in a plain hypo bath, wash, and dry.

The print tones may range from pinkish or reddish-brown to violet and purple. Their color can be improved by gold toning before fixing. For this process, print the image to a greater-than-normal density, wash it for about five minutes in running water, then treat it in the following toning solution:

Gold chloride	1 g
Calcium carbonate	20 g
Water to make	1 litre

The density is reduced as the color is neutralized somewhat; progress may be observed visually. Wash the print thoroughly to remove excess toner, fix it in a 10 to 20 percent hypo solution (100 to 200 grams hypo in water to make 1 litre), wash, and dry it as usual.

• *See also:* ARCHER, FREDERICK SCOTT.

Further Reading: Bruce, David. *Sun Pictures, The Hill-Adamson Calotypes.* Greenwich, CT: New York Graphic Society Ltd., 1973; Croucher, J.H. and Gustave LeGray. *Plain Directions for Obtaining Photographic Pictures by the Calotype and Energiatype, Also Upon Albumenized Paper and Glass, by Collodion and Albumen, Etc.* New York, NY: Arno Press, Repro. of 1853 ed.; Potonniee, Georges. *The History of the Discovery of Photography.* New York, NY: Arno Press, 1973.

"The Old Quadrangle at Brasenoge College," c. 1845, a calotype by William Henry Fox Talbot. Talbot patented the first negative-positive photographic process in 1841. The salted paper used for printing produces interesting colors and tones that range from pinkish or reddish-brown to violet and purple. Photo courtesy International Museum of Photography at George Eastman House.

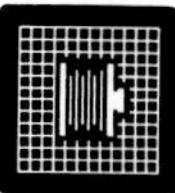

Camera and Lens Care

Most photographic equipment is designed to give long-term service without trouble. You can aid this service by proper handling and maintenance. Handling includes transporting and storing equipment, as well as putting it to use. The most important part of maintenance is keeping equipment clean and dry.

Handling

Vibration. Protect cameras and lenses from vibration and shock. Vibration occurs when traveling, whether by car, airplane, or motor-driven boat. It can cause tiny screws to loosen, fasteners and catches to open, meter movements to go out of balance, and a variety of other ills. Cushioning is the most effective protection. Use foam-padded cases or containers to transport equipment; the velvet linings of lens and camera cases really protect only against dents and scratches. Be sure to use padding between items of equipment, as well as along the outer walls, floor, and lid of cases. Place containers in protected spots. The seat beside you is excellent, if you can be certain that nothing will spill in case of a sudden lurch or stop. The floor is the worst possible place; it has the least padding, and motor vibrations—as well as the effects of rough roads, water, or air—are strongest there. It is also the dirtiest and, sometimes, dampest spot. If you place equipment in an overhead airplane compartment or the trunk of a car, try to put a spare pillow or a folded coat or blanket under it for protection. Do not use the dashboard (glove) compartment of any vehicle; vibration is usually accompanied by extremes in temperature.

Shock. Shock can be either a sudden severe jolt or repeated erratic bouncing that builds up an effect. To avoid jolts, set equipment cases down carefully. Whenever possible, carry them yourself, rather than leaving them to porters or baggage handlers. Do not run with equipment; it bounces severely as you move, and may be smashed if you fall.

When you carry equipment by straps around your neck or over your shoulder, keep a hand or arm on it so it does not repeatedly bounce against your body. An equipment bag can be strapped to your waist easily. A camera neck strap should be supplemented by one that passes around your back to hold the camera safely against your chest or body. Avoid carrying cameras by a strap over one shoulder. They swing too freely and can easily bang against other equipment, door jambs, people, and other things you pass. Long lenses seem to invite collisions because they stick out so far from a camera body. In addition, their weight puts a significant strain on the lens mount of the camera. A whack or jolt can damage both the lens barrel and the camera mount. As often as possible, carry a long lens in a separate case and mount it on the camera only when necessary.

Exposure meters can be seriously affected by jolts and shocks. Built-in meters receive whatever protection you give the camera. Separate meters should be carried in a pocket or on a secure belt clip. In addition, keep the cord or strap around your neck or tied to your waist in case the meter bounces free or is dropped.

Operating Equipment

When operating equipment, follow the manufacturer's instructions and approved procedures. Camera mechanisms in particular, are immensely complex and may be damaged by making settings out of sequence. Improper flash connections can cause shorts and arcing that will burn out a condenser or fuse sync switch contacts inside the camera. Whatever the equipment, do not snap controls into position or make abrupt changes; handle them with firm, smooth, but gentle, movements. Never force a control. If a film advance, a locking catch, a focusing ring, or any other control seems to resist adjustment or operates roughly, stop. Examine the equipment carefully. If you cannot determine the problem, consult a repair shop. Unless you have special training, do not attempt repairs yourself; you can easily turn a minor difficulty into major damage.

When removing a lens, grasp the barrel as close to the camera body as possible. Turning it by the outer end may start to unscrew various elements or sections. If a lens should separate, *do not* try to reassemble it. Lens sections have multiple-lead threads; only an experienced person can make sure that they engage in proper alignment.

Keeping Equipment Clean

It is only common sense to protect equipment as much as possible while it is being used. This includes keeping it shaded (if it's loaded) and protected from dirt and moisture. Do not leave camera cases in the direct sun, even for a short time. A white or light-colored covering will reflect heat and keep things several degrees cooler. It is often convenient to put several small equipment cases inside one larger insulated case of the type used for picnics.

In a dusty wind, or in rain or snow, slip a plastic bag mouth-downward over the camera. Your hands can reach up from below to operate the controls. The lens can stick through a slit in the side of the bag, protected by a deep lens shade and, if necessary, a colorless piece of glass in place of a filter.

Equipment is often dirtied by carelessness. No one consciously puts a camera in the mud, or places a thumb smudge on a lens. But few photographers take the trouble to brush or vacuum the inside of camera and lens cases even once a year. Many who carefully use front and rear lens caps and body caps on the lens mounts of their cameras unthinkingly put the caps in their pockets or purses while photographing. When replaced, they carry lint, dust, crumbs, and other unsuspected dirt directly onto the equipment. A small plastic bag, frequently changed, is a better place to keep caps when not in use.

Water Problems

One of the worst disasters equipment can encounter is falling into water. If this should happen, *do not try to dry it out*! There is no way you can dry the moisture from all the crevices of a camera, lens, or meter. Any traces of water left behind will start corrosive action as soon as air reaches them. Therefore, transfer the soaked equipment to a container of fresh water and get it to a repair facility immediately. If the equipment has fallen into salt water, flush it in two or three changes of fresh water—salt can cause corrosion in solution—and then keep it in fresh water. Do not delay in getting repair assistance. If a loaded camera falls into water, you may remove the film (if you can protect it from light) and the batteries, but the film must be kept wet until it can be processed, which must be within a few hours at the most. If film or equipment is allowed to dry immediately, disaster will be sure to result.

Storage

Choose a dry location with moderate temperature (not above approximately 24 C, or 75 F) to store equipment, even if it is just for a few days. Heat and moisture promote corrosion, mildew, and fungus growth. Some fungi can actually etch metal and coated glass surfaces. Excessive heat can cause anything made of rubber—foam, elastic bands, shutter curtain fabric, soft lens shades, for example—to deteriorate, and it may cause glues to run or crack. Room-temperature air should circulate through the storage area if it is not moist or dusty. In problem spots, seal equipment in airtight containers with some packets of desiccated silica gel, which will absorb air-borne moisture.

When bringing equipment in from the cold, let it warm up gradually before putting it away. Moist warm air causes condensation when it encounters cold surfaces. Leave equipment in a colder outer room before bringing it into a fully heated interior to avoid this problem, which is far more serious inside equipment and on the surfaces of film than on exterior surfaces.

Do not put equipment away for long periods with a lens on a camera, a filter on a lens, or otherwise assembled. If the parts should "set" to one another, it could be virtually impossible to separate them without damage. Aluminum, in particular, has a tendency to freeze to other metals as an oxide forms on its bare metal threads. A strip of soft leather or a wide rubber band may help you get a grip on a sticking lens cap or shade, or a filter ring. *Do not* try to use pliers or a wrench; even a little excess force can bend round metal parts or crack plastic, while a slip could be destructive. A qualified repair person has the proper tools and skills to disassemble sticking parts safely.

Always fire a shutter to release the tension on its spring before putting a camera or lens away. Leaving a shutter cocked can weaken the activating springs, causing a slowdown in the shutter speeds. Be sure all openings and optical surfaces are covered with properly fitting caps. Coil flash sync and power cords loosely, or wrap them around a tube about three inches in diameter. Avoid sharp bends and tight strapping; they can cause permanent kinks, cracked insulation, and broken strands of conductor wires. Similarly, do not bend cable releases. For long-term storage, remove all batteries from their containers or compartments. If they should corrode, the interior of the camera or flash unit could be damaged beyond repair.

Maintenance

Unless you are absolutely sure of what you are doing, you should not try to disassemble or repair equipment yourself. This is especially true in the cases of lenses, cameras, and electronic flash units with high-voltage condensers. However, you can do a great deal to maintain your equipment and keep it serviceable. The three primary things to do are to inspect, clean, and tighten.

Inspection

Inspect for dents, cracks, breaks, and especially for wear. It takes a strong blow to dent most equipment, and that may well cause interior damage, too. Shake the equipment next to your ear to check for the rattle of loose or broken parts. If you hear nothing, operate the equipment cautiously; if everything works smoothly, you may not need to have a repair person check further. But remember that a dent in a lens may mean that elements are out of alignment or that it will not mount precisely.

Inspect cable connectors to see whether they have been crushed or bent out of shape; flash cord PC connectors are especially susceptible to this kind of damage. Cracks and breaks in outer cable coverings or insulation are almost always a sign of further damage. They let dirt and moisture in and may be only the outer evidence of interior trouble.

Wear occurs with use; it is normal. You cannot avoid the eventual loss of some paint or the accumulation of some nicks and scratches on equipment (on a lens surface, they may be important, of course). But look for excessive wear wherever parts move together or across one another. Check lens mounts; even a small degree of wear may let a lens wobble rather than seat snugly in place. If a film-advance thumb-lever is scraping the camera body, either it or the shaft it turns is bent. Look at the metal rings on straps and the equipment lugs they fasten to. They can saw through each other rather rapidly when equipment is in constant use.

To inspect a bellows, stretch it out to full length, cover one end, and look through the other end as you move a light bulb all around the outside. You will see a flash or gleam wherever there is a break in the material. Then, in a darkened room, look at the outside of the bellows as you move a light inside it. Tiny leaks can be patched with bits of electricians' vinyl tape or black masking tape. Large leaks may require a new bellows.

Cleaning Kit

The following are a few simple items that will give you an efficient cleaning kit:

1. A bristle brush to clean exteriors. The kind attached to typing erasers or sold for use with library paste is fine, as is a soft, old toothbrush.
2. A soft brush, such as a camel's-hair brush, to dust lens and mirror surfaces. Never touch the end of this brush with your fingers or draw it across your face. It will pick up skin oils that can hold dirt or transfer the dirt to surfaces being cleaned. The kind that retracts into a case like a lipstick is easy to keep clean.
3. A squeeze-bulb syringe to blow away dust and dirt. The type sold as an ear syringe for babies is conveniently small

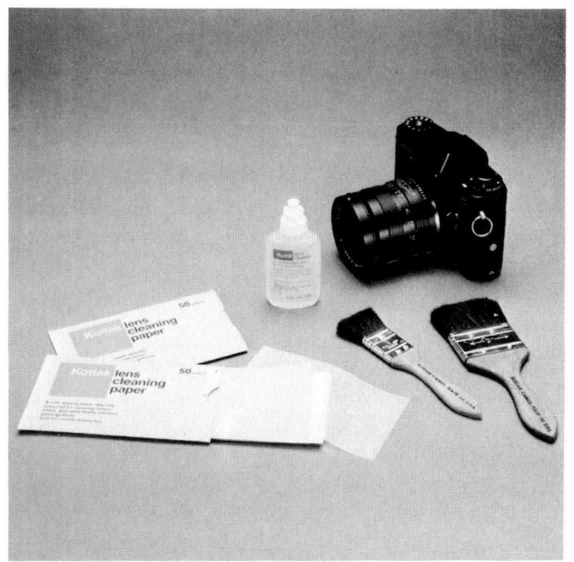

Contents of a camera-cleaning kit should contain (from left) lens paper, lens-cleaning solution, and camel's-hair brushes, both small and large, for interior and exterior cleaning.

(Near right) Clean interior of camera with soft, camel's-hair brush. Never let the brush touch your skin. (Center) Do not apply lens cleaner directly to lens; instead, use lens tissue moistened with cleaner. (Far right) Wipe lens dry with lens tissue.

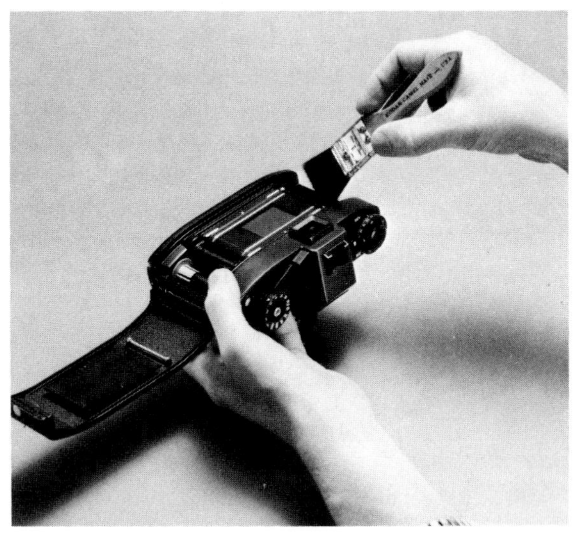

and gives about the right degree of air blast. Cans of compressed air or inert gas are popular for dusting off negatives in the darkroom; *do not* use them to clean cameras and lenses. The force of their blast is too strong; it can drive dirt firmly into inaccessible spots and can even damage delicate parts such as meter movements, if the nozzle is held too close.

4. Cotton swabs on both wooden and cardboard sticks. The wooden sticks give you a firm prod to help remove reluctant exterior dirt, if necessary; the cardboard sticks protect against damage from too firm pressure when working on delicate surfaces and parts.
5. Lens tissue. Be sure to use photographic tissue; the chemically impregnated and silicone tissues sold for use with eyeglasses will damage photographic lens coatings. Keep the lens tissue clean in an envelope or small plastic bag.
6. Lens fluid. A small squeeze bottle will last for years; you need only one or two drops at a time.

Cleaning Procedures

Exteriors. Always clean the exterior first so that nothing will fall inside when you open a piece of equipment. Use the stiff brush to dislodge surface dirt and corrosion; blow it away with the syringe. Try using the sticky side of a piece of tape to remove gummy deposits. Solvents may cause damage if they flow into crevices or under the edges of plastic or leatherette coverings. Some solvents will attack various plastics. If you use a bit of tape to make sure a flash connector does not pull out of the camera socket, remove the tape as soon as possible, and use some of the same kind of tape to remove any remaining stickiness.

Wipe bellows, cases, and straps with a cloth dampened with water (for plastics) or with a leather-treatment solution. Brush and vacuum the interiors.

Electrical Units. Discharge electrically powered units before cleaning. Be especially careful not to brush dirt into receptacles or sockets. A cloth should be barely damp so no moisture will enter. Do not use anything to clean a flash power pack that could cause a short circuit between terminals. You may ruin the batteries of a low-power unit or receive a severe shock from a high-power unit.

Camera Interior. To clean the interior of a camera, remove the lens and viewfinder and open the back (or remove the back panel of a view camera). This exposes the front-surface mirror of a single-lens reflex camera. Turn the camera so that dust will not fall inside, and blow off the mirror surface. Use the soft lens brush if necessary, or improvise one by rolling a piece of lens tissue into a cigarette-like tube and tearing it in half; use the torn ends like a brush. *Do not* touch the mirror surface or rub it with tissue, cloth, or cleaning fluid. The exposed reflective coating is very delicate, and scratches will soon interfere with viewing and focusing.

Raise the mirror and blow dust off the focal-plane shutter curtain; if you brush it, do so gently to avoid damage. Then open the shutter fully (on the "Time" setting, or locked on the "Bulb" setting), to protect it from being poked and to prevent dust from settling on it as you blow out the rest of the interior.

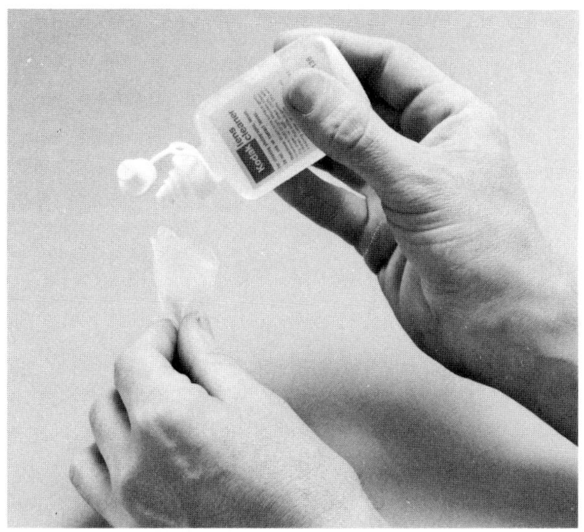

Use the squeeze bulb, and avoid directing air blasts in ways that will drive dirt into corners and crevices. Be sure to get all chips of film and emulsion out of the film channels and take-up compartments of roll-film and 35 mm cameras.

If the camera has a bellows, stretch it gently to full length. An old toothbrush can get at the interior folds, and a small hand-type vacuum cleaner is useful with large cameras. Wipe the bellows' interior with a slightly damp cloth, but allow it to dry before collapsing the bellows again.

Scratches on the black surfaces inside a camera may cause increased flare by scattering light. Touch them up with a dull black coating such as Kodak brushing lacquer, No. 4 dull black, or the equivalent.

As soon as you have finished cleaning, close the camera and put a body cap on the lens mount so nothing can enter the camera.

Pull the dark slides completely out of the sheet film holders and vigorously blow the dust out of them; be sure to get under the lips that hold the film edges. Vacuuming is helpful with large-size holders. You can make the vacuum cleaner more useful by running a small, flexible tube through a cork stuck into the vacuum's large hose or tube fitting. Wipe the interiors and the slides with an antistatic cloth before closing the holders.

Cleaning Lenses. Lens coatings are easily scratched, and many lens glasses are relatively soft. For these reasons, never directly rub or scrub a lens with a wad of lens tissue or a piece of cloth. Begin by blowing off surface dust and using a soft lens brush if necessary. Tear a tube of lens tissue into two short brush-like pieces for use. If surface dirt remains, moisten a cotton swab with lens cleaning fluid, squeeze it so that it is damp-dry, and gently clean the surface; wipe it dry with a second swab or some tissue, blowing gently to promote evaporation. Do not put drops of fluid directly on the lens surface; some may run down around the edges and affect the cement holding the element in place. *Do not* try to take a lens apart to get at interior dirt; *do not* try to clean or lubricate an iris diaphragm. These are things only an experienced person can do safely.

Tightening Screws

Small screws may occasionally work loose in your equipment. Use a set of jewelers' screwdrivers to tighten them. Be sure to use a blade that completely fills the slot in the screw head; too small a blade will gouge the slot, and the blade may jump out and scratch the equipment. Seat loose screws firmly, but do not try to tighten them as if you were assembling a steel bridge. The most important time to check screws is after an airplane or similar trip, when sustained high-frequency vibrations may have loosened small screws and parts.

Above all, remember that the more faithfully you inspect and clean your equipment, the more faithfully it will perform for you.

Once the basics of black-and-white photography have been mastered, a particular subject, such as composition, might be assigned to the participants.

Camera Clubs

A photographic club generally is started for one of three major reasons: A group of individuals want to show their pictures to one another and discuss them; they want to exchange information and learn new techniques in photography; or they want to pool their equipment and resources to obtain more extensive and sophisticated working conditions than they can achieve individually. Whatever the initial reason, most clubs soon embrace all three of these activities. A successful club administration will identify the major interests of the members and will provide varied programs, facilities, and activities that manage to touch all the interests over a period of time.

Photographic clubs attract different kinds of members:

1. Those who want friendly social contact as a kind of low-pressure way to learn how to take better pictures. Many such people are at a beginner's level in photography and are highly enthusiastic about learning photography.
2. Those who want salons, competitions, and exhibitions in which to show their work. They are interested in picture-

taking as an art, tend to be technically advanced, and are not interested in techniques for improving their first snapshots.

3. Those who want entertaining and somewhat informative programs presented to them. They tend to be somewhat passive, producing small numbers of pictures of their own, but will eagerly support programs that help them learn something without a great deal of effort.
4. Those who primarily want to take advantage of the club's facilities—darkroom, projectors, group discounts for materials, and the like. They work a great deal but may not be regulars at meetings.
5. Those who are essentially organizers. They may not take many pictures, but they enthusiastically want to belong to and help run a formal, well-organized group. Such people are few in number but are extremely valuable, for they make excellent committee heads and club officers.

General Programming

"Participation" is the magic word for successful meetings, and programs rather than business create participation. Outstanding programs usually bring everyone into the act, beginner and advanced member alike. All members must feel they are contributing to the club.

It's all too easy for a camera club to get into a programming rut. There is no reason to follow the pattern of other clubs. Boring programs are the chief reason people resign or lose interest in a camera club. Programs must offer what the members as a whole want. The club must activate and win the interest of beginners before they will become dyed-in-the-wool supporters. Varied program level is important. Nothing can kill the interest of a large number of members more quickly than three lectures in a row on "Advanced Sensitometry."

A club must provide a varied and live overall program geared to the interests of the majority of the group, inasmuch as attracting new members will increase available funds.

Small Groups

When there are two or three separate interests within the membership, perhaps the answer to programming problems is the formation of a small special-interest group, either as a separate club or as a "workshop" within the larger organization.

A special-interest group can enjoy unique features. The program provides for real participation by all the members, and a great deal of photographic

Many amateur photographers find children especially interesting and easily approachable subjects. Members might also want to learn how cropping techniques can turn their ordinary snapshots into interesting close-ups.

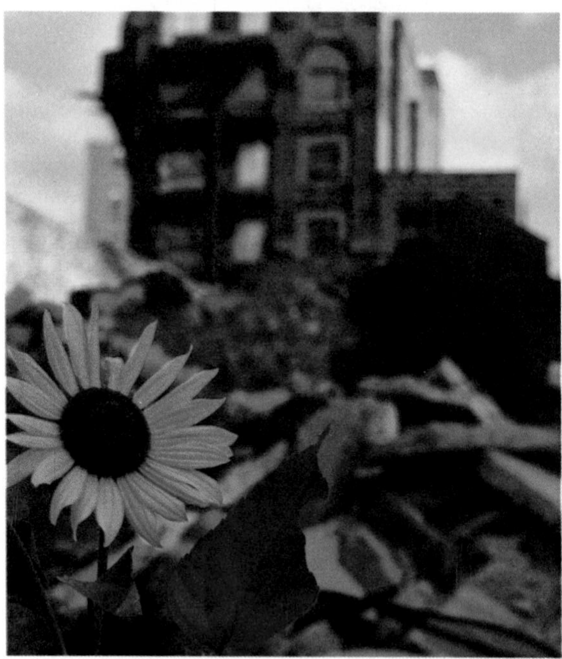

One area group members might want to explore is how to photograph flowers. This is a particularly interesting example because of the background, which throws the main subject into such interesting juxtaposition.

know-how can be gained in a most pleasant and informal manner.

There are several typical groups that might form small camera clubs, or perhaps sections within a larger organization. The following are some ideas.

Travel Group. A group interested in both local and worldwide travel might plan a series of meetings through the winter months, using the home of a different member every two weeks. In this way, twelve members could provide an interesting set of personal travelogues that would last through a six-month winter season. This sort of intimate group can discuss travel picture-taking and its members can help one another with related ideas and information, such as availability of film in different countries, slide-improvement suggestions, hotel accommodations, and good holiday spots.

Program Ideas. Ideas for programs will be largely unnecessary because of the very nature of the slide showings. But how about an evening devoted to the making of title slides? They certainly improve the average travelogue. Or one of the members could show others how simple it is to add a tape-recorded commentary and music to a slide show. Other ideas would be to invite an occasional "outsider," who may have recently taken an interesting trip, to enjoy the informal atmosphere and talk about a particular country. A travel agent could be asked to give a talk about Spain, for example, and an airlines person might be persuaded to discuss round-trip facilities and special, little-known holiday areas in the U.S.

Advanced Color Group. A regular meeting devoted to learning more about color photography would fill a real need for a group of people who have successfully mastered the production of good color slides, and who manage to win their share of awards in the average camera-club competitions. They could share the cost of color-film processing kits that they might not be able to afford otherwise. This is a perfect example of a benefit gained from membership in a camera club. The kits could provide materials for a series of uniquely practical programs based on trying a new color technique or process at every meeting.

Program Ideas. For an easy start, and for a program that could establish the level of interest required for membership, have each member take a

A special workshop on how to obtain truly fine color photographs will be of interest to many people. This photograph gives the impression of a painting.

Special techniques such as the making of multiple exposures are an area of study that will appeal to the more advanced club members.

flash exposure on the same roll of color film, such as Kodak Ektachrome 64 film, load it into a day-load tank, and go through the processing, step by step. This should make a really exciting program because many people will realize for the very first time how easy color processing is. The group will never forget that first roll of color pictures as it comes, gleaming wet, from the final stabilizing bath!

It doesn't matter if no one in the group has ever processed color film before. Just follow the step-by-step instructions packaged with the film-processing kit.

The next meeting follows naturally. The strip of dry film is cut into pieces, and all members mount their own pictures—lots of opportunity here for discussion and comparison of various slide mounts and mounting methods. Then the projector is switched on for an evaluation of the home-processed pictures.

An evening devoted to flash techniques, especially the more unusual methods such as bounce flash, off-camera flash, fill-in flash, bare-bulb techniques, and the use of two or more flashbulbs, would provide real practical know-how of great interest to color fans.

As a key to keeping meetings exciting, try things that no one in the group has yet attempted.

Advanced Salon Group. A group of pictorialists can meet once a month or so to discuss their most recent salon prints and slides. This is a typical specialized group with similar interests, which meets informally to consider more advanced photographic techniques.

Such a group may be made up of judges and advanced pictorialists who gain very little from average club membership—photographers who teach and lecture about the subject.

By associating with people whose artistic judgment they all respect, they can bring a print to a monthly meeting, have it thoroughly criticized, and come back the following month with a new print incorporating the suggestions made earlier.

Instead of dominating a larger club and overwhelming new hobbyists, and rather than constantly carrying prizes away from others in regular club competition or judging, these people can deliberately meet as a small group of experts in order to criticize their own prints in a very valuable and informal way.

Program Ideas. An advanced salon group will generally be able to provide a program for itself simply by discussing members' photographs. However, there are several sources of suitable program material.

The Photographic Society of America (PSA) has an international exhibits arrangement whereby member clubs can obtain print sets from foreign countries. Prints represent the work of photographers in member organizations of the Federation of

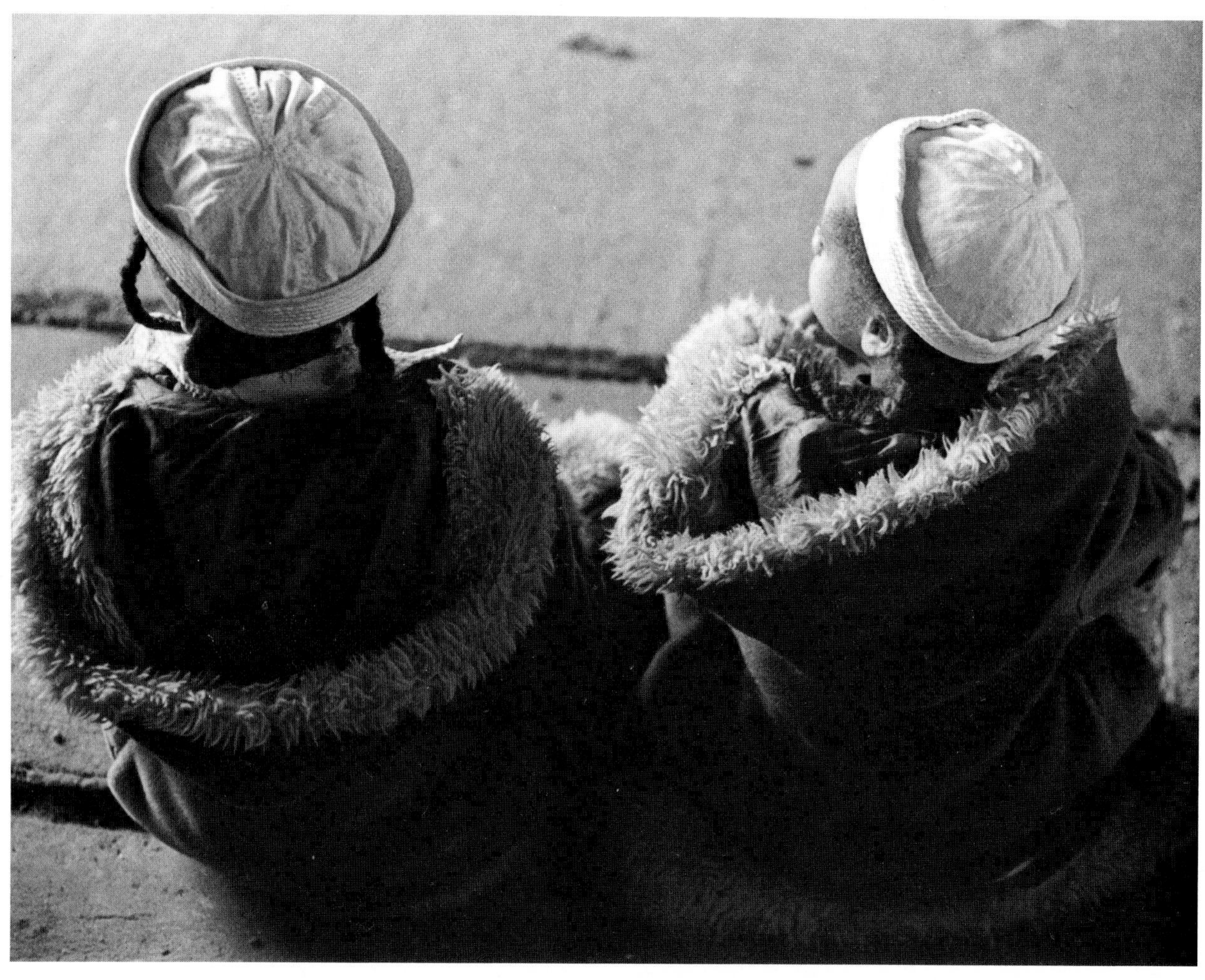

Workshops on what makes a good photograph should be a part of every club's agenda. These workshops should have an open format, as the subject is a very personal one.

International Artist Photographers (FIAP). Requests for this service are filled all year as print sets are available; the sets are changed from time to time so that material in use is constantly changing.

Other print sets are available from the Pictorial Division of PSA, and print portfolios can be exchanged with other, similar groups.

The PSA also offers an International Club Print Competition. Top prints from the club can compete for awards with others from clubs all over the world.

A club could also let it be known that it would be willing to judge and comment on groups of prints from other clubs.

Industrial Clubs. Industrial clubs are small groups within large industries. Many are very similar to regular camera clubs, but they receive some support from the company in the way of low-cost or no-cost meeting facilities.

All the ideas and program material suggested in this article can be used by the large industrial group. With an industrial group, the aim is to involve and interest the largest possible number of workers. The main thing to consider here is that although the majority of people in the organization take pictures at some time or other, few of those people belong to a camera club. Most of them have no particular interest in joining, and even if they were talked into joining under the pressure of a membership drive, they would not participate in, or even attend, most of the club's functions. Here is a fertile field for good programming.

The "One-Shot" Program

Members who will not get involved in a whole series of programs on a single topic will turn out enthusiastically for a program that promises to teach a specific skill in just one session.

All groups seem to have the same photographic inclinations and are capable of learning photography at about the same rate.

The easiest programs to prepare, and perhaps the ones evoking the most response, are the "how-to-do-it" sessions. A high percentage of members usually are interested in such topics as:

How to Photograph Babies
How to Take Vacation Pictures
How to Photograph Weddings
How to Light for Home Movies
How to Edit Home Movies
How to Make Simple Home Portraits
How to Photograph Hobby Activities
How to Make Sports Pictures
How to Expose Color Film
How to Photograph Children
How to Photograph Flowers

The sessions should include slides and demonstrations, and audience participation whenever possible. Handout sheets with pertinent facts emphasized and instructional helps clearly outlined will be popular and valuable.

Meetings

Much of a camera club's success depends on common sense in running meetings.

1. Plan everything well ahead of time.
2. Meet at regular intervals.
3. Start on time.
4. Dispose of necessary business quickly.
5. Let the planned program take up the majority of the meeting time.

Good, orderly procedures like these will keep members coming back for more.

Ability to instantly recognize good photographic possibilities requires long practice. This might make an interesting project for a group of members.

The lens board on a view camera can be moved to control the image on the film plane. The basic lens board movements are:
A. Rise *C. Shift*
B. Fall

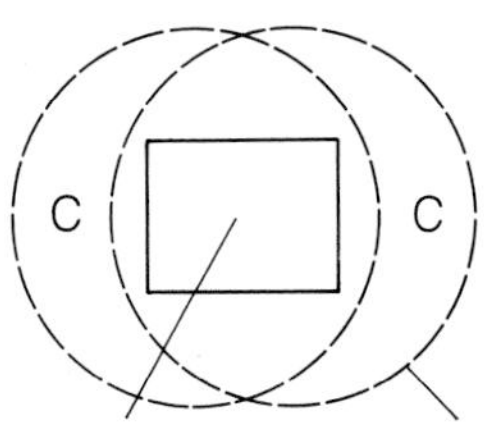

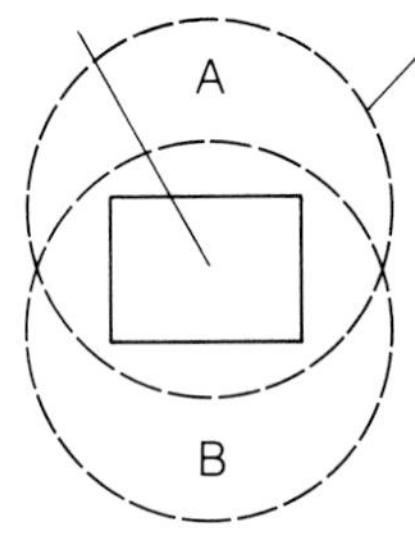

The following are still camera movements:
A. Rise *D. Swing*
B. Fall; Drop *E. Tilt*
C. Shift *F. Focus*

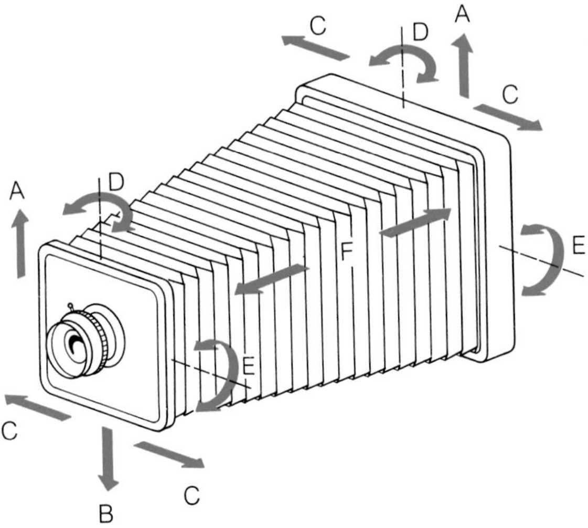

Camera Movements

In still photography, "camera movement" refers to changing the position of one part of the camera body in relation to another part of the body in order to adjust focus, picture coverage, overall sharpness, and linear distortion. In motion-picture and video photography, the term refers to moving the entire camera during a shot in order to change the field of view and to accommodate subject movement.

Still-Camera Movements

When the lens board and the back of a still camera are flexibly connected, as by a bellows, they can be moved independently of one another. (See accompanying diagrams.) They are moved toward or away from one another to adjust *focus.* A vertical movement is called a *rise* or a *fall* (or *drop*); a lateral movement is called a *shift.* A movement that pivots around a vertical axis is called a *swing*; a movement that pivots around a horizontal axis is called a *tilt.*

A lens-board rise, fall, or shift changes subject coverage because it moves the circle of coverage inside the camera with relation to the opening at the film plane. A lens tilt or swing moves the plane of sharp focus so that it will coincide with the most important subject plane.

A few special-purpose lenses for rigid-body cameras have an adjustable front element group to provide limited movements. Such lenses are often designated "tilt-shift," or, inaccurately, "perspective control" lenses.

A rise or shift of the camera back moves the location of the film within the lens circle of coverage. Some camera backs also have a falling or drop movement. A tilt or swing of the camera back changes the image size of various portions of the subject because it moves part of the film plane closer to the lens while moving another part farther away. It is commonly used to correct the linear distortion of a subject whose principal plane is not parallel to the film plane. A back tilt or swing also brings the film plane to coincide with the plane of sharpest focus in the image. The use of still-camera movements is further illustrated and explained in the article VIEW CAMERA.

Motion-Picture and TV Camera Movements

Hand-held camera movements are achieved directly by the camera person. In most cases, however, the camera is mounted on a wheeled tripod, pedestal support, or a dolly platform. Small supports may be moved by the camera person; large supports require a "dolly pusher" or other assistant.

A *pan* (panning, or panoramic) movement occurs when the camera remains in one place but pivots left, right, up, or down to change its field of view. A vertical pan is sometimes called a *tilt.*

Whatever support is used, a *dolly* movement carries the camera toward (dolly in) or away (dolly out, or back) from the subject. A curving dolly is an *arc.*

A horizontal movement of the camera accompanying a moving subject, produces a *trucking* shot. In a *leading* shot, the camera moves backward, at the same speed that a subject moves forward. In a *following* shot, the camera follows a subject moving away from the camera. A *tracking* shot is any movement in which tracks or rails have been laid down to guide the wheels of the camera support.

A *boom* movement raises or lowers the camera; the swinging arm, or boom, is usually mounted on a dolly. A *zoom* is not a camera movement at all; it is an optical change in image magnification caused by shifting the elements of a zoom lens, but the zoom takes the place of a dolly-in or a dolly-out camera movement.

• *See also:* VIEW CAMERA.

Cameras

A camera is essentially a lighttight box with a lens to form an image, a shutter and diaphragm to control entry of the image, a means of holding film to record the image, and a viewer to show the photographer what the image is. The capabilities of such a

The following are motion-picture/TV camera movements:
A. Pan *B. Tilt* *C. Dolly* *D. Arc* *E. Crab* *F. Truck* *G. Boom* *H. Follow* *I. Lead*

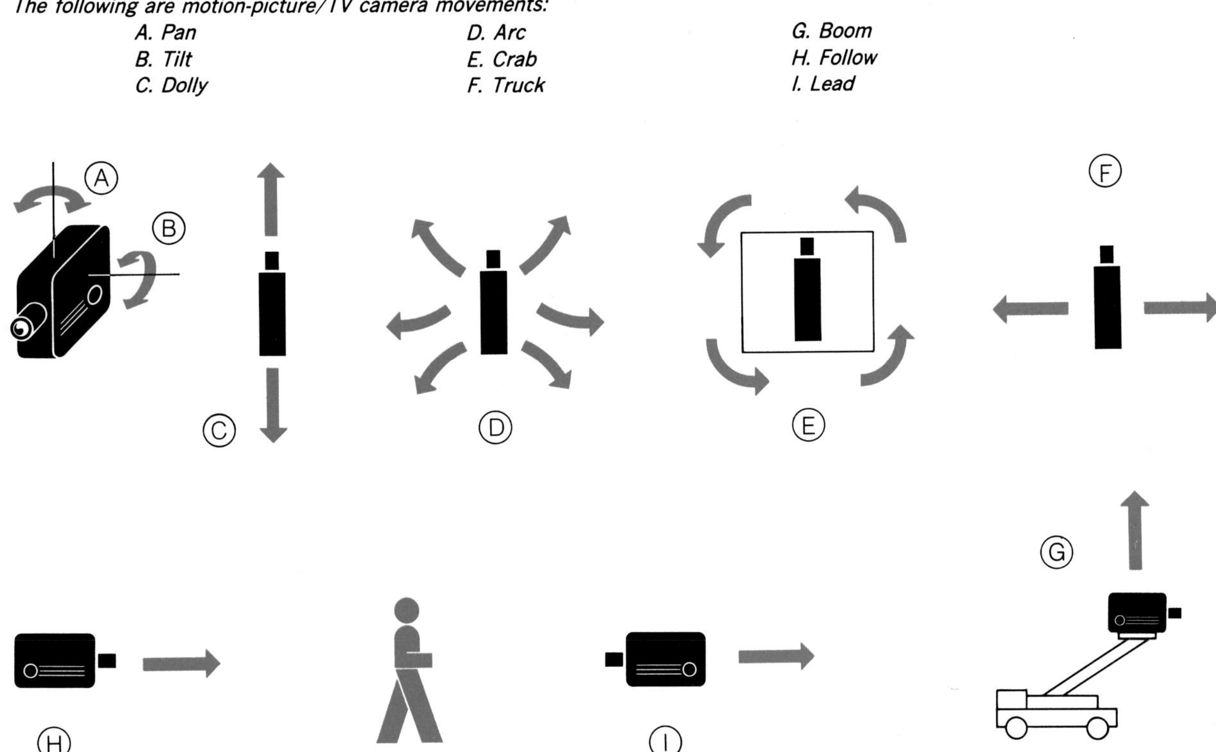

basic device are extended by features that permit the following:

1. Focusing on objects at various distances.
2. Changing to lenses of different focal lengths and fields of view.
3. Adjusting to correct linear distortion and lens focus coverage.
4. Adding attachments and accessories to use various size films or increase the technical capacity of the equipment.
5. Metering subject brightness and automatically controlling the lens opening, shutter speed, or both.

Camera Development

Cameras of a sort existed long before the materials for photographically recording the image were invented. The name comes from *camera obscura* (Latin for "dark chamber"), a device in use well before 1040 A.D. The chamber was a room with a small hole in one or more walls. Light rays passing in straight lines through a hole would project an image of the outside scene, which a person inside could view on a screen and perhaps trace or paint. By about 1560, a simple lens to provide a brighter image and a fixed diaphragm stop to improve sharpness had been added. Within another hundred years, artists were commonly using portable, box-like camera obscuras to make drawings of natural scenes that were precisely accurate in perspective and scale. Such a camera was fitted with a tubular focusing lens and an interior mirror to reflect the image up onto a ground glass for easy tracing. The original principle of the camera obscura survives in the pinhole camera; the furthest direct evolution of the artist's portable drawing box is the modern 120/220 film-size single-lens reflex camera.

The first photographic processes, introduced in 1839 and 1840, used a mirrorless, portable camera obscura with a viewing screen at the rear. The front and back were boxes that telescoped to adjust focus. After focusing, the viewing screen was replaced by a plate holder. Materials were so slow that no shutter was necessary; exposures were made by uncapping and capping the lens. Rigid-body cameras retained a box-like shape throughout the introduction of magazine loads for plates or sheet films and the first popular roll-film design, which Kodak introduced in 1888. A variety of improvements were made on the box camera, but the first significant change in body shape came in 1924 with the 35 mm Leica camera. Today's rigid-body cameras for 35 mm, 126, 110, and other film sizes have a great variety of shapes and features.

The collapsible-bellows camera was invented in 1839 especially for use in the new medium of photography and evolved along with other designs. This type of camera quickly developed into the following several forms:

Large, cumbersome studio cameras intended primarily for portraiture.
Large-format models that folded or packed conveniently for use in the field.
Practical cameras that folded to pocket size, yet used lenses long enough to cover a medium-size film format.
Folding cameras that used medium- and large-format films but could be operated hand-held.

Bellows have four main functions:

1. They allow the camera to be folded to a smaller size.
2. They permit focusing—even to very close distances—with lenses that do not have a built-in focusing capability.
3. They permit the use of interchangeable lenses of different focal lengths. For this and the preceding function, bellows have been incorporated in some rigid-body, reflex-viewing cameras and are available as an accessory in other designs.
4. They make possible adjustments to the lens and film planes (swings and tilts) for perspective control and for increasing the effective depth of field.

Camera Classifications

Cameras are commonly referred to or classified by (a) the size of the film they use or the format of the picture they produce, (b) their viewing/focusing

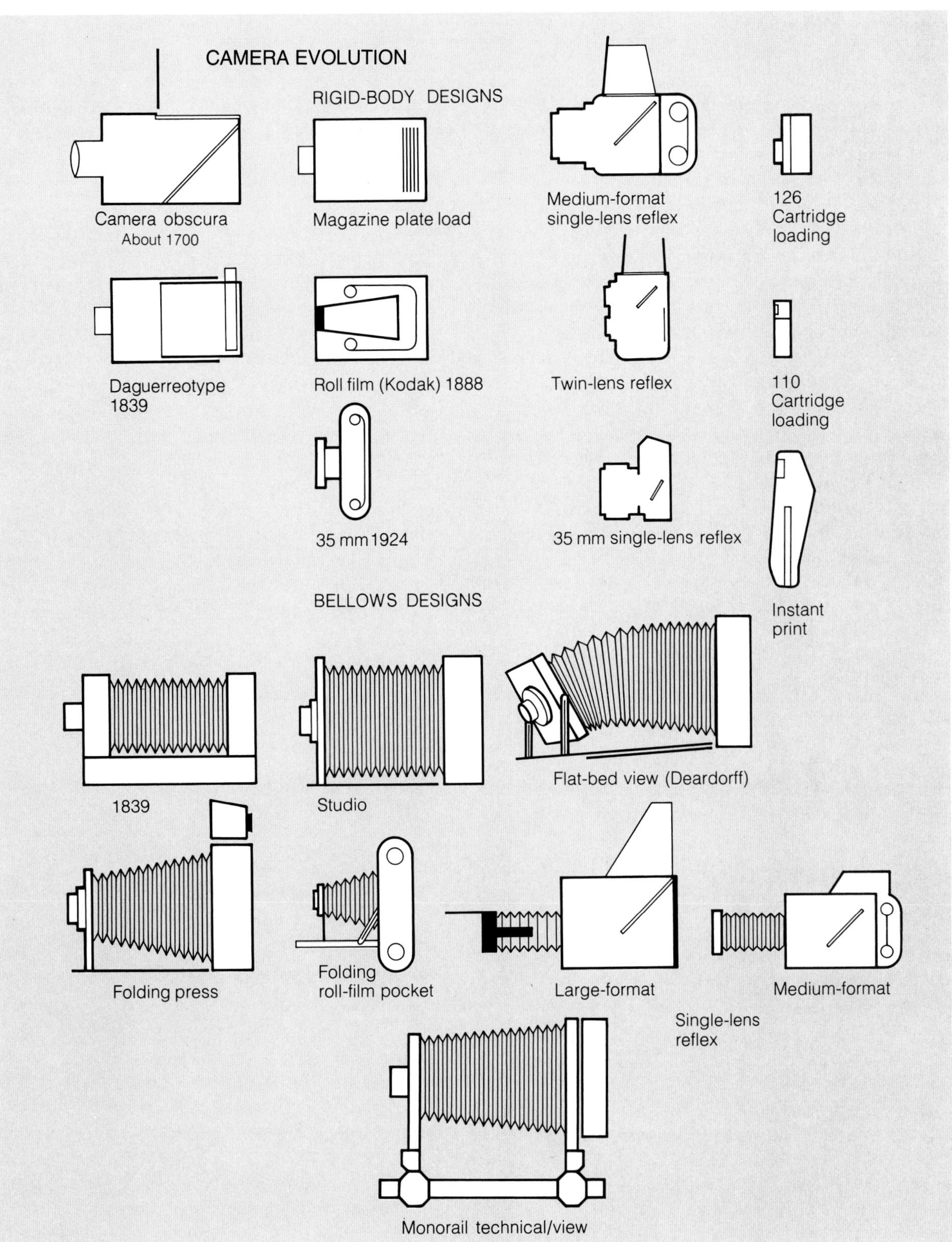
CAMERA EVOLUTION
RIGID-BODY DESIGNS
Camera obscura
About 1700
Magazine plate load
Medium-format
single-lens reflex
126
Cartridge
loading
Daguerreotype
1839
Roll film (Kodak) 1888
Twin-lens reflex
110
Cartridge
loading
35 mm 1924
35 mm single-lens reflex
Instant
print
BELLOWS DESIGNS
1839
Studio
Flat-bed view (Deardorff)
Folding press
Folding
roll-film pocket
Large-format
Medium-format
Single-lens
reflex
Monorail technical/view

systems, and (c) their overall design and function. Usually at least two of these categories are required to adequately identify a camera, for example, "a 35 mm single-lens reflex camera," or "a 4″ × 5″ camera."

Format. Most cameras in common use today variously utilize rolls or cartridges of film 16 mm to 70 mm wide, or sheet films up to 8″ × 10″ in size. Special-purpose cameras use even narrower or wider rolls, or larger sheet sizes. Many cameras designed primarily for one size film can accept smaller sizes or produce a variety of picture formats by means of magazine or adapter backs and film holders.

Large-Format Cameras. These cameras commonly use sheet films 10 × 12 cm (4″ × 5″) and larger. They are almost always bellows-type cameras, which allows them to accommodate the various focal length lenses required to cover the picture area. (A major exception is the aerial camera, which has a rigid-body design and uses roll film 5 or 9 inches wide.) Because of their size and consequently their weight, almost all large-format cameras are used on a stand or tripod. However, there are some folding press-type cameras using 4″ × 5″ film that can be hand-held.

Medium-Format Cameras. Most medium-format cameras use 120/220 or 70 mm roll film, or equivalent sizes of sheet film. They make pictures ranging in format from about 4.5 × 6 cm (1¾″ × 2¼″) to 6 × 9 cm (2¼″ × 3¼″). The full range of body designs is available in this size—studio or technical bellows type, rigid-body and bellows-equipped waist- and eye-level viewing types, and folding press cameras. Only the studio or technical type must be used on a tripod or stand; the others may be hand-held under a variety of conditions, although their performance is extended and improved by the use of a tripod.

Small-Format Cameras. These cameras use 35 mm and smaller film sizes (126, 110, 16 mm are common) contained in magazines or cartridges. At a time when most cameras were medium- or large-format designs, small-format cameras were called miniature (35 mm size) and subminiature (16 mm size). Such terms are inaccurate and essentially meaningless today because of the variety of small film sizes and camera-body styles in use. Small-format cameras are physically small and relatively lightweight; many are truly pocket size. They are readily used hand-held, and require accessory support only when used at slow shutter speeds, with long-focal-length lenses or heavy, bulky attachments.

Illustrated here are three of the most popular formats currently being used today. Left, 6 × 6 cm (2¼″ × 2¼″); above, 35 mm (photo by Editorial Photocolor Archives); and right, 110 format.

Camera Viewing and Focusing

The camera viewfinder shows how much of the subject will be included in the selected format using a particular lens. The simplest finder is a pair of wire frames, or a single frame with cross-wires to mark the center and an aiming post; it is used much like a gunsight. Wire frames are incorporated in some large folding cameras; they are most useful to follow fast action such as sports, with the lens focus preset to a certain range.

Optical Viewfinders. These viewfinders use a simple lens or lens system to present an aerial image of the subject to an eyepiece. They do not use the camera lens, but are designed to show the same field of view as the normal-focal-length lens for the format in use. Changeable masks or bright-line frames may be used to show the different fields of view of other lenses. Optical viewfinders are usually built into the bodies of small-format cameras. Some medium- and large-format folding cameras accept an accessory "universal" optical finder which can be adjusted to show the field of view of a number of different lenses.

The simplest cameras have fixed-focus lenses that produce acceptably sharp images of all objects from about 2 metres (6½ feet) from the lens to infinity. Other cameras with optical viewfinders provide for focusing by setting a distance scale on the lens barrel, or (in folding cameras), by moving the lens standard out to appropriate scale distances marked on the camera bed. For more precise focusing, a separate rangefinder may be mounted on the camera. But the most advanced optical viewfinders incorporate a rangefinder coupled with the camera lens so that viewing and focusing may be accomplished simultaneously.

To focus accurately at considerable distances, a rangefinder must be physically large. To overcome the limitations imposed by their small body size, some 35 mm cameras with optical viewing have a coupled rangefinder for use with lenses from about 35 mm to 135 mm focal length, but use an accessory reflex viewer between the camera body and lens for longer focal lengths. With shorter lenses, an auxiliary viewer shows the field of view, and close-distance focusing is achieved by setting the lens distance scale.

One difficulty with wire-frame and optical viewfinders is parallax. The finder and camera axes cannot be made to coincide, so the finder field and camera field match adequately only beyond a certain distance. This usually means that at close distances, the camera covers less at the top of the field and more at the bottom of the field than the finder shows, resulting in cutoff of the subject's head. Some finders have adjustments so that the finder shows the field being covered by the camera at close distances.

Ground-glass Viewfinders. This type of viewer presents an image on a screen at the rear or the top of the camera. The term "ground glass" is commonly used, even though today the screen may be etched plastic or other material. The image is formed either by the camera lens, or by a second lens of matched focal length so that framing and focusing can be adjusted at the same time.

A screen located in the focal plane at the rear of the camera shows the actual field of view of the camera lens; from this comes the general term "view camera." The image is upside down and reversed left-for-right; a dark cloth or light-excluding hood and a magnifier are usually required to see and focus the image clearly. View-camera focus is adjusted by

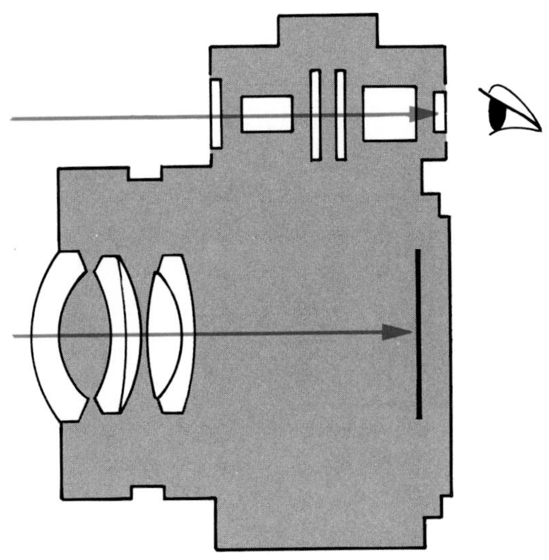

With viewfinder and rangefinder cameras, parallax is a problem because the camera axis and finder axis do not coincide.

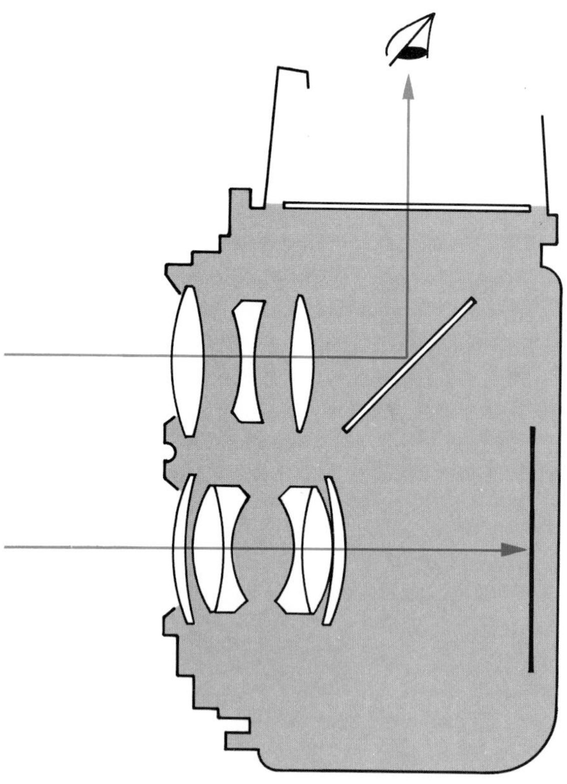

A twin-lens viewing system uses a separate, matched finder lens for image viewing.

In the viewing system of a single-lens reflex camera, an angled mirror reflects the image formed by the lens onto a screen at the top of the camera.

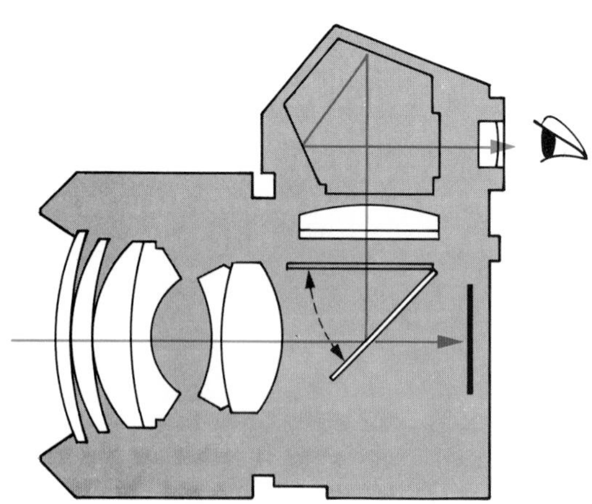

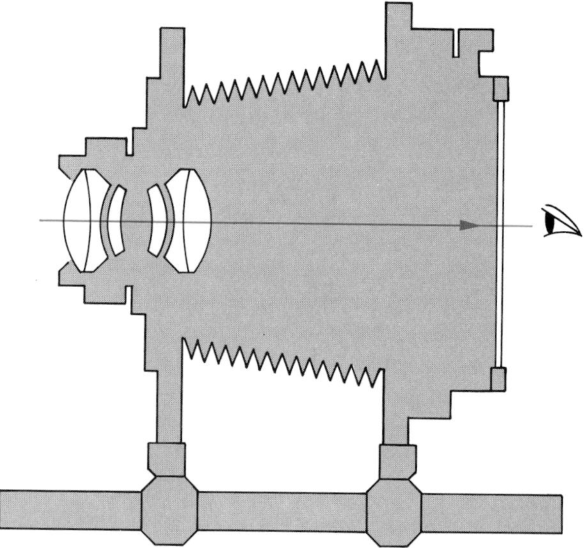

With a ground-glass viewfinder, the image is formed on a screen at the rear or top of the camera.

moving the lens standard toward or away from the focal plane; some designs also allow the camera back to be moved for focusing.

The Viewing System of Single-Lens Reflex Cameras. Single-lens reflex cameras have an angled mirror that reflects the image formed by the camera lens onto a screen at the top of the camera. When the screen is seen directly from above (so-called "waist-level" viewing), the image is erect but reversed left-for-right. When a prism is placed over the screen so viewing may be accomplished at eye-level from the rear of the camera, the image is both erect and not reversed. Single-lens reflex systems reflect the image of the camera lens to the screen; the mirror must move out of the way just before the shutter activates so that the image can fall on the film when an exposure is made. In many single-lens reflex cameras, the mirror returns immediately so that the image disappears, or "blacks out," only for the instant of exposure.

The Viewing System of Twin-Lens Reflex Cameras. Twin-lens reflex systems use a separate, matched finder lens to produce the image for viewing. Because the viewing system mirror does not have to move, such cameras operate quietly, with no vibration. However, at distances closer than about two metres, parallax affects the accuracy of the viewing system. Some cameras have a built-in adjustment coupled to the focusing system that tilts the viewing lens downward or moves a masking frame in the viewer to compensate for parallax error.

Camera Designs

Most cartridge, magazine roll-film, and some instant print cameras have rigid bodies. They are small enough in modern designs so that they do not have to fold, and are classified as *pocket cameras* and *hand cameras.* They include all small-format designs, and medium-format single-lens and twin-lens reflex designs.

Folding Hand Cameras. These cameras are primarily of bellows design, although some have telescoping rigid bodies. In most models, one side of the body opens to form a bed at right angles. The lens standard, attached to one end of the bellows, pulls out along tracks on the bed and either slides or is moved by a geared wheel (rack-and-pinion) mechanism for focusing. The bed often has double- or triple-extension tracks for close focusing, and can drop to a downward-slanted position so it will not be within the field of view of a wide-angle lens. The lens standard may rise, swing, tilt, and shift to a limited degree. So-called *press cameras* (from their widespread popularity for newspaper photography from about 1920 to 1950) and some modified technical cameras are of this design. The back of the body opens to load roll-film or sheet film holders up to a maximum size of 4″ × 5″. The back may provide a very limited tilt or swing movement, and may revolve to provide a vertical or horizontal rectangular format. There is both ground-glass and optical viewfinding, and often an accessory rangefinder.

Studio Cameras. Studio cameras for portraiture are large-format bellows designs with limited movements. A rising-shifting lens board is common, but front or rear tilts and swings are not required. Ground-glass viewing is used for careful adjustment of composition.

View Cameras. These cameras may have folding flatbed tracks for convenience in field use. But most view cameras today are composed of a single rail (monorail), which supports a lens-board standard and a back standard with a bellows connecting them. This is sometimes called optical bench design. Ground-glass viewing is used at the camera back. View cameras have complete lens and back movements, and are made in medium- and large-format sizes. A *technical camera* is a precision-engineered monorail view camera, capable of the maximum degree of corrective movements. This monorail view camera can be adapted for almost any kind of photography requiring the maximum technical control possible.

System Cameras. A system camera is a basic body design to which a great number of specially designed lenses, viewers, film backs, and accessories can be attached. It is the heart of an integrated set of equipment intended to give a photographer the greatest possible versatility without the need to own a large number of separate cameras. Some professional-quality 35 mm systems have hundreds of accessories to adapt them for scientific, technical, architectural, astronomical, underwater, and many other kinds of photography. Some large-format technical cameras have also been designed as system cameras.

Shutters

Camera shutters are usually located just in front of the film, or inside the lens. A focal-plane shutter opens completely and closes for long exposures, or produces a variable slit that moves across the film plane for shorter exposures. The width of the slit and speed of movement together establish the length of time each part of the film is exposed. Between-the-lens shutters are overlapping leaves that move outward to completely open the diameter of the lens (although the diaphragm setting may limit the actual diameter of the light path) and then close. The length of the exposure is controlled by varying spring tensions and gear trains.

Many simple cameras use some sort of leaf shutter directly behind the lens. They are often limited to one or two speeds, such as 1/40 or 1/80 sec., which are sometimes marked *I* ("Instantaneous"). Some have a second setting, labeled *B* ("Brief") or *T* ("Time"). However, many cameras provide a speed range of 1, 1/2, 1/4, 1/8, 1/15, 1/30, 1/60, 1/125, 1/250, and 1/500 sec., plus Time and/or Brief. *(B* originally meant "Bulb," because the shutters were air-activated, and a rubber bulb was used to open and close the shutter.) Many shutters also have speeds of 1/1000 and even 1/2000 sec., and may have various slow speeds from 1 to 10 seconds. Built-in self-timers in medium- and small-format

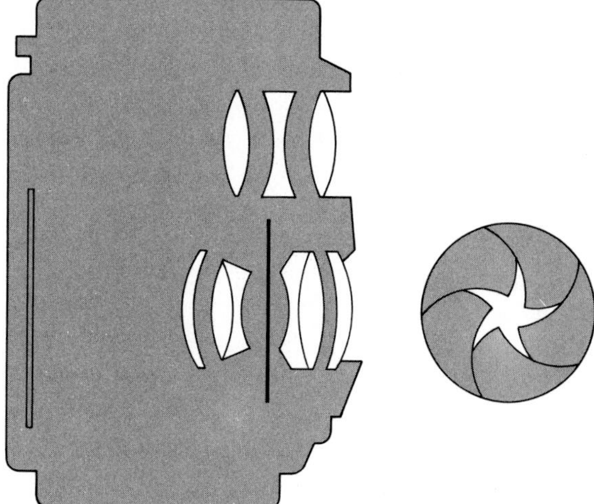

The overlapping leaves of between-the-lens shutters move outward to completely open the diameter of the lens and then close.

cameras provide a delay of up to 10 seconds before the shutter fires after the release is pushed.

In automatically controlled shutters, a coupled metering system varies the shutter speed according to the brightness of the subject or image. Most instant print cameras have completely automatic shutter and exposure control. The most sophisticated systems for conventional cameras control the shutter electromagnetically over a continuous range and can produce an intermediate speed such as 1/285 sec., if required.

The flash capability of a camera is linked to the shutter system. Because electronic flash is so brief (1/5000 sec. or less), the shutter must be fully open before the flash fires. Between-the-lens shutters generally achieve this at all speeds, but focal-plane shutters may be limited to settings slower than 1/125 or 1/60 sec. Otherwise, only a strip of film corresponding to the width of the shutter slit will be exposed. With a few special flash bulbs, faster focal-plane shutter speeds can be used because the peak light intensity lasts long enough for the traveling shutter slit to expose the entire film.

Large-format and twin-lens reflex cameras use lenses with built-in shutters. Some folding cameras in the press and modified technical sizes may use both between-the-lens and focal-plane shutters. The focal-plane shutter is left open when the lens shutter is used. In cameras with through-the-lens viewing systems, the lens shutter must be opened for viewing and focusing, then closed before a film holder is inserted in the camera and its dark slide removed to prepare for the actual exposure.

Most single-lens reflex cameras have focal-plane shutters that protect the film until the mirror has moved out of the way; then the shutter opens and closes for the exposure. A few medium-format models use between-the-lens shutters in order to obtain electronic flash synchronization at all speeds. They have an auxiliary capping shutter behind the mirror to protect the film. The sequence of operation is complex. The lens shutter is open for viewing and focusing. When the shutter release is pressed to take a picture, the following things occur:

1. The lens shutter closes.
2. The mirror rises (or drops) out of the way.
3. The capping shutter opens.
4. The lens shutter opens and closes.
5. The capping shutter closes.

The mirror may return and the lens shutter open again for viewing automatically, or those actions may be linked to advancing the film for the next exposure.

Interchangeable Lenses

The ability to use more than one lens greatly increases the versatility of a camera. Some pocket cameras have a built-in element that moves into position to convert the normal lens to a moderate telephoto lens, and most lenses can be fitted with supplementary or auxiliary lenses to change their effective focal lengths. True lens interchangeability is now available on most 35 mm and medium-format cameras. Lenses have screw or bayonet-locking mounts, and usually are designed so that their iris diaphragms couple to a camera's internal metering system. A single-lens reflex system permits viewing and focusing with any lens that can be fitted to the camera.

A focal-plane shutter produces a variable slit that moves across the film plane for shorter exposures, or opens completely and closes for long exposures.

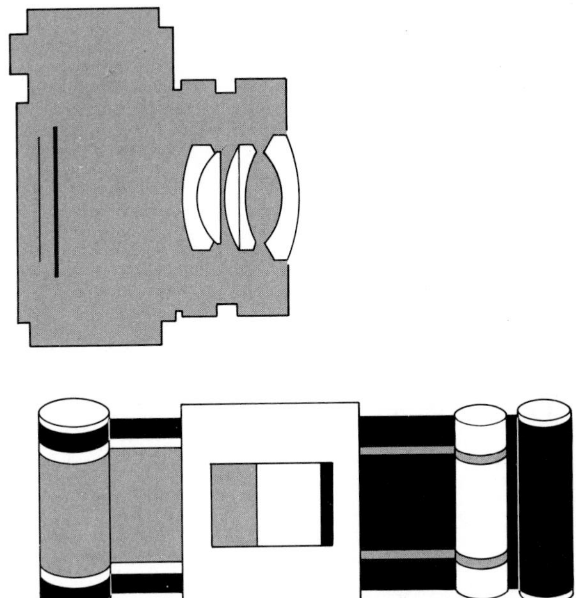

In a twin-lens reflex camera that has interchangeable lenses, both the viewing and taking lenses must be changed. Usually the entire front panel is removed, to be replaced by another with a matched set of lenses of the desired focal length.

Medium- and large-format bellows-type cameras accept lenses mounted on lens boards (made of plastic, metal, or wood) that lock into the front standard. Lens boards are easily released and changed. The choice of a lens with such a camera is limited by the bellows draw, or length. It must be at least as long as the lens focal length to focus objects at infinity, and even longer to focus objects at closer distances. For life-size (1:1) images, the bellows must extend enough to place a lens twice its focal length from the film plane. Triple extension bellows are relatively common on view cameras.

Film Changing

In small- and medium-format cartridge and roll-film cameras, the film is advanced by moving a lever, or turning a knob or crank. A coupled counter advances to show how many exposures have been made. In most such cameras, the shutter is simultaneously cocked as the film is advanced. However, some medium-format roll-film cameras advance the film with a forward movement of the knob or crank, and cock the shutter with a half-turn backward. A number of 35 mm and roll-film cameras can be fitted with motors that automatically move the film after each exposure. Depending on the camera, more than two exposures per second are possible with a motor-drive film advance. An auxiliary film chamber holding a much longer-than-normal roll of film is a useful accessory to a motor-driven camera.

Sheet-film cameras accept double film holders. Each side of the holder contains one sheet of film and is fitted with a dark slide, which is pulled out to uncover the film for exposure after the holder has been loaded into the camera. The dark slide is replaced, the holder removed and turned over, and returned to the camera to expose the other sheet. In addition, most such cameras also accept adapter backs for smaller sheet-size holders, roll-film holders, sheets or packs of instant print materials, or film packs. In some cameras, the ground glass is spring-loaded, and the film holder is inserted between the back and the camera. In these types, the ground glass is removable, and the film holder replaces the ground glass on the camera back.

Built-In Meters

Meters are now incorporated in most small-format and instant print cameras, and meter-controlled lenses are available for large-format cameras. Mass-market and amateur cameras frequently have totally automatic exposure control coupled to the metering system; the photographer cannot control the exposure. More advanced cameras provide manual as well as semi-automatic or fully automatic exposure control. There are two types of semi-automatic control. In an *aperture-preferred* system, the photographer chooses a lens *f*-stop setting, perhaps to control depth of field, and the camera metering system selects the appropriate shutter speed according to the subject or image brightness. In a *shutter-preferred* system, the photographer chooses a shutter speed, for example, to provide capturing movement without blur, and the metering system closes the lens diaphragm to the required aperture when the exposure is made. (*See:* AUTOMATIC EXPOSURE SYSTEMS.)

When the photographer chooses to set both aperture and shutter speed manually, he or she may use the camera meter simply to take readings of various subject brightnesses, much as he or she would use a separate meter.

Camera Choice

In selecting a camera, you must consider what kind of work you want to produce, and what you will need in the way of maneuverability, versatility, and control. The following are some examples.

If your primary aim is color slides, or if you must be free to move easily or travel, a 35 mm camera is the obvious choice. A single-lens reflex camera has greater versatility in terms of the variety of lenses and accessories that can be fitted to it. A coupled-rangefinder model operates more quietly (because there is no mirror movement) and provides a brighter viewfinder image for positive focusing under low-light conditions.

For volume portraiture on location, such as for school yearbooks, a medium-format roll-film camera may be best—one that uses 220 or 70 mm film to cut down on reloading.

For studio portraiture, a large-format studio or view camera provides negatives large enough to be retouched easily.

For architectural work, a medium- or large-format technical camera provides full movements to correct perspective and control the placement of depth of field.

For color illustration and product photography, a large-format technical camera is best, because the major demand is for large color transparencies, usually 4″ × 5″ or 8″ × 10″.

For fashion photography, a small- or a medium-format hand camera is essential to capture models in motion; a large-format camera is required for carefully posed illustrations, both in the studio and on location.

For scientific work, facsimile copying, and other jobs requiring the greatest technical excellence, a medium- or large-format technical camera is the preferred choice.

Whatever kind of camera you decide upon, compare features, construction, and handling procedures before deciding. Then buy the very best quality you can afford; a mediocre camera is expensive in the long run because it may turn out poorer work and is usually replaced sooner or later with a better quality model.

Specialized Cameras

Many jobs that can be accomplished only with difficulty using conventional cameras are easily done with specialized cameras. Such work includes: aerial photography; identification and fingerprint photography; cathode-ray tube recording; panoramic, high-speed, and stereoscopic photography; racing finish-line records; color separation and photomechanical reproduction photography; photography of eyes and internal organs; x-ray, stress analysis, and other kinds of scientific photography. The use of cameras designed for these kinds of work requires specialized training, and seldom will an individual photographer be purchasing the equipment.

• *See also:* AUTOMATIC EXPOSURE SYSTEMS; BELLOWS; FORMATS; LENSES; RANGEFINDER; SHUTTERS; VIEW CAMERA; VIEWING AND FOCUSING SYSTEMS.

Further Reading: Clerc, L. *Camera and Its Function.* Englewood Cliffs, NJ: Prentice-Hall, Inc., 1974; Editors of Time-Life Books. *The Camera.* New York, NY: Time-Life Books, 1971; Emanual, W.D. *All in One Camera Book,* 66th ed. Garden City, NY: Amphoto, 1973; Gaunt, Leonard. *The Photoguide to 35 mm.* Garden City, NY: Amphoto, 1976; *Photography with Large Format Cameras.* Garden City, NY: Amphoto, 1973.

Camera Supports

A camera support is a device to hold a camera firmly and steadily primarily to avoid the effects of vibration or movement during an exposure, and when view cameras are being used, to make viewfinding and operation easier. Some cameras can only be used on a support because of their size, weight, or complex operation. But the picture sharpness of any camera-lens combination can almost always be improved by the use of an appropriate camera support. Even fast shutter speeds can seldom overcome the vibration that results from hand-holding a camera—the results may be acceptably sharp, but they could be even better. It is obvious that support is especially required when slow shutter speeds, long-focal-length lenses, or heavy or bulky photographic accessories are used.

Illustrated here are four typical camera supports. In the foreground, a unipod and a Kodak compact camera stand model 2. In the background, a medium format camera on a clamp-pod and a 35 mm SLR on a tabletop tripod.

Camera supports consist of tripods, studio stands, and a number of miscellaneous devices. They usually attach to a camera by means of a ¼″ × 20″ thread bolt that screws into the camera's tripod socket or bushing. On some camera supports, quick-release attachments fasten to the camera and engage locking key slots; they permit mounting or unmounting a camera from the support in a second or two, rather than the 30 or so seconds it might take to accomplish the result without the attachment.

Tripods

The collapsible tripod with telescoping legs is familiar to every photographer. It ranges in size from pocket and tabletop models to studio designs capable of supporting hundreds of pounds at heights of up to about ten feet. The size and weight of a tripod must be sufficient to support a given camera without the slightest movement. It is hardly possible to get too solid a tripod for a camera, in terms of achieving steadiness. But because compact transportability is so attractive a feature, many photographers get too small or lightweight a tripod for effective support.

To test a tripod, set it up with the legs fully extended. Grasp the top and press down firmly while rotating your hand from side to side. There must be no movement at the individual leg joints or at the top where they join together. Repeat the same test with a camera in place. If there is movement, you need a better-made tripod, and probably one that is larger.

Useful features in a tripod include large knobs for positive locking and unlocking of controls and adjustments and, for additional elevation, a gear-driven center post that will not slip. Provision for reversing the post or attaching the camera to the lower end permits photography at very low elevations. Spiked feet are useful outdoors to prevent legs from slipping; they must convert to rubber or plastic padded ends for indoor use. A "pan head" makes it easy to tilt and pivot smaller cameras. Most ball-and-socket and friction-locking heads are suitable for very lightweight cameras. A gear-driven head is a great convenience for use with large cameras. Built-in spirit levels are a distinct aid in setting up for such things as architectural, panoramic, or precision photography.

Using a Tripod. Extend all three legs to the same length; then spread them out. Firmly plant one leg; then shift the other two individually until the tripod is level. Be sure all pan head and center post controls are locked before mounting the camera. When you attach the camera, keep a firm grip on the

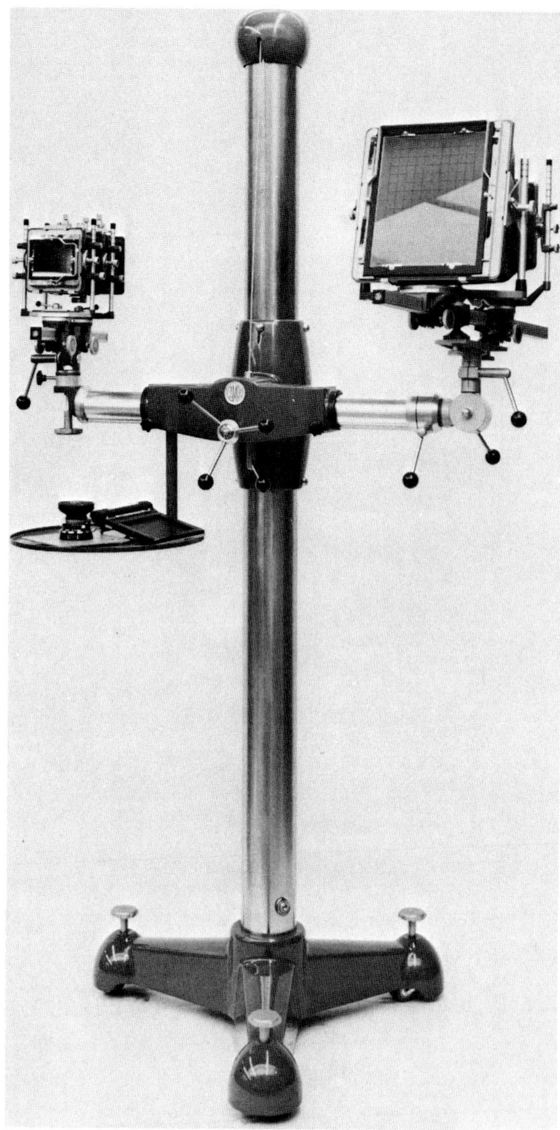

Large, heavy camera stands are ideal for use in studios. They occupy little floor space and cannot be easily upset, as they are very sturdy. This monopod has two view cameras mounted on side arms.

camera with one hand until the connection has been completed.

When possible, set up the tripod with one leg pointing directly toward the subject; this will allow you to stand comfortably between the other two legs, behind the camera, and makes it easier to level and to change the vertical angle of the tripod. If you straddle a leg, you risk kicking the tripod out of position. On a slope or a stairway, put two legs on the downhill side. You will have to shorten the single uphill leg to level the setup.

When adjusting ball-and-socket or ungeared heads and ungeared center posts, keep one hand on the camera to steady it if anything slips. Do not raise a center post up to the point where wobble develops.

Keep telescoping legs clean; wipe off all dirt and moisture before closing them—anything that gets inside can cause jamming, slippage, or corrosion. In wet or muddy locations, slip small plastic bags over the tripod feet to keep them clean.

A small tripod should be used with hand cameras on top of tables and other flat surfaces, or turned sideways so its legs can brace against a wall. All three legs should be used close together at full extension as a kind of monopod in crowded conditions. Another way to use a tripod to steady a hand-held camera is to shorten the legs and place one over each shoulder, and the third into your belt. Still another way is to group the shortened legs together so you can put them over one shoulder, and use the camera somewhat like a gunstock.

Above all, *never leave a tripod unattended or turn your back on it outdoors or indoors in a group session*—someone is sure to bump into it and knock it over. Damaged cameras are either impossible or very costly to repair.

Camera Stands

Camera stands are primarily used in the studio. There are three major types:

1. A large-diameter pedestal on wheels with a telescoping center tube. The camera mounts on a platform or tilt head on top of the center tube. This kind of stand is ideal for the heaviest, most cumbersome cameras.
2. A square or H-section vertical post on a wheeled base. The camera mounts on a cross arm that travels up and down the post. The arm may be counterbalanced if required, or can have lighting units attached to it. This design is especially useful for supporting a camera at very low elevations.

3. A pipe frame or scaffold-like rack mounted on wheels with an elevated platform large enough for the photographer and the camera. The camera may mount to the rail, or a tripod may be used on the platform. This is the preferred stand when the camera must be more than about seven feet above the floor.

In all stands, the wheels lock or lift out of the way so there can be no movement once a position has been chosen.

Other Supports

A monopod is a single, telescoping pole with a tripod thread at the top on which the camera mounts. It is useful with lightweight hand cameras. Keep it vertical, directly below the camera, with its foot between your own feet.

A chainpod is another hand camera device. It is a length of chain with a crossbar that you stand on, or a loop that you place one foot into. The other end screws into the camera. You pull up, against the chain, pulling it taut to gain some steadiness. A similar device can be made from rope or nylon cord (for ease of cleaning).

A chestpod is a short monopod that fits into a socket hanging around your neck.

A gunstock support lets you hold and aim a camera as if it were a rifle. It is especially helpful when you need to handhold very long-focal-length and zoom lenses.

While all these devices help steady a camera more than hand-holding, when it comes to picture sharpness there are no substitutes for a sturdy tripod. However, there are many situations where the use of a tripod is too slow, or it is too heavy a device to carry. It is then that monopods, chainpods, chestpods, and gunstocks come into their own.

There are various styles of screw clamps that can grip flat things such as the top of a park bench, or tubular things such as pipes, railings, and tree branches. Often they will solve a problem in a location where a tripod cannot be used.

Vacuum- or suction-base supports will grip firmly to clean, smooth surfaces. They do well with small cameras on horizontal surfaces. They should not be trusted on vertical surfaces such as doors, walls, or windows. There is no way of ensuring that unseen dust or grease will not cause them to lose their grip at a critical moment. Slightly moisturizing the vacuum cup with glycerine water (or saliva in an emergency) will improve the grip.

• *See also:* TRIPODS.

Candid Pictures

A candid photograph is a visual record of a moment in time, an image of a person or persons made from life as it was really happening, an honest instant caught on film by a photographer who did not directly intrude on or interfere with the situation he or

A candid photo is an honest instant caught on film by a photographer who acts only as an observer and recorder. He or she may, however, select the occasion and the subject.

she was witnessing. The subjects of candid photographs are not posing or acting. They are simply being themselves and behaving as they would if the photographer were not there. These subjects might be anyone: grade-school children in their classrooms, a group of men shooting a game of billiards in a basement recreation room, a one-year-old getting his or her first haircut, or a bride waiting nervously at the rear of a church just before her wedding. It is the genuineness, the warmth, and the truth of such photographs that give them their great appeal.

Candid Subjects

Potential candid subjects are all around us. Indeed, the ability to select meaningful images from the constant stream of people and events in our everyday lives is what really counts in getting good candid photographs. To probe for, and to extract, evocative pictures from a seemingly ordinary scene, a candid photographer must have a real ability to see, to interpret, and most important, to feel.

Familiarity with, and empathy toward, the subject is a basic requirement for getting good candids. As a starting point in slice-of-life picture-taking, family and friends will provide a wealth of subject matter—people being themselves.

Equipment

Any camera is capable of becoming a candid camera. A simple model may be limited in the range

Candid photographs taken at special occasions, such as weddings, are often more valid recordings of the true feeling of the event than the more formal, posed pictures. The candid photos make treasured possessions for years to come.

Certain facial expressions are almost impossible to "fake" for a posed picture. To probe for, and to extract, evocative pictures, a candid photographer must have a real ability to see and to feel. The photographer must also be very fast and adept at handling equipment.

of picture situations it can handle when compared with a more advanced camera, but even a simple camera can make candid photographs of happenings around the home, which can provide rewarding results for the family photo album. It's the photographer's ability to take a discerning and selective look at what's going on that really counts.

More advanced cameras, with their fast, interchangeable lenses, are admirably suited to candid photography in a much wider range of locations and lighting conditions. A small single-lens reflex camera provides ease of handling, and the large number of exposures per roll of film lets you keep on shooting when with other cameras you might have to stop for reloading. Fast lenses make it easy to shoot pictures indoors without flash, which might destroy the mood and distract the subject. Wide-angle and telephoto lenses provide control of viewpoint and perspective at the camera, without interfering with the subject or imposing on the situation.

Whatever camera and accessories are used, handling must be practiced and smooth. A fast-moving human-interest situation does not allow time for fumbling with camera controls, flash equipment, exposure meters, or loading techniques. Presetting the shutter speed, aperture, and distance for the prevail-

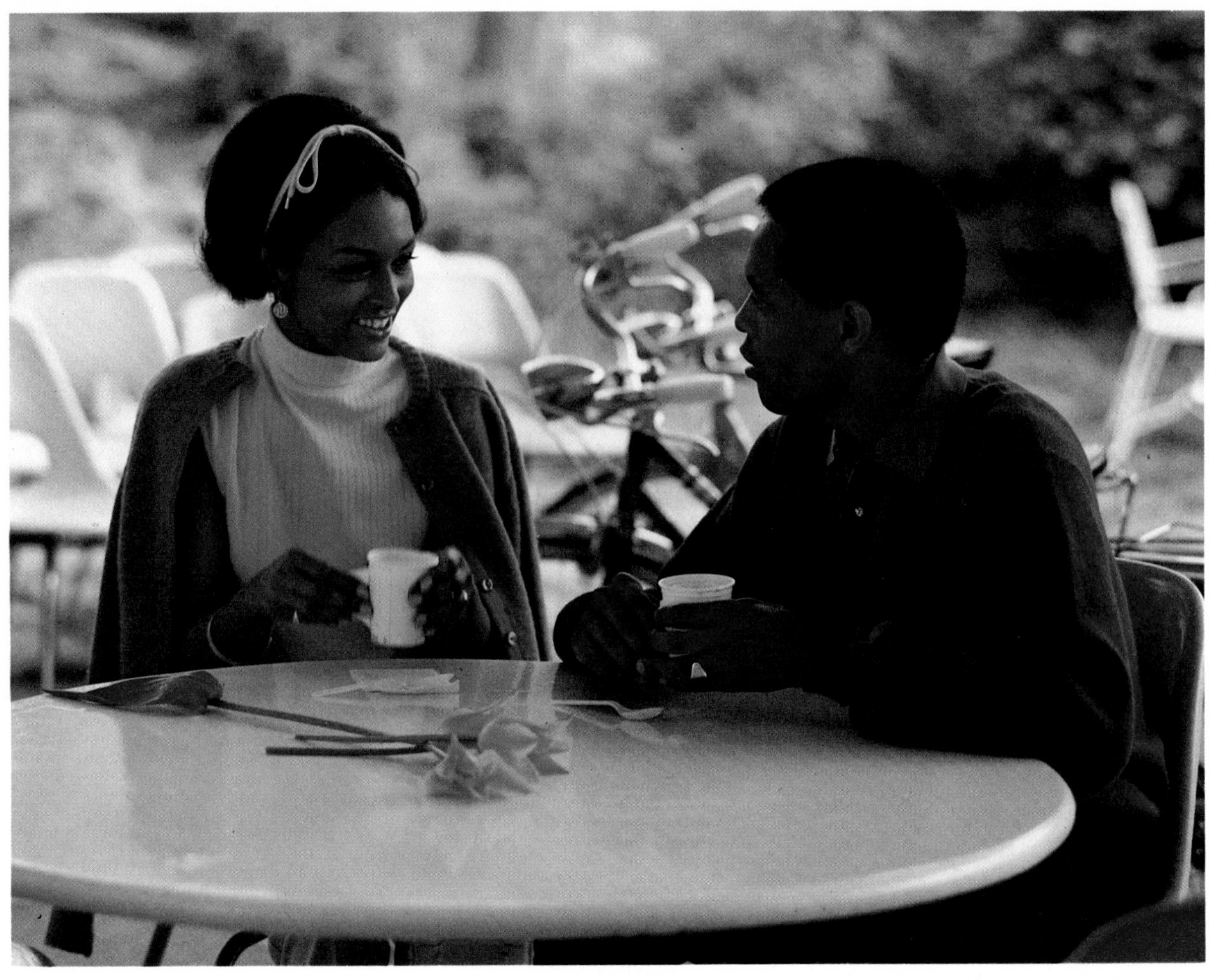

In candid photography, using existing light, the ability to determine correct exposure quickly and accurately is essential. It would have been easy to underexpose the dark faces of this young couple seated in a shaded spot with a brightly lighted background.

ing conditions will keep you ready when the decisive moment arrives.

Shooting by Existing Light

Existing-light photography is taking pictures using only the light found at the scene. It might be light from fixtures in a room, daylight from windows, light from a streetlamp, or candlelight. There's nothing new about this technique. It's been used successfully for years by photojournalists and other photographers to give pictures a believability and realism that would be virtually impossible by any other method. Such pictures appear so natural that the mode of lighting used will probably never enter your mind.

Today's high-speed films, such as Kodak Tri-X pan film for black-and-white prints and Kodak Ektachrome 200 film for color slides, make existing-light photography possible with any camera that has an *f*/2.8 or faster lens. By using a Kodak special processing envelope, ESP-1, you can obtain special processing that doubles the speed of Kodak Ektachrome 200 film (daylight). This means that hand-held existing-light color pictures are possible under all but the dimmest lighting conditions. For existing-light pictures with color films, use a tungsten film, such as Kodak Ektachrome 160 film (tungsten) with tungsten light, and a daylight film with existing daylight.

When existing light and candid photography get together, beautiful, compelling, and more natural-looking pictures can result. But if you're not using a camera with automatic exposure control, you must be able to determine the correct exposure quickly and accurately. There is no *one* right way to do this. Use an exposure meter you feel comfortable with and that gives you consistent results, follow the manufacturer's recommendations for its use, and *practice* with it until using it, like using your camera, becomes second nature. Some existing-light situations are impossible to measure with a meter; tables and dials that give starting exposures for such situations are readily available in publications from manufacturers of photographic materials.

At the slow shutter speeds and large lens openings used in existing-light photography, accurate focusing and a very steady camera are a must. Practice holding the camera steady, and squeeze—don't jab—the shutter release. Whenever possible, brace the camera against a doorjamb, lamppost, the back of a chair, or anything that is handy to help avoid camera movement.

This evocative photo of a sad or pensive child was taken entirely by light from the window. Any attempt to use flash or reflectors would have totally spoiled the mood.

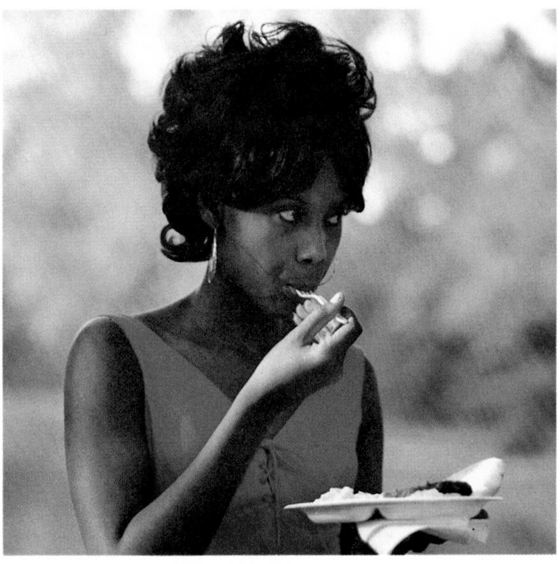

While hardly a classic pose, this is an excellent candid photo; had the photographer waited for the subject to stop eating, this thoughtful and solitary moment would have been lost.

The Unobtrusive Photographer

No matter what camera or lighting techniques you use, the real secret to getting good candid photographs comes from being able to photograph without calling undue attention to yourself. In some cases, the people you are photographing may be so engrossed in what they are doing that they are virtually oblivious to your presence; on the other hand, the situation could be so relaxed that you can't help being noticed. In such an instance, get in there and start shooting. Many times, after the first dozen or so shots, the people will be used to your shooting and may begin to ignore you.

With children as subjects, it is often effective to tell them to pretend that you are not there, and not to look at you or your camera. Both the cooperation and the results have been amazing. The same approach could be used with a group of adults, say, at a small gathering at home. Just ask them to ignore you.

The photographer must always be ready for the significant facial expression or interesting gesture, such as the look of deep concentration on the face of this young dancer.

Above all, keep looking and keep shooting. Be ready for the significant facial expression or interesting gesture. Move around. Look for interesting camera angles. Watch for the relationship of one person to another. Frame the principal subject with someone or something in the foreground that will help tell what's going on. If your equipment permits, use selective focus to isolate the prime subject from its background or foreground. Existing light too dim? Try bounce flash to simulate or augment the existing light.

Don't try to save film. In the long run, it's the least expensive item you're using. You will miss some shots by the very nature of the fleeting subjects you're photographing, and being stingy with film won't increase your percentage of good pictures.

Shoot to make pictures that are mirrors of the people and events around you; they will have a compelling authenticity that posed pictures never equal.

Further Reading: Editors of Time-Life Books. *Photojournalism.* New York, NY: Time-Life Books, 1971; Gatewood, Charles. *People in Focus.* Garden City, NY: Amphoto, 1977; Wooley, A.E. *Photography, A Practical and Creative Introduction.* New York, NY: McGraw-Hill Book Co., 1974.

Carbon and Carbro Printing

The carbon process derives its name from the fact that the pigment originally used in it was carbon, although one of the chief characteristics of the process is that it makes use of a great variety of pigments, affording almost unlimited choice of color. It is a long-scale process, reproducing quite faithfully the gradations of almost any negative. Carbon is a development of the process communicated to the Society of Arts for Scotland by Mungo Ponton in 1839, by which he secured images of drawings and dried flowers by printing through them onto a sheet of paper sensitized by a solution of potassium bichromate. The first practical method of pigment printing was introduced by Sir Joseph Wilson Swan in 1864, improved by J. R. Johnson in 1868, and brought to its final form by J. R. Sawyer in 1874.

The bichromated and pigmented gelatin is made insoluble in warm water in proportion as it has been acted upon by light, which means in practice, according to the densities of the different parts of the negative under which it is printed. The soluble pigment is then washed out, revealing the image. As the insolubility proceeds from the front of the coating, where it is in contact with the negative, the parts under the shadows and halftones are still soluble after printing and would be washed away, taking the image with them, if development proceeded from the front. For this reason the *tissue,* which consists of a sheet of thin paper coated with the sensitized, pigmented gelatin, is transferred, face down, upon another support. The paper is stripped off, and development proceeds from what was the back of the emulsion when it was being printed. This leaves the picture in reverse, and to bring it the right way about, it is again transferred to a *final support.* If the negative has been reversed in the making, or if it is immaterial which way it appears, it can be left upon the so-called *temporary support* and the final operation dispensed with. As this materially shortens and simplifies the process, it is generally resorted to. Alternatively, a reversed negative may be made from a regular negative by projection, by facing the emulsion away from the lens in one of the operations. This method has the added advantage that the negative can be made any desired size, regardless of the size of the taking camera. Negatives upon film may be printed through the thickness of the film, with the image reversed, with very little loss of definition, especially if artificial light is used and it is kept at considerable distance, so that the rays tend to become parallel. Before printing, the negative should be provided with a safe edge, which need be no more than a quarter-inch wide. It is conveniently made by sticking a strip of black photographic tape, or opaque paper, along all four edges of the negative. If the tissue is printed clear to the edges, it is difficult to handle it without damage.

Making the Tissue

The gelatin mass is prepared with hard and soft gelatin in the ratio of 3:1, or the finest pale carpenter's glue may be used, with an admixture of rock candy; in very hot, dry climates, add a little glycerin. The latter addition is not advisable under ordinary circumstances. A typical formula for the gelatin mass is:

Gelatin	200 g
Rock candy	50 g
Water	1 litre
Coloring pigment	4–10 g

Soak the gelatin and candy (granulated sugar will do as well, if rock candy is not available) in the water for about 30 minutes and melt in a water bath. The pigment should be the finest powdered colors, as used by artists. It should be worked up with a muller on a sheet of glass with a little of the gelatin solution, and added to the remainder of the solution, stirred well, and strained through linen.

The Colors

The colors can be mixed in various proportions, so that any shade may be obtained, and these should be judged by their appearance when mixed with a little of the gelatin solution and dried.

Chocolate brown. India ink 6, English red 4, alizarin 1, dissolved in a little soda solution, purpurin 1 part.

Engraving black. Lampblack 19, carmine lake 10, indigo 10 parts.

Warm black. Lampblack 6, carmine lake 6, burnt umber 4, indigo 2 parts.

Dark brown. Indigo 2½, Indian red 6, carmine 1¼, Vandyke brown 4, lampblack 30 parts.

Red brown. India ink 6, carmine 8, Vandyke brown 8 parts.

Sepia. Lampblack 4, sepia 35 parts.

Pure black. India ink 15, Vandyke brown 2, Venetian red 2 parts.

Violet black. India ink 20, indigo 2, carmine 1 part.

Red chalk. English red 10, Italian red 5, lampblack 0.03 parts.

Transparency tissue for enlarged negatives and positives. India ink 2, Indian red 3, carmine lake 5 parts.

To Coat by Hand

Strain the warm mixture into a flat dish standing in warm water, and clear the bubbles off the surface with a strip of paper or thin card. Hold the paper to be coated upright at the farther end of the dish, its lower edge just touching the liquid, and gently lower it onto the surface. Float for two minutes, then raise with a steady motion; allow to drip and hang up to dry.

Single-transfer paper

Brush over plain paper:

Soft gelatin .... 60 g
Water .... 875 ml

Soak the gelatin for 30 minutes, dissolve in a water bath, and raise nearly to the boiling point; add with constant stirring:

Chrome alum .... 1.25 g
Water .... 125.00 ml

The mixture must be rapidly used and kept hot, or it will gelatinize.

Flexible temporary support

Gelatinized paper is coated with a resinous solution. As a rule, a baryta-coated paper is used, either matte or glossy, which may be prepared as follows:

Gelatin .... 100 g
Barium sulfate .... 30 g
Glycerin .... 5 ml
Water .... 940 ml

Soak the gelatin in water, dissolve by heat, and add the baryta rubbed into a cream with the glycerin. Add very carefully, almost drop by drop, with constant stirring:

Chrome alum .... 1.6 g
Water .... 60.0 ml

Paint the mixture thickly over the paper, or float it twice, hanging up by opposite ends each time.

Waxing solution

The temporary support has to be waxed prior to use, and the following may be used:

Beeswax.......................... 20 g
Powdered resin .... 20 g
Turpentine .... 1 litre

Melt the wax in a water bath, add the resin, and stir until dissolved; then add the turpentine gradually with constant stirring. This should be applied to the paper with a pad, polished off with a dry pad, and then hung up to dry. It takes from 12 to 24 hours to dry; if ether is substituted for the turpentine, it will dry in a few minutes.

CAUTION: Because both turpentine and ether are highly explosive and can be ignited by a flame, even at some distance, the water bath or double boiler should be brought to boiling temperature and the flame extinguished, or the vessel removed to a safe distance from the heat source, before the solvents are uncapped and poured into the upper container.

Alum bath for clearing bichromate stain

Alum .... 62.5 g
Water............... 1.0 litre

Collodion for double transfer from glass

This gives an extremely fine matte surface, without any glaze, if matte surface glass is used; if polished opal is used, a high gloss is obtained:

Pyroxyline.................... 8.5 g
Alcohol .... 500.0 ml
Ether .... 500.0 ml

Opal glass, ivory, or wood as final support

Coat with the chrome-gelatin mixture given above under single-transfer paper. For canvas, the surface paint should be removed by scrubbing with hot soda solution, about ten percent, until nothing but the priming is left. Paint freely with the chrome-gelatin mixture, dry thoroughly, rub down smooth with fine sandpaper, and repeat the operations about four times. The print should be finally soaked in the gelatin solution, and squeegeed into contact, patting it down with the hand if the surface is rounded.

Substratum for transparencies

Either of the following may be used:

A. Gelatin ....40 g
   Water ....1 litre
   Potassium bichromate ....4 g

Coat the glass thinly, dry, and expose to light for 30 minutes; then wash and dry. Or the glass may be coated with the following, which keeps well:

B. Gelatin .... 7.0 g
   Glacial acetic acid .... 34.0 ml
   Water .... 270.0 ml

Soak the gelatin in acid and water for 30 minutes.

Dissolve by heat, and add slowly, with constant stirring:

Alcohol ....680 ml
Phenol (carbolic acid) ..10 ml

Then add, with constant stirring a solution of:

Chrome alum ...... 0.75 g
Water.................. 14.00 ml

Sensitizing

The tissue has a pronounced tendency to curl, which sometimes makes it difficult to handle. If this tendency, which grows with the age of the tissue, should be too pronounced, it can be overcome by suspending the tissue for a few minutes before sensitizing over a vessel of boiling water.

The standard sensitizer is:

Potassium
  bichromate ......21–63 g
Water ....1 litre
Ammonia.................. see below

Enough ammonia should be used to make the solution smell distinctly, which may require up to about 200 minims for the above amount of solution, depending upon the strength of the ammonia. For soft negatives, use the smallest amount of bichromate; for normal negatives, the mean; and for contrasty negatives, the greatest amount. From the same negative, a weak bath will give stronger prints, and a more concentrated bath softer prints. The temperature of the bath should be within a few degrees of 16 C (60 F). This is quite important because bichromated gelatin swells more readily than plain gelatin. Sensitizing may be done in full light, but the tissue must be dried in the dark, as it becomes sensitive while drying, which takes from 3 to 8 hours, depending upon humidity and drying conditions.

Immerse the tissue in the sensitizing solution for 3 minutes, keeping it moving all the time and handling it to prevent it from curling and keeping any part of it out of the solution. Break any air bells that may form on it with a soft brush or with the fingertips. Drain it for a couple of minutes and then suspend by one corner to dry.

Drying can be accelerated by laying the sensitized tissue face up on a sheet of glass and wiping off the surplus solution with a soft rubber squeegee. The squeegee must be as long as the shortest dimension of the tissue so that the whole surface will be included at one stroke, otherwise the end of the squeegee is likely to make a dent on the tissue, which will persist through all subsequent manipulations. This operation is risky because the emulsion is very soft and easily injured, and it is safer to allow the tissue to dry naturally. Results are likely to be unsatisfactory if the air is so moist that drying takes more than eight hours.

Tissue is in best condition for printing as soon as it is dry, but it may be kept in a cool, dry atmosphere for two or three days with little deterioration, or for a much longer time in airtight tin containers with a lump of calcium chloride, or wrapped in old newspapers that have been thoroughly dried by heat.

A formula containing citric acid will keep the tissue in good condition longer than the regular sensitizer and is used by many occasional workers.

Citric acid sensitizing solution

Potassium
  bichromate ....20 g
Citric acid ....5 g
Ammonia...................... see below
Water ....1 litre

Dissolve the bichromate and the acid first in the water and then add ammonia gradually until it has changed the color of the solution from orange to lemon-yellow and the solution smells distinctly of ammonia. Printing time and contrast increase with the amount of citric acid used.

Quick-Drying Sensitizer

A spirit sensitizer has the advantage that the tissue will be dry within half an hour.

Stock solution

Ammonium bichromate ..60 g
Water ....1 litre

This stock solution can be kept, like all the sensitizers mentioned above, for an indefinite time if protected from the light by wrapping the bottle in black paper. For use, take equal parts of the stock solution and of alcohol. The working bath should be used immediately, as it will not keep after the addition of the alcohol. This is applied to the tissue with an atomizer or with a Blanchard brush. In five minutes, it will be surface-dry; then apply another coating and then hang it up to dry. Drying of tissue, however sensitized, can be hastened by gentle heat and the use of a fan.

Printing

Carbon may be printed by daylight, arc, mercury-vapor, or sunlamp. As there is no visible image, prints must be timed by an actinometer. As a rough guide, the time for tissue sensitized in a four percent bichromate bath is about one-third that of printing-out paper. The printing time increases with the strength of the sensitizing solution, and it varies with the density of the negative and with the color of the pigment used. Accepting black as normal, blues, purples, and greens will require less printing time, and browns, reds, and yellows more.

The printing frame for making carbon prints should be supplied with strong springs to keep the negative in good contact with the paper against its decided tendency to curl. In damp weather, the frame should include a sheet of rubber or plastic film behind the paper to keep out moisture.

After tissue has been sensitized and dried, it gains in sensitivity for a short time and then begins to lose it. Allowance must be made for this, in timing prints, as printing times are not comparable except at the same interval after sensitization. The effect of light also continues for a time in the tissue after printing is stopped, even if it is stored in the dark, and the printing time must be adjusted to the interval that will intervene between printing and development. These two factors at their maximum may have considerable influence upon the character of the print. They can hardly be estimated, as they vary with conditions and so have to be learned by observation. It is well for the worker to standardize his procedure in this respect by printing at a fixed interval after the tissue is dry, and developing either immediately or at a fixed interval after printing. These intervals do not have to be calculated so closely as in terms of hours, but a day's difference in the operations may have a noticeable effect.

Development

After printing, the tissue is soaked in cold water until it becomes limp. Assuming that the print is to be made by single transfer, a sheet of single-transfer paper is thoroughly soaked in cold water, which may take an hour for thick, rough papers, and this time does no harm to smooth papers, which may be conditioned in less time. The gelatin side of the transfer paper should be marked by pencil before it is soaked, as it is sometimes difficult to identify it when it is wet. The gelatin side of the transfer paper and the pigmented side of the tissue are brought together under water and the two papers in contact are withdrawn and placed on a sheet of glass or other hard, smooth surface and squeegeed into perfect contact to exclude all air and water. Place between hard blotters under a light weight of a pound or so to keep them from curling, for about 20 minutes. The bichromate stain showing through on the back of the transfer paper is an indication that this process is complete.

Immerse the adhering papers in water between 38 and 41 C (100 and 105 F). Very soon the pigment can be seen oozing out between the two papers, which are then gently stripped apart, keeping them all the time under water. The pigment paper is then thrown away and development commenced upon the transfer paper, to which most of the pigment has adhered. Agitate and gently splash the paper under the warm water until all the soluble pigment has been washed away, leaving the image in insoluble pigment on the paper. When the image is clear, transfer the print to cold water, and then to a five percent solution of potassium alum in which it should be left until the yellow stain disappears. A final rinse in several changes of cold water completes the process, and the print is hung to dry.

Double Transfer

In the double-transfer process the print is developed upon a temporary support, which has a waxed surface to which the pigment will not adhere so strongly that it cannot be pulled off by the final support. Development upon the temporary support is similar in all respects to that in the single-transfer method, and the developed print is given the alum bath and hung up to dry. The final support, which must be larger than the print, but smaller than the temporary support, should be soaked in cold water, then placed for two minutes in water at 32 C (90 F), and then returned to the cold water. The dry print upon the temporary support is placed in cold water until limp, then the two are squeegeed into contact and hung up to dry. When they are dry, the temporary support is pulled off, leaving the print upon the final support.

Some workers use celluloid sheets as temporary supports; these must be waxed before each use, otherwise the image may stick and tear. Vinyl plastic sheets can also be used; some types of plastics do not require waxing.

Carbro

This is a development of the *Ozotype* process patented by Thomas Manly in 1899, in which a sized and bichromated paper was printed under a negative until a visible image appeared. After this had been washed to remove the bichromate stain, a "pigment plaster" was squeegeed into contact with it. The plaster consisted of pigmented gelatin that had been sensitized by immersion for about one minute in:

Glacial acetic acid	4 ml
Hydroquinone	1 g
Copper sulfate	1 g
Water	1 litre

After from 30 to 60 minutes in contact, the papers were separated and the print developed by washing away soluble gelatin in water at about 43 C (110 F).

Ozotype was followed by *Ozobrome,* which Manly patented in 1905, using a bromide print instead of the printed image of the previous process, thus obviating the necessity for an enlarged negative. With improvements by Howard Farmer in 1919, this became the carbro process, which gives a carbon print equal in all ways to one made by direct printing except in the matter of critical sharpness. In direct carbon, the bichromated, pigmented tissue is made insoluble by the action of light through a negative, while in carbro, a similar effect is obtained by the reaction between the tissue and a bromide print with which it is placed in contact.

The advantages of carbro are that it does not require a large negative, that daylight is not required, that all the work except the making of the bromide enlargement can be done in full light, and that the image is not reversed by the process.

Trays for the carbro process should preferably be of rubber, glass, or porcelain. Enameled iron trays can be used if the coating is intact and not porous, but for safety, they should be painted with a chemical-resisting varnish.

Smooth, semi-matte bromide papers are best adapted to carbro. Glossy papers usually give trouble. Chloride and chlorobromide papers are likely to give a faulty first print, but good ones subsequently. They can be conditioned by bleaching them in:

Potassium bromide	3 g
Potassium ferricyanide	9 g
Water	300 ml

and then washing until the yellow stain disappears, redeveloping, and washing again, after which they are all right for carbro. Rough paper is likely to trap air in the irregularities of the paper and prevent good contact with the tissue. Prints should be fully developed. If part of the shadow detail is buried by full development, the carbro print will still show it. Printing under a mask that leaves a white margin all around the print provides an area of soluble gelatin that will prevent frilling.

The single-transfer papers of the carbon process are used for carbro. The commercial product is better than any that can be hand-coated, but any bromide paper with a soft emulsion can be used for a transfer paper by fixing-out the silver emulsion in plain hypo and then washing. The back of the transfer paper should be marked by pencil when it is dry, so that it can be easily distinguished when it is wet.

Sensitizing. Sensitizing is usually performed in two operations for which baths are prepared by diluting the following stock solutions.

Carbro stock solution No. 1

Potassium bichromate	30 g
Potassium ferricyanide	30 g
Potassium bromide	30 g
Water	600 ml

For *working solution,* dilute 1:3. The stock solution is so nearly saturated that it sometimes crystallizes out in cold weather, in which case it should be heated until it is all in solution again before use. The working solution may be rebottled afterward and kept for future use, as it keeps for a long time if protected from light.

Carbro stock solution No. 2

Glacial acetic acid ....30 ml
Hydrochloric acid, C.P. ..30 ml
Formaldehyde,
40% solution.............660 ml
Water...............................45 ml

For *working solution,* dilute 1:32. The stock solution gradually precipitates a white sludge, which may be ignored if the solution is poured off from the top without disturbing it. The second bath is short-lived under working conditions and must be prepared fresh at the time of use, and not more than a dozen 8″ × 10″ prints should be processed in 32 ounces of the working bath. Both the stock solutions will keep well if protected from the light.

Working Directions. The bromide print and the transfer paper, which must be large enough to overlap the print all around, should be put to soak in cold water about an hour before commencing work, so that they will be in condition when needed. Thin papers, prints and transfer, may not need this much time, but the longer time will do no harm.

The tissue, which is the same as that used for carbon printing, is sensitized by immersion for 3 minutes in the No. 1 working bath, then drained for a few seconds and placed for about 20 seconds in the No. 2 working bath. The temperature of both baths should be the same, and between 16 and 18 C (60 and 65 F). Care should be taken to keep the tissue completely immersed all the time, in spite of its tendency to curl, and to break any air bells that may form on either the front or the back of the tissue.

The time of immersion in the second bath varies with conditions and can be learned only by experience. It may run from 10 to 60 seconds. Other things being equal, shorter times give harder prints. Different papers require different times for similar results. Soft water shortens the time, which should never be less than 10 seconds. If less time than this seems to be indicated, the working bath should be further diluted with an equal amount of water.

While the tissue is in the first bath, the print is withdrawn from the water and placed upon a sheet of glass in a level position. A squeegee is passed lightly over the print to make it adhere to the glass so that it will not slip during subsequent operations, and its surface then covered with water again. With the print thus ready and waiting, the tissue is taken from the first working bath at the end of 3 minutes, placed in the second bath for the predetermined number of seconds, and then withdrawn and immediately squeegeed into contact with the print. This must be done quickly and carefully, first putting one end of the tissue in contact with an end of the print and then lowering the rest of the tissue down onto the print in such a way as to force out any air and water from between them. The tissue is then made to adhere to the print by several strokes with a soft rubber squeegee. If the print and the tissue slip after coming in contact, a double image will ensue. Instead of the glass support, professional workers use a board with a hinged strip of wood across one edge. The edge of the print and of the tissue are placed in contact under the strip, which is then pressed down onto them, holding them immovable in relation to each other during the rest of the operation. Just sufficient force should be used in squeegeeing to make the tissue adhere to the print. If too much pressure is applied, the tissue and the bromide print cannot afterward be separated without tearing one or the other of them. If the pressure is too light, it will result in a light print or in lack of contact, which will cause an imperfection in the print.

The print and the adhering tissue are placed between waxed papers to exclude the air, so that they will not dry unevenly, and left under light pressure, just enough to keep them in contact, for 15 minutes. At the expiration of this time, they are gently pulled apart. The bromide print is dropped into a tray of water and left to be redeveloped later for making more carbros. The tissue is laid, face down, onto the transfer paper, which has previously been withdrawn from the water in which it had been soaking, and laid face up on the sheet of glass. The two are then squeegeed into contact and left between blotters, this time without the waxed paper, for about 20 minutes. Movement between the two papers in this operation does no harm.

Development. At the end of 15 minutes, the adhering papers are placed in a tray of water at about 135 C (95 F). There should be a considerable volume of water so that the temperature will not fall off much in a few minutes. After a few seconds, pigment will be seen oozing out from between the two papers, which are then pulled apart with a steady movement, taking care to keep them under water all the while. The tissue is then discarded, and the image is developed in the pigment on the transfer paper by gentle laving, during which some control can be exercised, as during the development of a carbon print, by directing the water against parts that need to be lightened.

When development has been carried as far as desired, the print is transferred to a five percent solution of potassium alum to harden it and to clear the bichromate stain, and then washed in two or three changes of cold water and hung to dry.

The original bromide print is thoroughly washed, redeveloped, and, without fixation, washed again, when it is in condition to make further carbros. Or the redeveloped print may be dried and used at any later time. Succeeding prints from the same bromide show increasing contrast, and this should be allowed for in the timing in the second sensitizing bath if identical prints are desired.

Combined Bath. The process is sometimes shortened by combining the two sensitizing baths into one. To 16 parts of stock solution No. 1, add 60 parts of water, and when thoroughly mixed, add 1 part of stock solution No. 2. This bath decomposes rapidly. It should not be used more than once, and will not give satisfactory results for more than 4 hours after mixing. The average time of immersion in this bath is about 2½ minutes, but like the second bath in the regular process, the time has to be learned by practice, as it varies, under different conditions, between 1½ and 4 minutes. The concentration of the bath may be changed if satisfactory results cannot be obtained within these time limits. Shorter time or greater dilution gives more contrasty prints, while a longer time or less dilution results in softer prints. Results with the combined bath are not so certain as with the two baths, and its use is not advised for beginners.

No Transfer. Instead of transferring the print to a separate support, it may be developed directly upon the bromide print. In this case, the sensitized tissue is left in contact with the print for 30 minutes, and then instead of stripping the papers apart, they are placed in water at 35 C (95 F) until the pigment begins to ooze, when the tissue is stripped off, under water, and discarded, and the carbro print developed upon the bromide print.

After the final hardening of the carbro print in alum, the underlying silver image must be dealt with. This is now in an unstable state, and it can be removed entirely by fixing in hypo, or by Farmer's Reducer, or it may be redeveloped under the carbon image to reinforce and strengthen it if it is weak. Whether the silver image is to be removed or redeveloped must be planned from the beginning so that the carbro print can be made strong enough to do without assistance, or left light enough so that it will need the reinforcement of the redeveloped silver image. Very interesting two-tone effects can be secured by using different colors of tissue over the black silver print, or the two colors may be matched so that they blend into one tone. If the carbro image comes out somewhat lighter than desired, the silver image may be only partly redeveloped, stopping development when sufficient strength has been secured, but the stability of the image cannot be guaranteed under these conditions.

This method is quite popular, the labor of making a bromide print for each carbro being offset by the labor and hazard of the transfer. The cost of the bromide paper and of the transfer paper being about the same, there is practically no difference in cost, while the opportunity of using the underlying image makes it possible to save some prints that would otherwise be lost.

Because the pigment image is as permanent as the pigment chosen, carbro prints were generally very long lived. The degree of control offered is great, both in the making of the bromide print and in the later stages of the process. The carbro process is still suitable for making artistic prints.

There is some difficulty today in obtaining proper bromide paper for the original prints. Most papers available today have a protective overcoat of gelatin, and very few paper emulsions are made with silver bromide as the only silver salt. Most papers are made with a mixture of silver bromide and silver chloride. Even so, some fast enlarging papers made today will work satisfactorily.

Tricolor Carbro

Tissues pigmented with cyan, magenta, and yellow pigments were made for many years for the making of natural color prints from separation nega-

(Left) Nickolas Muray (d. 1963), one of the best-known proponents of the carbro process. Muray was widely noted for his portraits of film stars (see opposite page) and even better known for his food photography. At the height of his career, he and his associates produced an average of three full-page color advertisements per week in Life *magazine alone. (Below) Muray's A & P coffee ad (1953), made with an 8″ × 10″ camera on Kodak Ektachrome film, is a combination of three photographs: the background and fruit, the coffee in the cups, and the coffee "pour" itself. The first two photographs were made with tungsten lighting exposed between 10 and 20 seconds; the "pour" was made on daylight film with strobe lighting. After separation negatives were made, the pigmented tissues of all three shots were hand-applied, layer by layer, and aligned by eye. A print such as this might require two days to produce.*

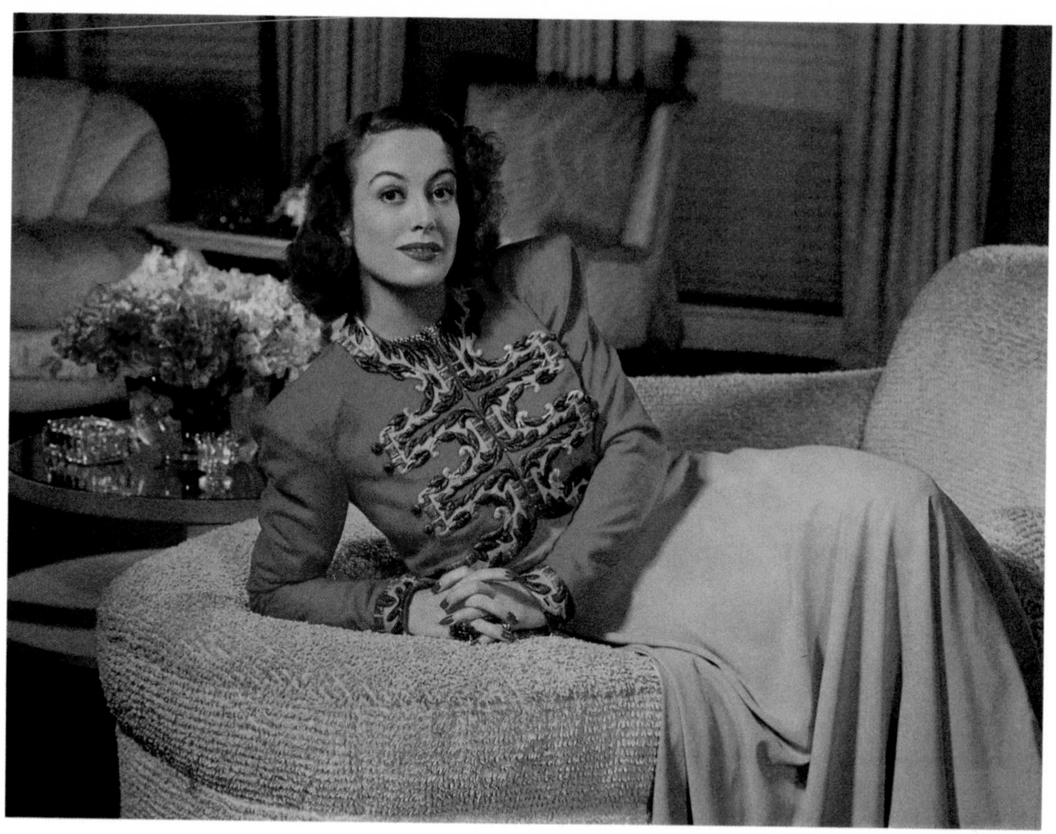

The carbro process is particularly appropriate in portraiture, where archival color—color that will never fade—is desired. The colors are earth pigments, not dyes, and have the same lasting qualities as oil paints. Muray's portraits of Joan Crawford (above) and Carole Lombard (right), made in the late 1930s or early 1940s, and that of Muray himself, made in the early 1950s, were photographed with a Devon One-Shot Camera, a color separation camera that produced three color plates in one shot. This camera used Super Panchro-Press Type II glass plates; the glass filters on the camera reduced the ASA to 2. In such a situation, the lighting was a crucial factor and was carefully controlled. Exposure was between 1/25 and 1/50 second. Aside from the lasting quality of the color pigments, the carbro process also produces a color quality and density range superior to most other methods. The highlights, which are matte, glow rather than shine; the shadows, which are glossy, have a depth and richness unequaled elsewhere. Although the carbro process is drawn-out and painstaking, a revival is presently under way among still photographers seeking superb and lasting color for their fine photographs. All four photos courtesy International Museum of Photography at George Eastman House.

tives from the time that panchromatic emulsions became available. The carbro process had been used since about 1865, but the tricolor carbro process was not developed until the early 1900s.

In this process, three bromide prints matched for size, density, and contrast were made from separation negatives exposed through red, green, and blue separation filters. The cyan, magenta, and yellow tissues were contacted to these bromides and the images placed in succession, and in register, on the transfer paper. Very high quality color prints could be made by this process and it was a favorite with professional photographers up to the advent of sheet color transparency films and the negative-positive processes.

WARNING: The carbon and carbro printing processes are extremely hazardous. Individuals attempting these processes should heed the precautionary warnings found on the product labels of the chemicals and dyes used.

Further Reading: Burbank, Rev. W.H. *Photographic Printing Methods.* New York, NY: Arno Press, 1973 (rep. of 1875 ed.); Lietze, Ernst. *Modern Heliographic Processes: A Manual of Instruction in the Art of Reproducing Drawings, Engraving, Manuscripts, Etc., by the Action of Light.* Rochester, NY: Visual Studies Workshop, 1974 (rep. of 1888 ed.); Vogel, Dr. Hermann. *The Chemistry of Light and Photography.* New York, NY: Arno Press, 1973 (rep. of 1875 ed.).

Carbonates

Carbonates are metal salts of a hypothetical acid, carbonic acid (H_2CO_3). Actually, the acid never exists in the free state, only in the form of its salts, but these latter follow all the rules of salts of other acids. That is, it is possible to make a carbonate of sodium by substituting the sodium for both atoms of hydrogen in the acid; thus we get sodium carbonate (Na_2CO_3). Or we can substitute sodium for only one of the two hydrogen atoms and get sodium bicarbonate ($NaHCO_3$). The same applies to other metals, such as potassium, which also form a carbonate and a bicarbonate, as does lithium. Calcium, however, having a valence of 2, forms only the carbonate $CaCO_3$.

Other metals also form carbonates, but they have little or no interest to photographers. Sodium carbonate is the most commonly used alkali in print developers; being the salt of a strong base and a weak acid, it is highly buffered and has a fairly high pH. It is for this reason that sodium carbonate is most often used as the accelerator in black-and-white paper developers; it produces a fairly high pH with a large reserve alkalinity. Potassium carbonate is used occasionally where higher pH is required. Lithium carbonate could also be used, but has no advantage and is much more expensive. Calcium carbonate is insoluble in water, hence is not useful. The bicarbonates are also highly buffered but have lower alkalinity, hence are seldom used except in combination with the carbonates to attain a somewhat lower alkalinity midway between the two.

Sodium carbonate is seldom used today as the activator in black-and-white film developers because when the film is put in an acid stop bath after development, the action of the acid on the carbonate is to release bubbles of carbon dioxide. As this occurs within the gelatin emulsion, pinholes can be caused in the emulsion, which remain after the film is processed. The same reaction occurs in prints, but the bubbles are tiny and are not visible. In negatives that are enlarged, they appear as visible black spots on the print.

• *See also:* POTASSIUM CARBONATE; SODIUM CARBONATE.

Carbon Tetrachloride

Tetrachloromethane, perchloromethane

Used mainly as a solvent and grease remover.

Formula: CCl_4

Molecular Weight: 158.83

Clear, colorless liquid with a characteristic odor, slightly soluble in water, mixes freely with alcohol, benzine, benzol, chloroform. Mixed with benzine, or purified gasoline, it forms a nonflammable cleaning fluid sold under trademarks such as Carbona. Carbona no longer contains CCl_4.

DANGER: Carbon tetrachloride is extremely poisonous; breathing the fumes or vapors for any appreciable time can cause severe liver damage and death. Since other, less dangerous cleaning fluids are now available, the use of carbon tetrachloride should be avoided.

Careers in Photography

Photography plays a vital role in our daily lives. As a leader in communications technology, photography offers a wide variety of career opportunities. Business and industry rely heavily upon photographers and technicians in advertising, public relations, marketing, research, quality control, and training. Photographers and technicians are employed in education and graphic arts; in federal, state, and local governments; and in the military services. Camera stores, photofinishing plants, newspapers, magazines, television stations, and the fields of freelance and commercial photography offer additional opportunities.

In many fields outside photography, photographic knowledge and skills are an asset and a key to career advancement. Such fields include educa-

PHOTOGRAPHIC CAREERS FOR TECHNICIANS AND PHOTOGRAPHERS

Career Field	Photographic Opportunities
Advertising	Fashion, TV commercials, exhibits, newspapers, magazines, direct mail.
Aeronautics	Research, publications, exhibits, TV and movies for education and training.
Agriculture	Journalism, research, publications, slides, motion pictures, exhibits, television.
Art and Illustration	Documentation, reporting, fashion, teaching.
Business and Industry	Selling photographic equipment and supplies, photofinishing, microfilming and information storage, audiovisual training, document reproduction, photoinstrumentation, cataloging, research, public relations, publications, promotional films, sales training, documentation, and reporting.
Education	Teaching photography, preparing photographs for training manuals, making audiovisual aids and training films, curriculum development.
Entertainment	Motion pictures, TV, animation, sports, recreation, travel.
Journalism	TV, newspapers, magazines, sports, social events, politics, fashion, national or local events.
Medicine	Photomacrography, pathology, x-ray, surgery, laboratory research, photomicrography.
Military	Aerial, combat training, research, news, public relations, documentation.
Oceanography	Underwater scientific photography—black-and-white and color, still and motion-picture.
Portraiture	Children, adults, notables, animals.
Printing	Photoengraving, photomechanics, photolithography, rotogravure, stripping.
Safety and Public Health	Detection and identification, reporting, training.
Space Exploration	Research, reporting, publications, exhibits, photoinstrumentation.
Transportation	Photo mapping, recording, traffic control, instrumentation, safety, training, public relations, maintenance.

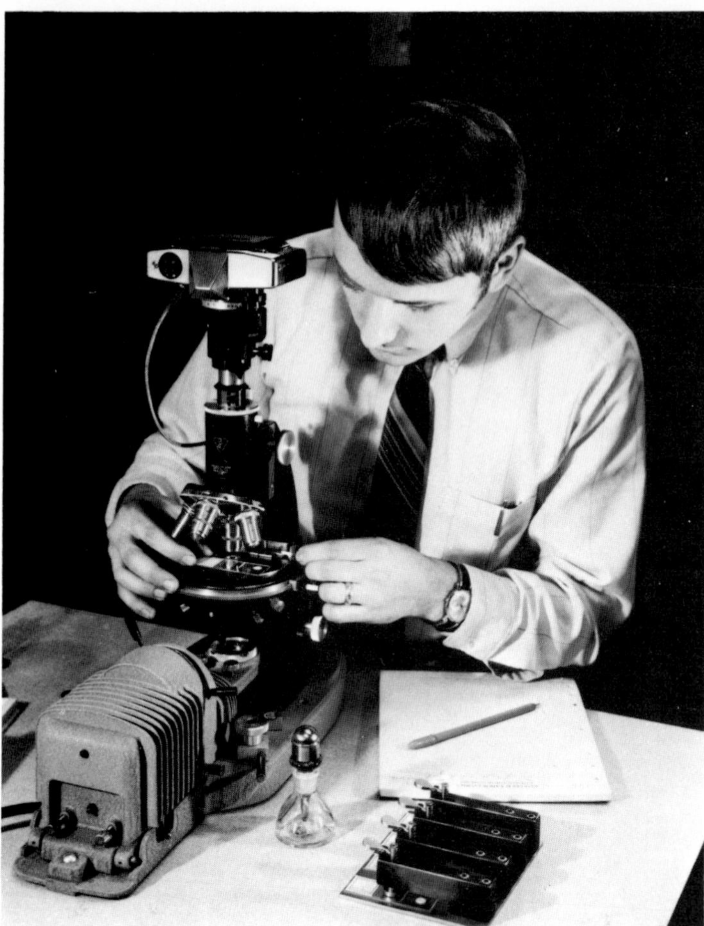

In the field of scientific research, photomicrography—photography through a microscope—is essential for the recording and classification of data. The technique is currently learned through apprenticeship, but it might soon be taught as part of a formal photography course.

tion, medicine, engineering, public safety, and research.

Many Careers are Open

The foundation for the entire structure of photography is the business of supplying cameras, film, papers, chemicals, and a wide variety of specialized apparatus and services. This is what makes up the photographic industry. In thinking about a possible career in this field, many people assume that their ability to make a good photograph gives them an advantage. Actually, photographic skill is a requisite for only a *few* jobs in the photographic industry. The people who make film, cameras, and equipment must be first-class technicians, engineers, chemists, machinists, draftsmen—almost every trade is needed in photographic manufacturing and marketing.

Research workers must be well-trained physicists, chemists, and mathematicians. It doesn't matter whether they are clever photographers, since their work lies in the fields of pure and applied science. Jobs in manufacturing go to the people who can offer the kinds of skill needed in the production operations.

The business of selling photographic merchandise is somewhat different. The prime requirements are a pleasing personality and a good appearance as well as a firsthand knowledge of what the customer is doing with photography. Photographic retailing offers splendid opportunities in itself but has also been used by many people as a stepping-stone to another job.

Photofinishing is closely associated with retailing. It offers some job opportunities that require relatively little technical training. The top positions go to those who have business and executive ability. The increased demand for photofinishing services, especially in color photography, means more and more job opportunities for qualified technicians and people with administrative abilities. For supervisory jobs in the field of color photography, a thorough knowledge of high-school chemistry, physics, and mathematics is needed.

The fields of commercial and portrait photography are highly competitive, but there is still room at the top for the person with real ability. Good training in an accredited school will provide an even start with others looking for similar careers. Good training will also help in the motion-picture field. But school training is only a foundation on which to build with experience. Practically all the top photographers have come up through the ranks. Almost any position that will bring you in touch with work in photography is valuable. Then work your way up by taking every opportunity to learn and demonstrate your skill.

The number of people employed in various kinds of photographic positions is significant. Perhaps the largest number are employed in the audiovisual or nontheatrical film field. This is the field which produces and distributes motion-picture films for education, business and industry, government, churches, and medicine. There are opportunities for technicians and photographers in film production, in

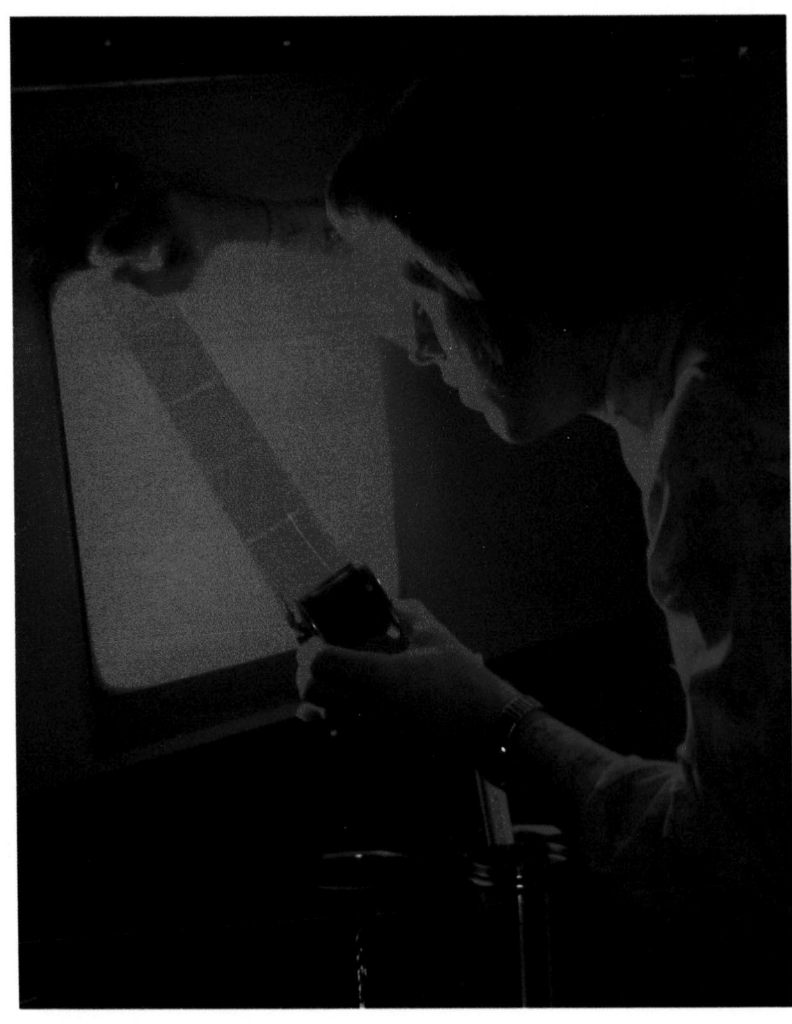

Darkroom technicians are highly skilled workers who are often photographers in their own right. Here, a technician inspects a strip of negatives to determine which are of sufficient quality to print. Skilled darkroom workers can produce excellent prints from mediocre negatives, while unskilled technicians can produce poor prints from even top-quality photographs.

laboratory work, in distribution, and as communication specialists or audiovisual coordinators.

In the medical field, countless people are employed full-time as x-ray technicians. Many others work part-time, serving also as medical receptionists, nurses, and the like. Many people specialize in biomedical photography, an interesting career for which the chief training is apprenticeship.

There are thousands of professional photographers. This includes self-employed photographers and those employed in studios, industry, and the press.

Photography plays a vital role in the printing industry. There are many opportunities for technicians and cameramen.

After film has been exposed, it must be processed. There are a great many companies that specialize in the professional quality of photofinishing that is required by illustrators and professional photographers. The several thousand processing laboratories in the United States include commercial photofinishers, custom laboratories specializing in work for professional and industrial photographers, and laboratories in business and industrial firms.

There are some 12,000 photo retailers selling photographic goods and more than 50,000 drug-

Biomedical photography offers a range of opportunities for career openings. Here, the photographer makes a movie of a surgical procedure. Photo by Bob Simmons; © Herbert R. Smith.

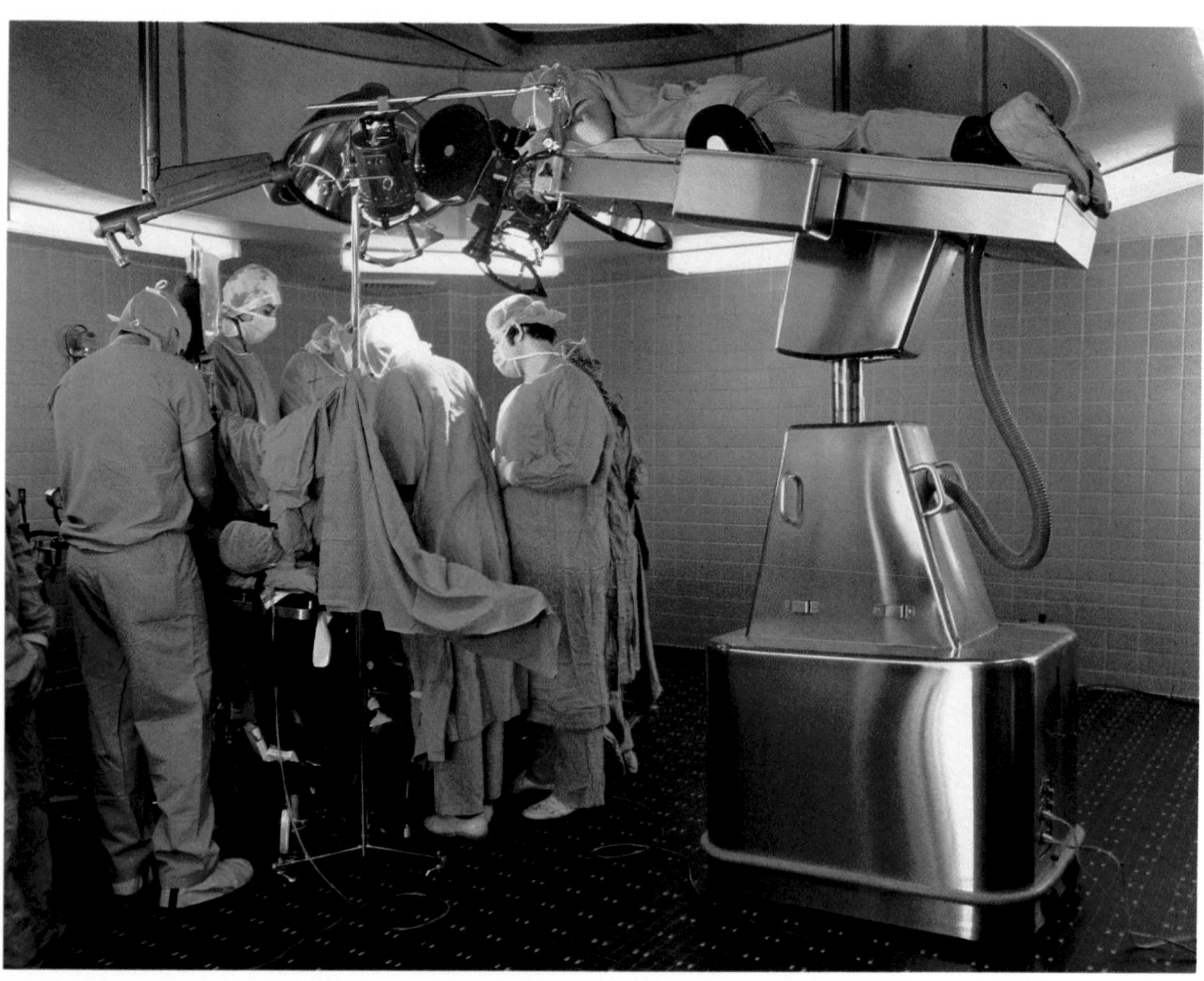

Teachers, photo editors, art directors, lecturers are all involved in the selection and inspection of photographs to be used for publication and audiovisual aids. Such jobs require a good understanding of both the technical and artistic aspects of photography.

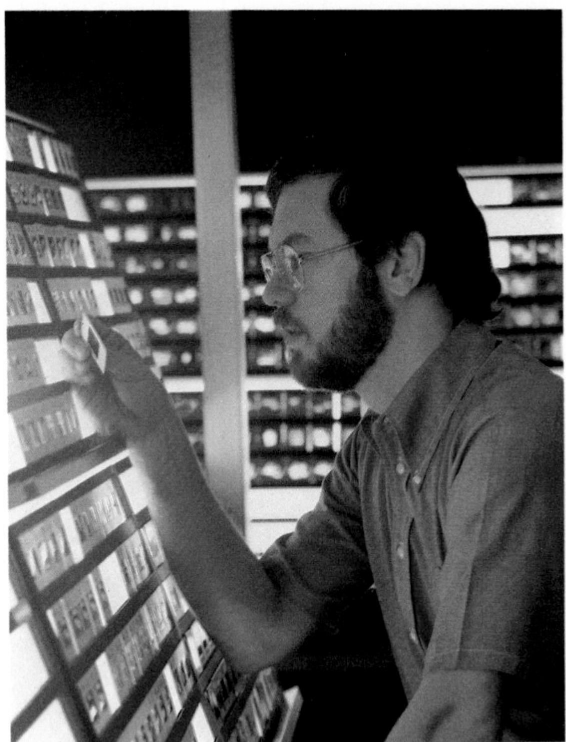

stores selling photo products or having photo departments.

Education and Training

The type and extent of training you need depends upon the photographic career you intend to enter. Conversely, the kind of work for which you can qualify depends upon your photographic education and experience. Photography courses in some high schools may prepare you for a career opportunity. However, you will need additional training in college, technical school, or the military services for most careers.

Almost every state has colleges, universities, or technical schools that offer courses in some phase of photography. Many colleges and universities have four-year programs leading to a bachelor's degree with a major in photography. Some colleges and universities offer a master's degree with a major in a specialized area, such as color photography. Other institutions offer a two-year curriculum leading to a certificate or associate degree in photography.*

Some high-school graduates prepare for careers as professional photographers through two or three years of on-the-job training in a portrait or commercial studio. Many of these trainees are part-time students. A trainee gets darkroom experience by learning how to develop film and make enlargements. He often assists an experienced photographer in setting up lights, cameras, and props.

If you plan to enter industrial, news, or scientific photography, you will need considerable training after high school. Photographic work in scientific and engineering research requires a good background in science or engineering as well as in photography.

As a prospective photographer, you should be manually dexterous and have some artistic ability. Imagination and originality are helpful assets for commercial and freelance photography. Press photography demands a good knowledge of news values and the ability to act quickly. If you plan to go into business for yourself, you should have good business sense and a pleasant personality.

Pursue Your Interest

Write down the career opportunities that appeal to you, and explore the following aspects of each one:

1. The educational background or training required.
2. The employment outlook for this field.
3. The earnings and employment conditions.
4. The nature of the work.
5. The equipment and techniques used.
6. The advantages and disadvantages of this type of work.
7. Personality traits suited to this type of work.

**A Survey of Motion Picture, Still Photography, and Graphic Arts Instruction*, T-17, is a listing of the colleges and universities that offer courses in photography. Write to Department 412L, Eastman Kodak Company, 343 State Street, Rochester, New York 14650. There is a minimal charge involved.

A phototechnician adjusts a light integrator used to control multiple exposures for halftone generation. Halftones, which reproduce photographs, drawings, and other pictures made up of shading and tone, are widely used in the graphic arts and publishing industries.

You can find out about these aspects by consulting the following sources:

1. A guidance counselor.
2. Publications in the Sources of Further Information section of this article, school and public libraries.
3. Specialists in your field of interest.
4. Commercial, industrial, and governmental photographic installations.
5. Family members and others in whom you have confidence.

Look Before You Leap

Starting your own photographic business is a venture which should receive a great deal of consideration. Being a good photographer does not ensure success, especially as an owner of a studio or other photographic business. When you start earning your living by photography, you become a professional, and your work will be judged by professional standards. You will be competing with photographers who may be well-known, who have had years of experience, and who do good photographic work consistently, not just occasionally.

It is not unusual for a beginning photographer to go into business for himself, but it is unusual for him to stay in business. It is better to start out as an employee in the kind of photographic business you'd like to own, and learn as much as possible that way.

Sources of Further Information

More in-depth information on careers in photography is available from sources such as Eastman Kodak Company, U.S. Government Printing Office, U.S. Department of Labor, photographic societies, and universities that offer courses in photography. You may contact places such as these for books and pamphlets regarding photographic careers.

Further Reading: Bennett, Edna. *Careers in Photography.* Garden City, NY: Amphoto, 1962; Bensusan, Arnold E. *So You Want to Be a Photographer.* New York, NY: British Book Center, 1975; Johnson, Bervin A. *Opportunities in Photographic Careers.* Louisville, KY: Vocational Guidance Manuals, Div. of Data Courier, Inc., 1969; Keppler, Victor. *Your Future in Photography,* 2nd ed. New York, NY: Arco Publishing Co., Inc., 1974.

Carte-de-Visite

A carte-de-visite is a small photograph mounted on a card approximately 2½″ × 4″, the standard size of a calling or visiting card (French: *carte-de-visite*) in the nineteenth century. It was introduced as a portrait novelty and as a means for quantity production of low-priced portraits, usually a full-length pose. Eventually, it was also used for souvenir, memento, and advertising photographs. Millions of cartes-de-visite were made from the 1850s to the 1890s. They have survived in great number and are one of the least costly collectible items from the history of photography.

The method of producing cartes-de-visite was patented in 1854 by the Parisian photographer André Adolphe Disdéri, who made a fortune after

Napoleon III visited his studio to have carte portraits taken. A full-size (6½″ × 8″) wet collodion plate was exposed in a camera with four, six, or eight lenses. A mask in the camera divided the focal plane into separate small rectangles, one for each lens. Exposures were made by uncapping one or more lenses at a time; the subject could change position or pose between exposures. In the case of a four-lens camera, half the plate was exposed, then a shifting back brought the unexposed portion of the plate into position for four more pictures.

The developed plate was contact-printed onto a single sheet of albumen paper; the selected poses were cut out and mounted on cards. An experienced photographer would uncap two or more lenses simultaneously to record a pose he thought the customer would particularly like. This gave him duplicate negatives on the plate, which would reduce the work of printing quantity orders. The unwanted poses were masked off during printing.

When two lenses located side by side were uncapped at the same time, the result was a stereo-

Front and back of carte-de-visite dating from the late nineteenth century. (Left) Front shows a sepia-tone portrait photograph, mounted on board with a gold edge. (Right) Back of card gives photographer's name and location. Card shown actual size.

graphic pair of images. However, this aspect of carte-de-visite production was largely ignored, and a dual-lens camera was employed when stereographs were desired. The multiple-lens camera was also adopted for the production of ferrotypes ("tintypes"), which gave lesser-quality direct positive images that were cut apart with metal shears.

• *See also:* ALBUMEN; FERROTYPE; WET COLLODION PROCESS.

Cathode-Ray Tube Recording

The cathode-ray tube (CRT) is common to a number of instruments—oscilloscopes, image-converter cameras, radar indicators, flying-spot scanners, and so on. Of these, the oscilloscope is the most common. However, the photographic techniques dis-

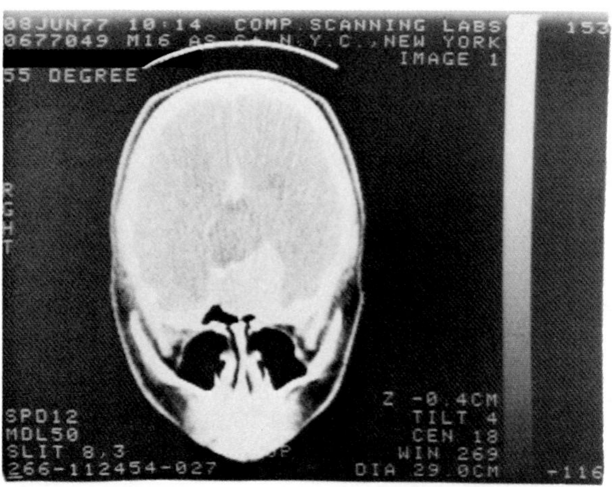

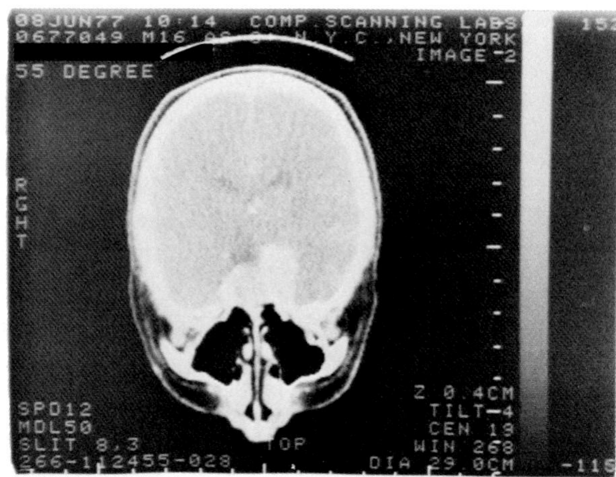

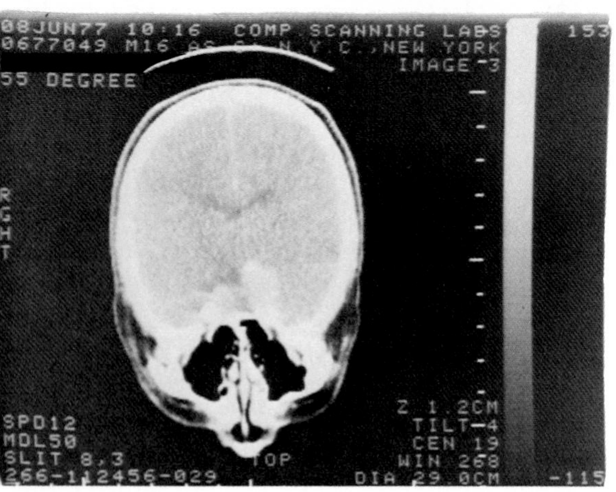

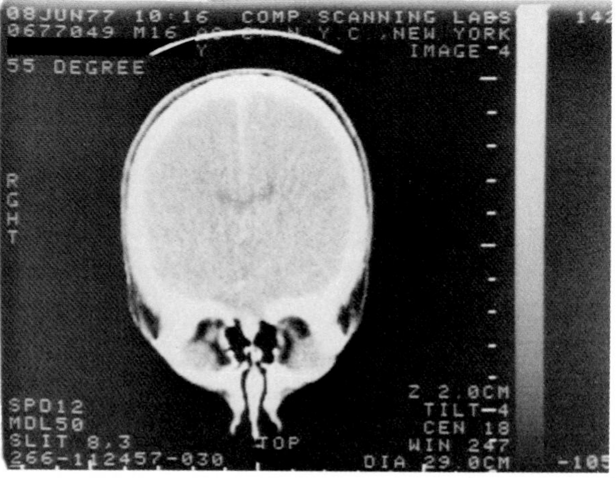

Four cross-section views of a skull taken on a computerized axial tomograph scanner, which produces images via a cathode-ray tube. The x-ray tube and detector rotate around the patient's head. Only a few moments were required to photograph and process this series. Photos courtesy J. M. Weinraub, M. D.

USE OF SUPPLEMENTARY LENSES FOR A CRT

35 mm Camera and 50 mm Lens (24 × 36 mm format)				2¼″ × 2¼″ Roll-Film Camera and 80 mm Lens			
Size of CRT Face (inches)	Use Close-Up Lens	Focus Scale Setting (feet)	Front of Lens to Tube Face Distance (inches)	Size of CRT Face (inches)	Use Close-Up Lens	Focus-Scale Setting (feet)	Front of Lens to Tube Face Distance (inches)
3	+3 plus +2	15	7¾	3	+3 plus +3	3½	5¾
5	+3	15	12¼	5	+3 plus +2	4	7
7	+2	6	15¼	7	+3 plus +1	inf	9¾
10	+1	6	25½	10	+2	4	14
16	+1	10	30	16	+1	3	22

cussed here apply to all CRT recording, regardless of instrument type.

The three basic types of cathode-ray tube photography are:

1. *Single-Frame Recording*—used when specific displays of data must be photographed. Most any still camera can be used, since the photographic material will remain stationary during the exposure.

2. *Continuous-Motion Recording*—used when data must be photographed continuously over a period of time (e.g., the duration of a test). In this case, a special camera is needed because the photographic material is moving during exposure.

3. *Repeated Single-Frame Recording*—with many single frames of rapidly formed images, automatic still cameras synchronized electronically with the output are used to record CRT images. This is the fastest way of getting printout data from computer storage of alpha numeric information.

A cathode-ray tube is similar to a black-and-white television tube. Instead of displaying pictorial images, however, it displays the output of electrical measuring devices and computers.

BELLOWS CORRECTION FOR 35 mm CAMERAS

Size of CRT Face (inches)	Increase in Lens Opening (stops)
3	⅔
5	⅓
7	⅓
10	⅓
16	None

This table is based on the full diameter of the CRT filling the short (24mm) dimension of the 35mm frame (24 × 36 mm). Increase the lens opening by the amount indicated for the size of the CRT face being photographed. No exposure correction is needed when using close-up lenses. However, when using bellows, extension tubes, or macro lenses, the above table applies.

Setup for Single-Frame Recording

If there is a special camera designed for the oscilloscope to be photographed, use it. If not, then most any camera can be used to make an acceptable record of a CRT. Use the following procedure.

First, get the camera close enough to the face of the CRT to get a big image on the film. This is most easily done with press-type or view-type cameras, but a 35 mm or other roll-film camera will work equally well if you add supplementary close-up lenses. (See the tables on the use of supplementary lenses with these cameras.) The 35 mm or roll-film camera also offers the advantages of greater film supply and a larger relative aperture for recording fast transient phenomena.

Second, to prevent background fog and reflections, make sure that stray light is not reaching the

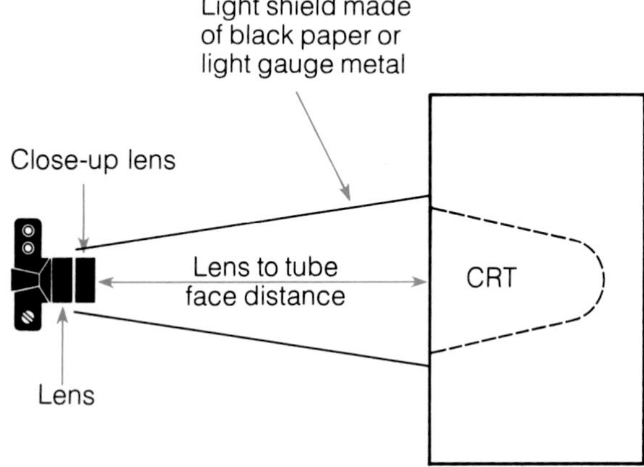

Setup for single-frame cathode-ray tube recording. Camera position must be close enough to the face of the CRT to produce a large image on the film. Make sure that stray light does not reach the CRT face.

face of the CRT. A simple shield made of a cone of black construction paper or a light-gauge metal can be used (see accompanying diagram). Or, you might be able to use a focusing cloth and some coat-hanger wire to make a cone to eliminate stray light. Alternately, you can work in a darkened room, but this should be considered as an emergency measure only.

Adjusting the Oscilloscope

Even though you probably won't need to understand all about oscilloscopes, you should have at least a rudimentary understanding of what the various oscilloscope controls do. Therefore, have someone who does understand oscilloscopes help you make some trial exposures before recording any actual tests.

Focus, astigmatism, and *intensity* controls must be adjusted for the sharpest trace of useful intensity. Be certain that these adjustments are made at the sweep rate (the rate at which the trace moves horizontally across the face of the CRT) that will be recorded, because many oscilloscopes require different settings for high and low sweep speeds, and also for single sweeps.

Make the initial focus and astigmatism adjustments at a low-intensity setting. There will probably be several pairs of settings that make the spot appear sharp, but careful checking will often show one combination to be best. The object is to make the spot as near to a point source of light as possible.

Once the focus and astigmatism controls are set, make a few trial exposures at various intensity settings to determine which will be best for your setup. Most work will probably require an intermediate-intensity setting. Be sure to use the same film type for each test and to note the intensity and lens settings used. You might also want to make these trial exposures with several different kinds of phenomena, such as stationary patterns and single sweeps.

Recording Stationary Patterns

Stationary patterns of recurrent phenomena are the easiest to photograph. With a between-the-lens shutter*, the minimum exposure time (in seconds) that can be used for oscilloscope recording is:

$$\frac{1}{\text{sweep rate in Hertz (cycles per second)}}$$

For example, if the sweep rate is 500 Hz (cycles per second), then 1/500 sec. would be the *minimum* shutter speed that could be used to record one complete trace or a single sweep of a recurrent phenomenon. Unless you are certain of your shutter's calibration, however, it would be safer to select a slower shutter speed (say, 1/250 sec., as in our example above). You may want to use a shutter speed that will record five to ten consecutive sweeps. Five consecutive sweeps in our 500 Hz example would require a shutter speed of 1/100 sec.

NOTE: Many oscilloscopes will give the sweep rate in terms of time (seconds, milliseconds, and microseconds). The accompanying table translates common shutter speeds into either Hz or milliseconds.

For radar indicators, the shutter should be opened for the time it takes for one complete sweep, and then closed. Video images are best recorded when the shutter is open for the time it takes for the entire tube face to be scanned. In most TV systems, this is 1/30 sec.

*For focal-plane shutters, do not use a shutter speed faster than that recommended for synchronizing with electronic flash. Most 35 mm cameras have focal-plane shutters.

Recording Single Sweeps

There are several ways to record a wave form that appears for only one sweep. If the oscilloscope has a triggered sweep, the shutter can be left open until the event occurs, and the resultant wave form can then be photographed (assuming that a light-tight shield or a darkened room is used). If the event is cyclic in nature, it is sometimes possible to trigger the sweep generator with the flash contacts on the camera shutter (use "X," or zero-delay, synchronization). Don't forget to turn off the graticule illumination if the oscilloscope is so equipped.

A method of recording one sweep cycle of a continuously varying pattern is to arrange a brightening gate on the z-axis input of the oscilloscope. Such an arrangement permits one cycle to be traced brightly since all other cycles have too low an intensity to be recorded. A pulse generator is a good source to trigger the brightening gate.

CONVERSION TABLE SHUTTER SPEED TO SWEEP TIME OR SWEEP FREQUENCY

Shutter Speed in Seconds	Sweep Time in Milliseconds	Sweep Frequency in Hz (cycles per second)
1	1000.00	1
1/2	500.00	2
1/4	250.00	4
1/5	200.00	5
1/8	125.00	8
1/10	100.00	10
1/15	67.00	15
1/20	50.00	20
1/25	40.00	25
1/30	33.00	30
1/50	20.00	50
1/60	16.00	60
1/100	10.00	100
1/125	8.00	125
1/200	5.00	200
1/250	4.00	250
1/400	2.50	400
1/500	2.00	500
1/800	1.25	800
1/1000	1.00	1000
1/2000	.50	2000

PHOSPHOR CHARACTERISTICS

JEDEC Designation	JEDEC Persistence Class*	Color of Fluorescence and Phosphorescence	Types of Film Sensitivity: Pan	Ortho	Blue
P1	Medium	Yellowish-green	x	x	
P2	Medium-short	Yellowish-green	x	x	
P4 (sulfide)	Medium	Violet	x	x	x
	Short	Greenish-yellow	x	x	
P5	Medium-short	Blue	x	x	x
P7	Medium-short	Violet	x	x	x
	Long	Yellowish-green†	x	x	
P11	Medium-short	Blue	x	x	x
P12	Long	Orange	x		
P14	Medium-short	Violet	x	x	x
	Medium	Yellowish-orange†	x		
P15	Very short	Near ultraviolet	x	x	x
	Short	Green	x	x	
P16	Very short	Near ultraviolet	x	x	x
P20	Medium to Medium-short	Yellowish-green	x	x	
P31	Medium-short	Green†	x	x	

*JEDEC (Joint Electron Device Engineering Council) persistence classifications (based on time for phosphorescence to decay to 10 percent of initial brightness:

Very long—1 sec. and over
Long—100 millisec. to 1 sec.
Medium—1 millisec. to 100 millisec.
Medium-short—10 microsec. to 1 millisec.
Short—1 microsec. to 10 microsec.
Very short—Less than 1 microsec.

†Phosphorescence may last for a minute or longer.

Selecting a Photographic Film

The spectral emission of the display on a CRT will vary, depending upon the type of phosphor that is coated on the inside of the tube face. Thus the film selected must have a spectral sensitivity that includes the spectral output of the phosphor. Blue phosphors can be recorded by any film, green phosphors by orthochromatic or panchromatic films, and orange phosphors by panchromatic films only.

If you don't know which phosphor a CRT has, then find out the tube designation number. (The instrument manual should give this.) A number might read "3RP1," "5UP11," or "7VP31." The last part of the number, starting with the "P," indicates the phosphor. The three tubes listed have a P1 (yellowish-green), P11 (blue), and P31 (green) phosphor, respectively. Some phosphors (P4, P7, P14, P15) have more than one color component.

There are many Kodak films that can be used for CRT recording. The best one to use for a particular application would depend not only on the type of phosphor being photographed, but also on the type of signals to be recorded. Kodak Tri-X pan film is a high-speed, panchromatic film and will do a fairly good job of recording any phosphor output.

If a higher speed film is needed (for recording very high-speed transients—particularly a single-sweep transient), try Kodak Royal-X pan film or Kodak recording film.

Developer Choice

Perhaps the best all-around developer for CRT work is Kodak developer D-19. It yields sharp images and high photographic speed. If a continuous-tone image is required (as in TV recording), then Kodak developer D-76 is a good choice.

Development

Expose and process the film so that the CRT traces on the negatives have a density between 0.3 and 1.5. Higher densities will probably yield traces that are not as sharp. Lower densities may be all right in some applications, provided they can be seen, but they do not leave much room for exposure error.

As a starting point, follow the suggestions in the accompanying development table. Keep in mind that the times and temperatures given may need to be modified, depending on the type of CRT recording being done and processing equipment and techniques used.

DEVELOPMENT FOR CRT RECORDING

Kodak Film	Type of Development	*Kodak* Developer/ Time/ Temperature
All *TRI-X* pan films	For normal speed	*D-19*/4min./20C (68 F)
	For increase in speed of 2 to 3 times	*D-19*/15min./20C (68 F)
Royal-X pan, *Royal-X* pan (*Estar* thick base), or Recording 2475 (*Estar-AH* base)	For highest speed (for most phosphors) Gives 6 to 10 times speed of *Tri-X* pan films (normal processing)	*DK-50*/8min./20C (68 F) or *D-19*/15min./20C (68 F)

Helpful Hints—Pitfalls

Colored Filters and Graticules in the Optical Path. They can seriously modify or attenuate the output of the phosphor.

Ultraviolet Attenuation in the Optical Path. Many materials (lenses included) have poor transmittance in the ultraviolet or near-ultraviolet region of the spectrum, where many phosphors have their most photographically useful output.

Cathode Glow. Panchromatic films (which are sensitive to red radiation) sometimes record an out-of-focus image of the cathode. Unless you need the red sensitivity, you can eliminate recording of cathode glow by (a) switching to an orthochromatic or blue-sensitive film or (b) adding a green or blue filter to the optical path. Be careful not to eliminate the useful output of the phosphor.

Room-light Phosphorescence. Most phosphors will phosphoresce slightly for several minutes after exposure to room light. If the CRT face has been exposed to room light, wait several minutes before making the first exposure, to avoid an overall fog on the film.

More Information

If cathode-ray tube recording is being done as a regular matter, and optimum results are required, it is preferable to use films made especially for this purpose and with characteristics to match the various types of cathode-ray tube screen phosphors. Individual data sheets are available from Kodak on most of the films available for this purpose.

Celsius

The Swedish astronomer Anders Celsius (1701–1744) devised a temperature scale of 100 equal intervals between the freezing point of water (0 C) and its boiling point (100 C). The scale is extended by measuring increase or decrease in the same size units. The scale is also known as the centigrade scale, a term no longer used in order to avoid confusion with various *centi-* units in the International System (SI) of measurement.

The Kelvin scale uses units identical to those of the Celsius scale, but begins at absolute zero (−273.15 C). Thus conversions between the two scales are:

$$K = C - 273.15$$
$$C = K + 273.15$$

The ° symbol is not used when temperature is expressed in Kelvins.

The Fahrenheit scale uses a smaller unit of measurement, such that 9 Fahrenheit degrees equal 5 Celsius degrees. This scale places the freezing point of water at 32 F, the boiling point at 212 F. Conversions are accomplished as follows:

$$C = \tfrac{5}{9}(F - 32)$$
$$F = \tfrac{9}{5}C + 32$$

• *See also:* FAHRENHEIT; KELVIN; WEIGHTS AND MEASURES.

Centigrade

An obsolescent term for the Celsius scale of temperature, which places the freezing point of water at 0° and the boiling point at 100°.

• *See also:* CELSIUS; FAHRENHEIT; KELVIN; WEIGHTS AND MEASURES.

Changing Bag

A large bag made of several thicknesses of opaque material, used for handling sensitized materials in daylight. Its most common use is for loading film into camera magazines when working on location. It also can be used when a darkroom is not available for loading or unloading film holders, loading film into a developing tank, and similar purposes.

The usual changing bag is actually two bags, one inside the other. One side of each bag can be opened to insert or remove film, reels, holders, and the like. The openings close with lightproof zipper flaps. The other side of the bag has sleeves for reaching inside. Elasticized sleeve openings close tightly around the forearms to prevent light leaks.

Only a little practice is required to get the knack of using a changing bag; it is essentially the same as working in total darkness. However, too small a bag will restrict movement excessively and

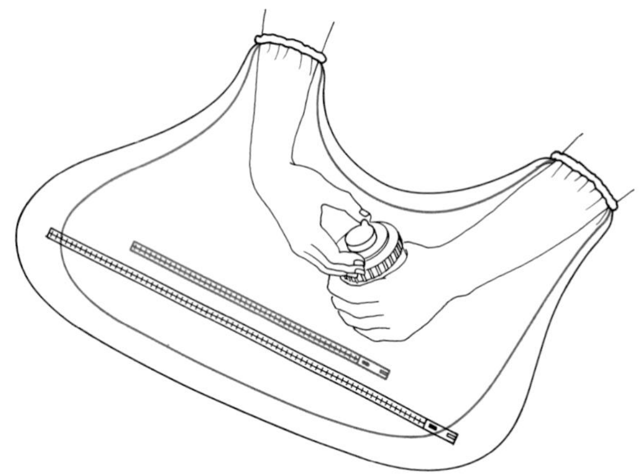

A changing bag is used for handling sensitized materials in daylight. It is two bags, one inside the other, with openings to insert materials and sleeve openings to insert hands.

make it difficult to handle film without spoiling it. In hot weather, hands may quickly begin to perspire because there is no air circulation in the bag.

Characteristic Curve

The way a photographic emulsion responds to exposure and development is seen most clearly by plotting a graph called the characteristic curve.

To obtain the characteristic curve of a film, a section of the material is given a carefully controlled exposure through a step tablet in an instrument called a sensitometer. The step tablet produces a series of exposure steps in the film, each one of which differs from the preceding step by a constant factor, such as 2 or the square root of 2 (1.41). The exposed sample film is developed under very carefully controlled conditions to yield a test film with a series of steps that differ in density.

Density is a measure of the light-stopping attribute of an area in a photographic image, and is largely dependent on the amount of metallic silver developed in the image.

To produce a curve that is easy to interpret, density is plotted versus the *logarithm* of exposure.

The characteristic curve made from readings taken from a test film exposed and processed, as in the accompanying illustration, is an absolute or real characteristic curve of a particular emulsion, processed in a particular developer, in a particular manner, and so on.

To make a *relative* characteristic curve, photograph a transilluminated film step scale or an illuminated paper gray scale, and plot the densities of the test film versus the transmission densities of the original film step scale or the reflection densities of the original paper gray scale. This produces a *relative* characteristic curve, which provides relative speed information.

Representative characteristic curves are those which are typical of a product, and are made by averaging the results from a number of tests that are made on a number of production batches of photographic films.

Curve Shape

Because of its shape, the characteristic curve is generally divided into three distinct regions. In the

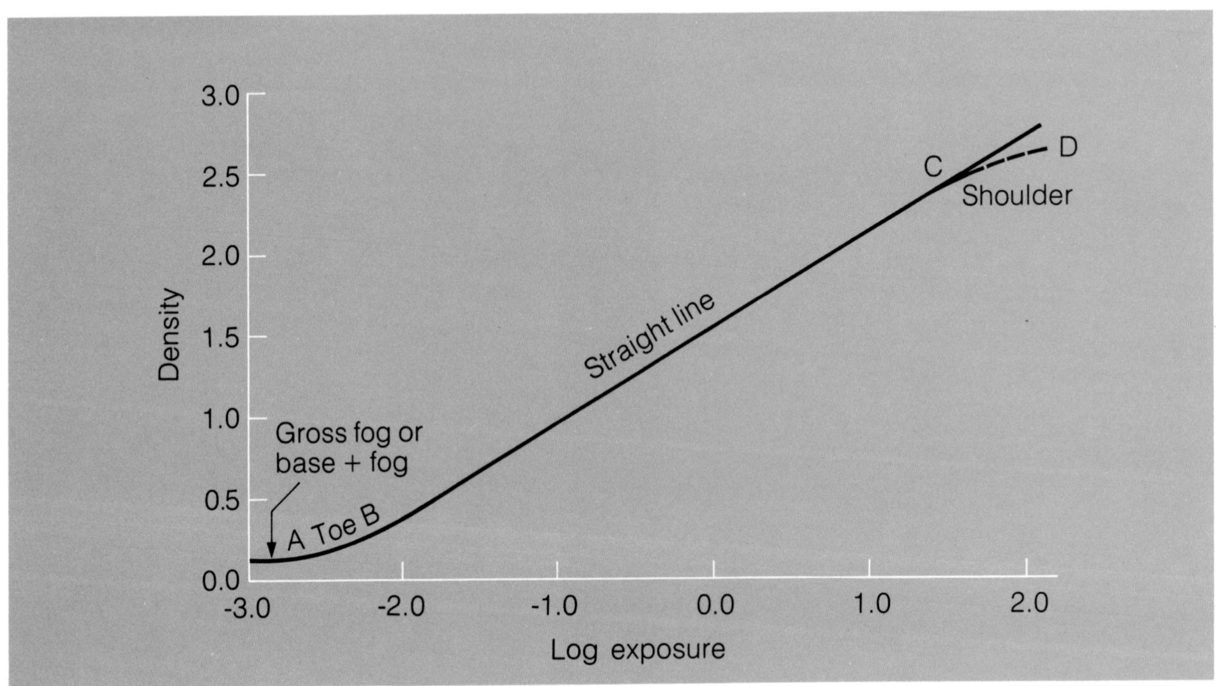

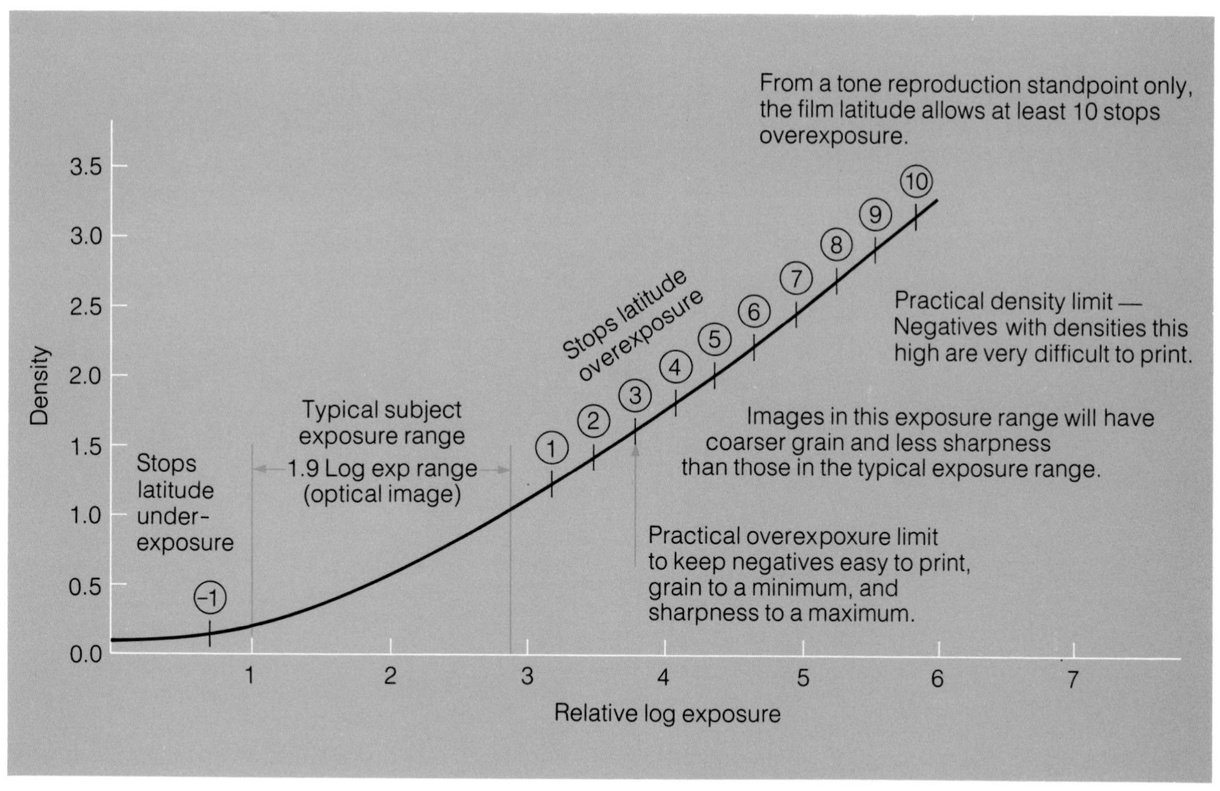
From a tone reproduction standpoint only, the film latitude allows at least 10 stops overexposure.
Density
3.5
3.0
2.5
2.0
1.5
1.0
0.5
0.0
Stops latitude under-exposure
Typical subject exposure range
1.9 Log exp range (optical image)
Stops latitude overexposure
Practical density limit — Negatives with densities this high are very difficult to print.
Images in this exposure range will have coarser grain and less sharpness than those in the typical exposure range.
Practical overexpoxure limit to keep negatives easy to print, grain to a minimum, and sharpness to a maximum.
-1
1
2
3
4
5
6
7
8
9
10
Relative log exposure

(Left) This typical characteristic curve is divided into the toe (AB), the straight line (BC), and the shoulder (CD). The shape of the curve is dependent upon the response of the emulsion to exposure and development. (Above) Characteristic curve of a long-toe film developed to a contrast index of 0.53. In this curve, the straight-line part of the curve is an extension of the toe and does not shoulder off even at 10 stops overexposure.

illustration of the typical curve, section AB is called the toe, BC is called the straight line, and CD, the shoulder.

The shape of the characteristic curve varies with different emulsions. The toe may be short or long. The straight line may be long, or it may be a straight line in name only. With some films, the curve may continue upward, like an extended toe, throughout the entire useful range of the film.

The Toe

The section to the left of A in the illustrated curve is a horizontal straight line. This represents the region of exposure in which the film gives no response. The unexposed edge of a processed film has this density. It is sometimes called the gross fog or base-plus-fog density.

From A to B is the toe, the crescent-shaped lower part of the characteristic curve. In this region, the tones are compressed, and the density change for a given log-exposure change increases continuously. As a practical matter, this means that the separation of thin shadow densities in the negative becomes progressively less as the lower end of the toe is approached, and densities less than about 0.10 density units greater than the gross-fog level usually print as black. The toe region varies in length and shape with different films. Toe shape is an important factor in the choice of a film for a particular use.

The Straight Line

In films that have a straight line in the characteristic curve, the midsection of the curve (B to C) has a constant slope, rise, or gradient for a given log-exposure change. The relationship between density and the log exposure is constant. The tonal scale is compressed *evenly.*

Some films have a long straight line; others have little or no straight line. When the direction of the line changes only a few degrees, this usually does not change the tone reproduction to a visible extent. In other words, the line may be considered straight even though it has a slight bend or curve in it.

The differences in curve shape affect choice of a film, exposure, and development latitude, and can be used to advantage in various picture-taking situations. The slope of the straight line (a measure of the angle it makes with the horizontal axis) is an important measure of contrast and is determined both by the emulsion characteristics and the development. The actual slope of the straight line is called *gamma.* A more useful measurement is *contrast index,* which is the slope of a line between precisely defined minimum and maximum printable densities.

The Shoulder

As shown by the dotted line in the upper part of the curve (C to D), the shoulder is the region where the slope of the characteristic curve decreases and the curve finally becomes a horizontal line again. With most films, the shoulder is never reached in practical picture-making. Negatives would have to be 10 to 15 stops overexposed before the shoulder would be reached. With some films, such as Kodak high speed infrared film, the shoulder is reached within the highlight region of the exposure. For best results, such films must be exactly exposed, because when highlights are exposed on the shoulder of a film, tone separation is lost, and the highlights are "blocked"; this means poor highlight tone separation. However, most film emulsions for general use are designed with extremely long or almost straight lines, which result in excellent tone separation in the highlights, even in grossly overexposed negatives.

The illustration on the previous page shows the characteristic curve of a long-toe film. Note that the straight-line portion might be considered an extension of the toe, and that there is no tendency to shoulder off even at 10 stops overexposure.

However, factors harmful to photographic reproduction become evident with gross overexposure—negatives become difficult to print because of the high density levels, and the graininess is increased while the sharpness is decreased. For these reasons, three stops of overexposure should be considered a practical limit. The characteristic curves are sometimes called the H & D curve, after Hurter and Driffield, who started the science of sensitometry in 1890. Another name is the D–Log E (Density-Logarithm of the Exposure) curve—the names of the two axes of the curve.

• *See also:* CONTRAST INDEX; DENSITOMETRY; SENSITOMETRY.

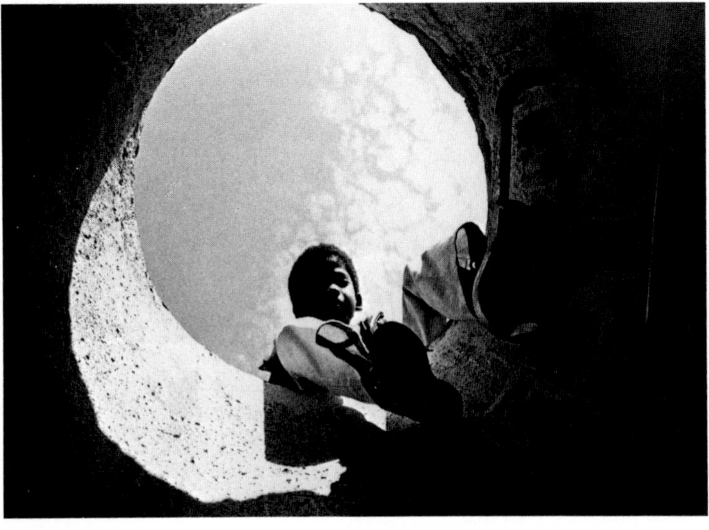

Short-toed films are ideal for high-flare conditions usually encountered outdoors; such films also possess especially good tone reproduction characteristics. For low-flare studio conditions, long-toed films are suitable.

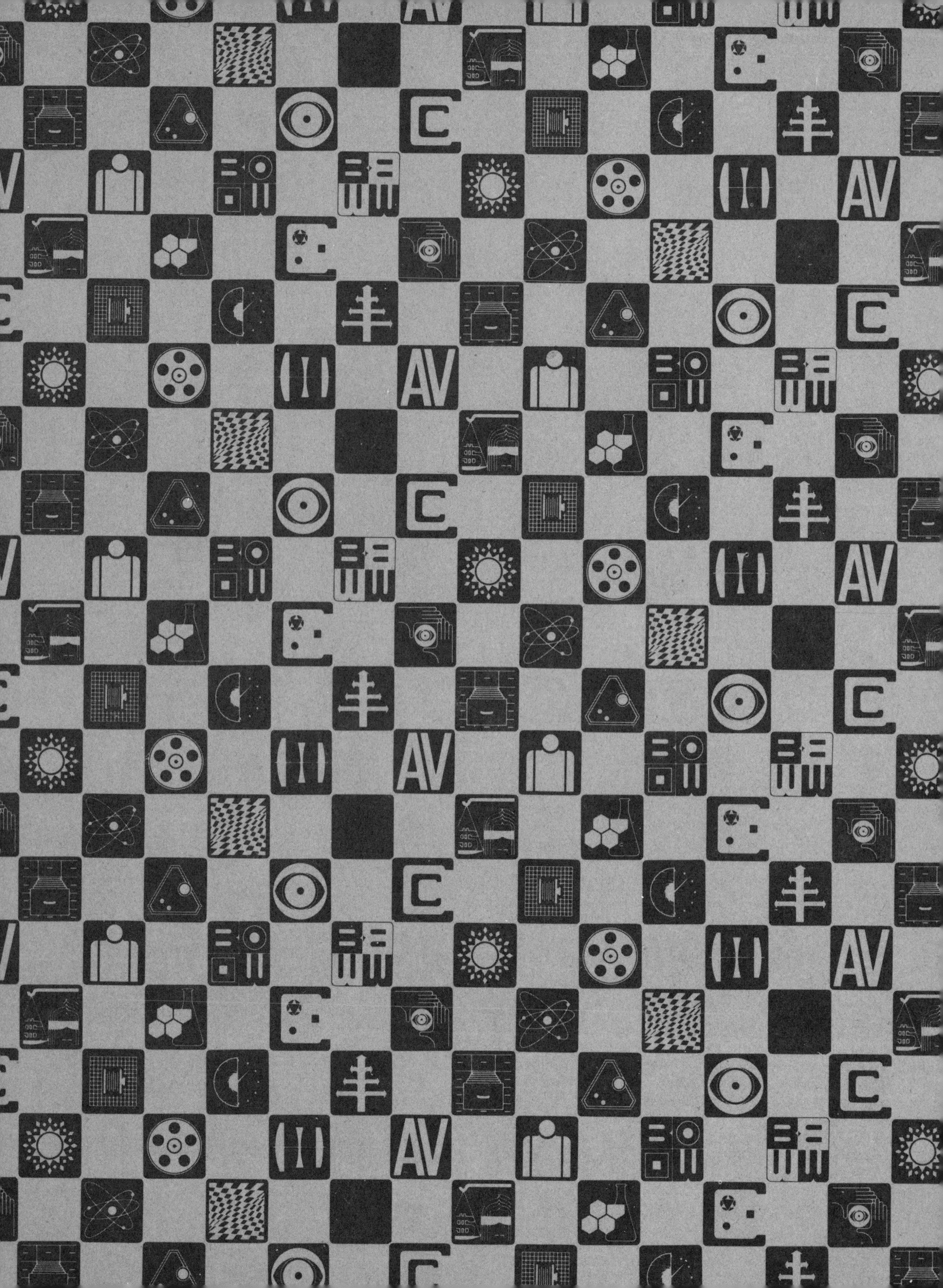